Vol. 2

Created & Illustrated by
Sho-u Tajima

Created & Written by
Eiji Otsuka

cmx

Jim Lee
Editorial Director

John Nee
VP—Business Development

Jonathan Tarbox
Group Editor

Paul Levitz
President & Publisher

Georg Brewer
VP—Design & Retail Product Development

Richard Bruning
Senior VP—Creative Director

Patrick Caldon
Senior VP—Finance & Operations

Chris Caramalis
VP—Finance

Terri Cunningham
VP—Managing Editor

Dan DiDio
VP—Editorial

Alison Gill
VP—Manufacturing

Rich Johnson
VP—Book Trade Sales

Hank Kanalz
VP—General Manager, WildStorm

Lillian Laserson
Senior VP & General Counsel

David McKillips
VP—Advertising & Custom Publishing

Gregory Noveck
Senior VP—Creative Affairs

Cheryl Rubin
Senior VP—Brand Management

Bob Wayne
VP—Sales & Marketing

Michael Niyama
Translation and Adaptation

Michael Heisler
Lettering

John J. Hill
CMX Logo & Publication Design

Ed Roeder
Additional Design

MORYO SENKI MADARA VOL. 2 © SHO-U TAJIMA 1996 © EIJI OTSUKA 1996 (OTSUKA EIJI OFFICE)
First published in Japan in 1996 by KADOKAWA SHOTEN PUBLISHING CO., LTD., Tokyo.

MADARA Volume 2, published by WildStorm Productions, an imprint of DC Comics, 888 Prospect St. #240, La Jolla, CA 92037. English Translation ©
2004. All Rights Reserved. English translation rights arranged with Kadokawa Shoten Publishing Co., Ltd., Tokyo, through Tuttle-Mori Agency, Inc.
The stories, characters, and incidents mentioned in this magazine are entirely fictional. Printed on recyclable paper. WildStorm does not read or
accept unsolicited submissions of ideas, stories or artwork. Printed in Canada.

DC Comics, a Warner Bros. Entertainment Company.

ISBN: 1-4012-0530-5

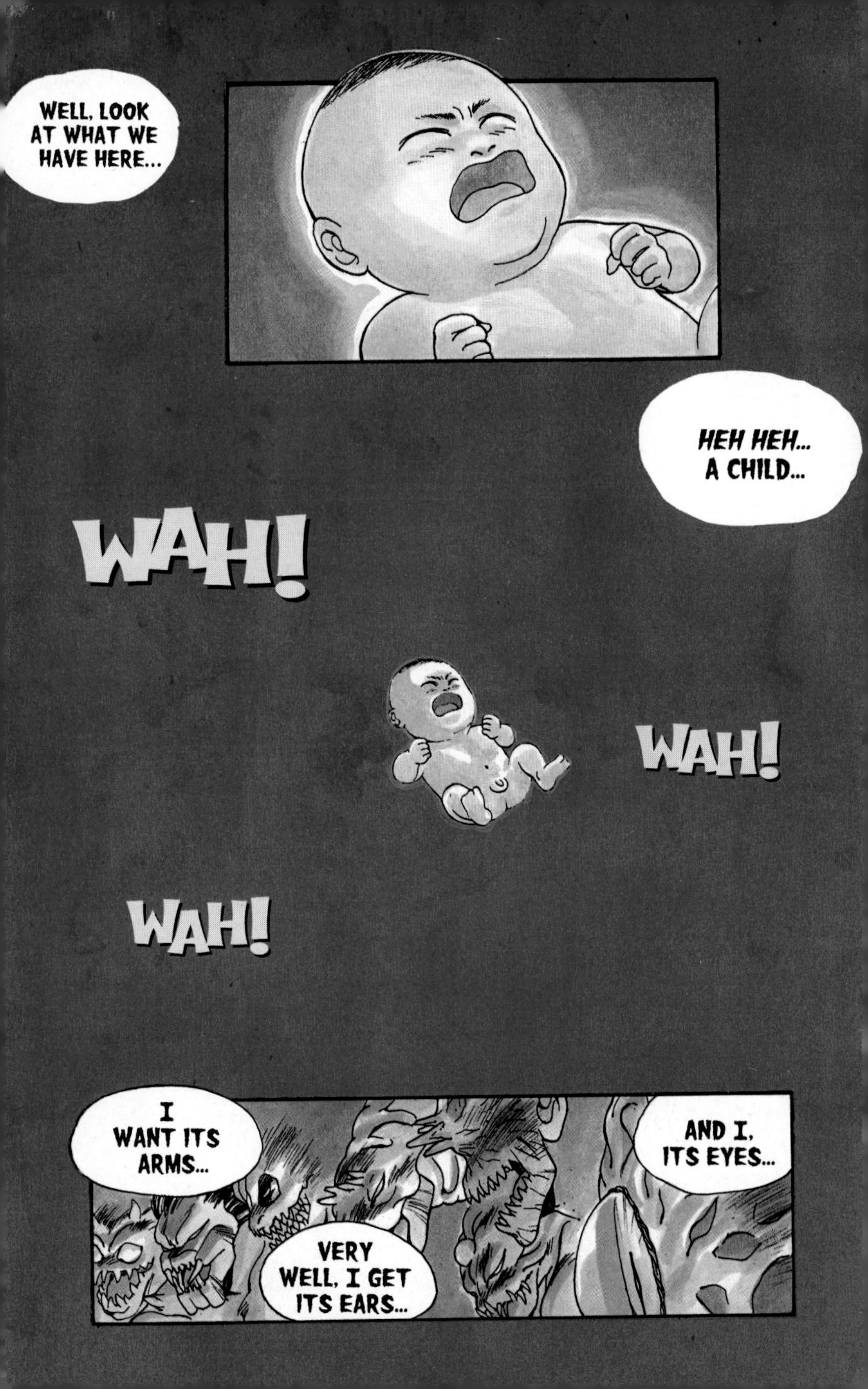
WELL, LOOK AT WHAT WE HAVE HERE...
HEH HEH... A CHILD...
WAH!
WAH!
WAH!
I WANT ITS ARMS...
VERY WELL, I GET ITS EARS...
AND I, ITS EYES...

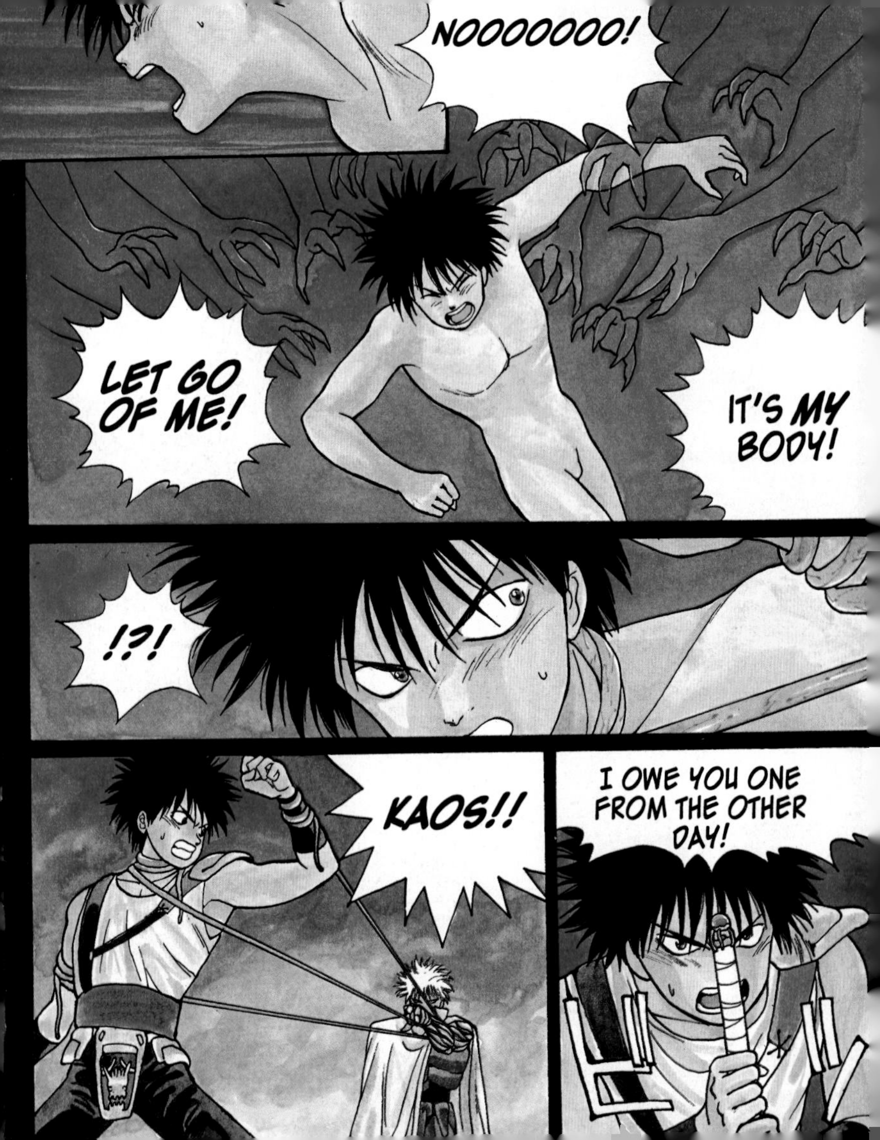
NOOOOOOO!
LET GO OF ME!
IT'S MY BODY!
!?!
KAOS!!
I OWE YOU ONE FROM THE OTHER DAY!

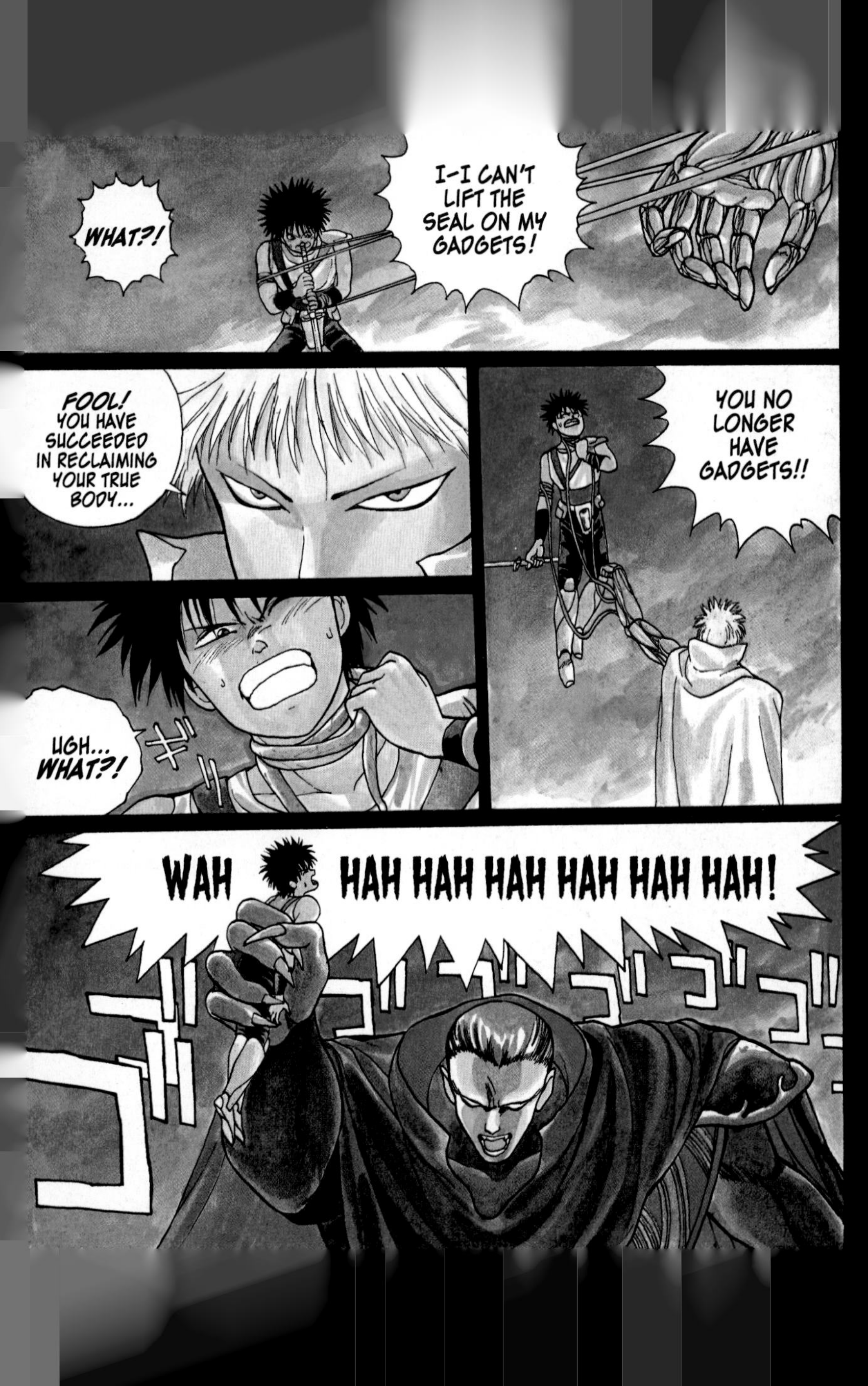
WHAT?!
I-I CAN'T LIFT THE SEAL ON MY GADGETS!
FOOL! YOU HAVE SUCCEEDED IN RECLAIMING YOUR TRUE BODY...
UGH... WHAT?!
YOU NO LONGER HAVE GADGETS!!
WAH HAH HAH HAH HAH HAH HAH!

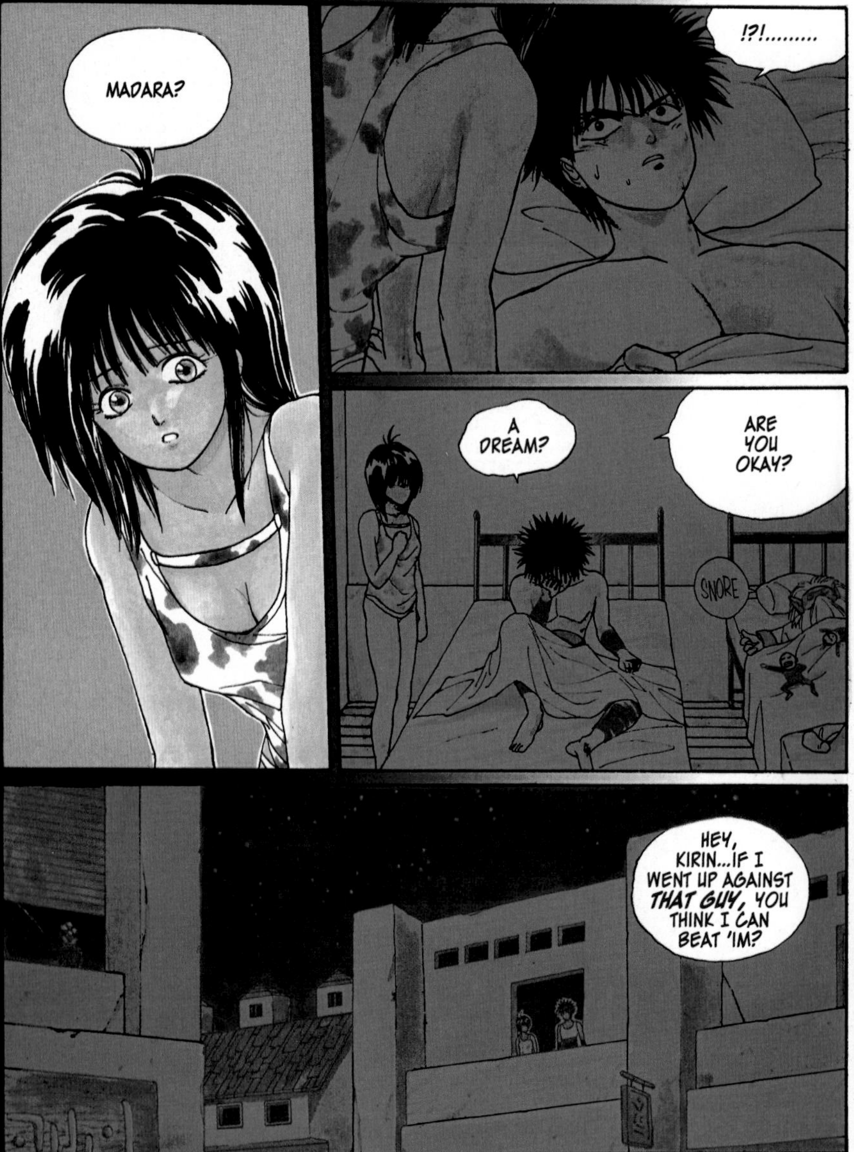
MADARA?
!?!.........
A DREAM?
ARE YOU OKAY?
SNORE
HEY, KIRIN...IF I WENT UP AGAINST THAT GUY, YOU THINK I CAN BEAT 'IM?

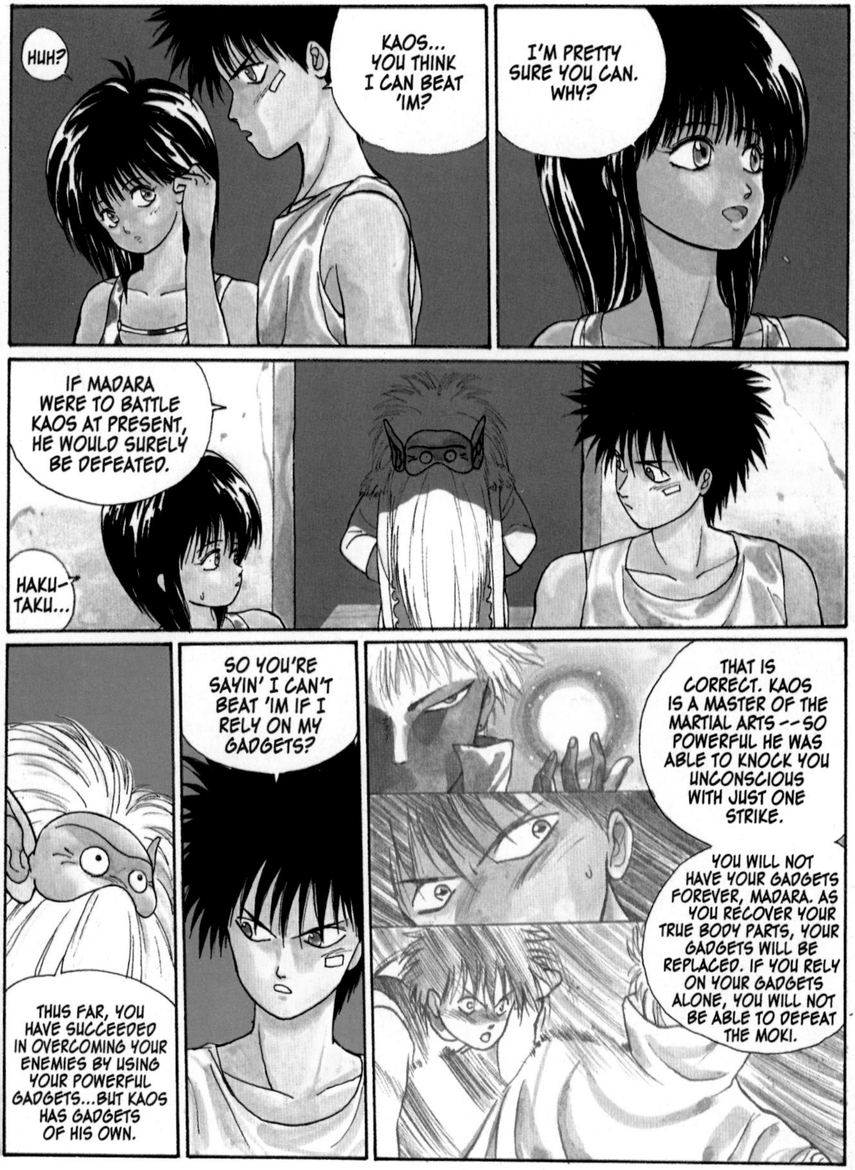
HUH?
KAOS... YOU THINK I CAN BEAT 'IM?
I'M PRETTY SURE YOU CAN. WHY?
IF MADARA WERE TO BATTLE KAOS AT PRESENT, HE WOULD SURELY BE DEFEATED.
HAKU-TAKU...
THUS FAR, YOU HAVE SUCCEEDED IN OVERCOMING YOUR ENEMIES BY USING YOUR POWERFUL GADGETS...BUT KAOS HAS GADGETS OF HIS OWN.
SO YOU'RE SAYIN' I CAN'T BEAT 'IM IF I RELY ON MY GADGETS?
THAT IS CORRECT. KAOS IS A MASTER OF THE MARTIAL ARTS--SO POWERFUL HE WAS ABLE TO KNOCK YOU UNCONSCIOUS WITH JUST ONE STRIKE.
YOU WILL NOT HAVE YOUR GADGETS FOREVER, MADARA. AS YOU RECOVER YOUR TRUE BODY PARTS, YOUR GADGETS WILL BE REPLACED. IF YOU RELY ON YOUR GADGETS ALONE, YOU WILL NOT BE ABLE TO DEFEAT THE MOKI.

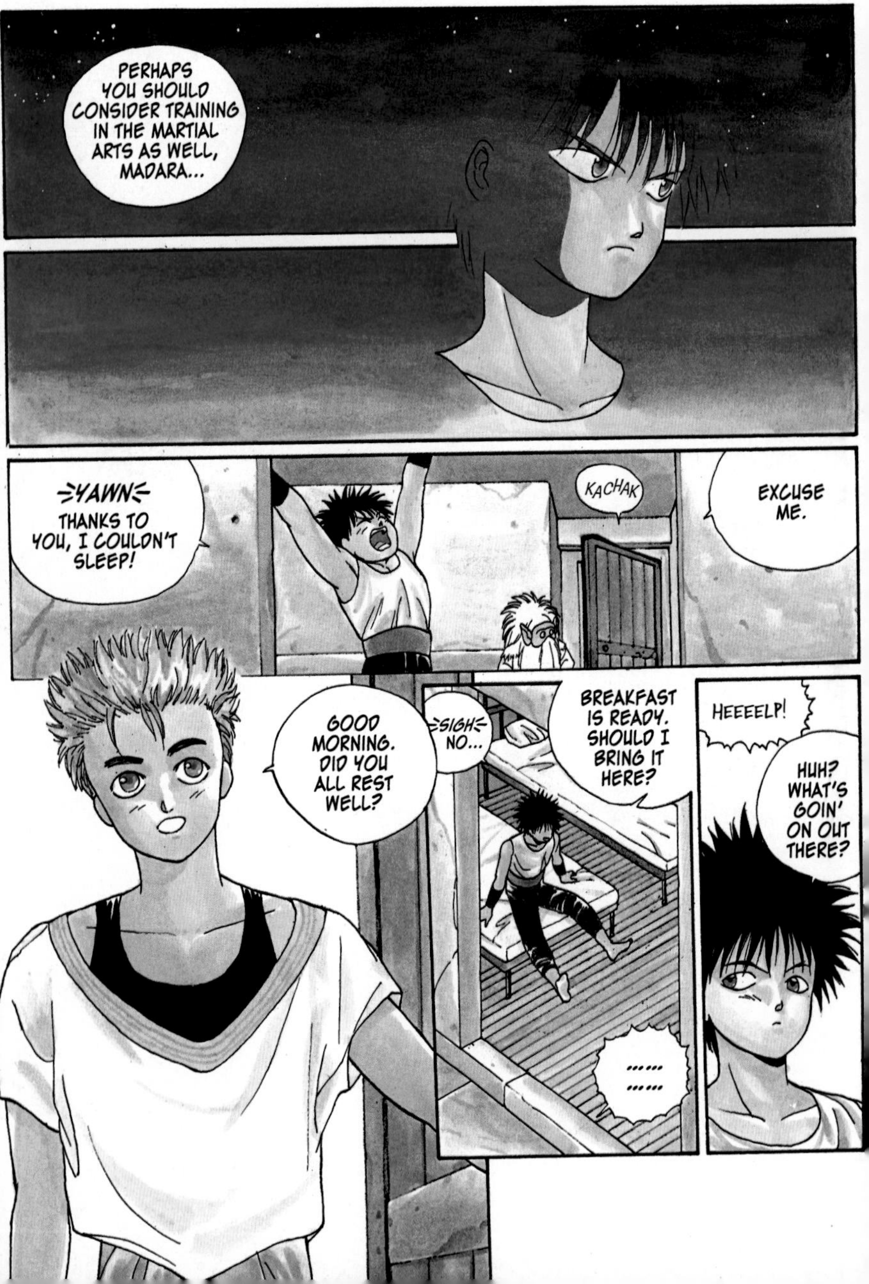
PERHAPS YOU SHOULD CONSIDER TRAINING IN THE MARTIAL ARTS AS WELL, MADARA...
=YAWN= THANKS TO YOU, I COULDN'T SLEEP!
KACHAK
EXCUSE ME.
GOOD MORNING. DID YOU ALL REST WELL?
=SIGH= NO...
BREAKFAST IS READY. SHOULD I BRING IT HERE?
......
......
HEEEELP!
HUH? WHAT'S GOIN' ON OUT THERE?

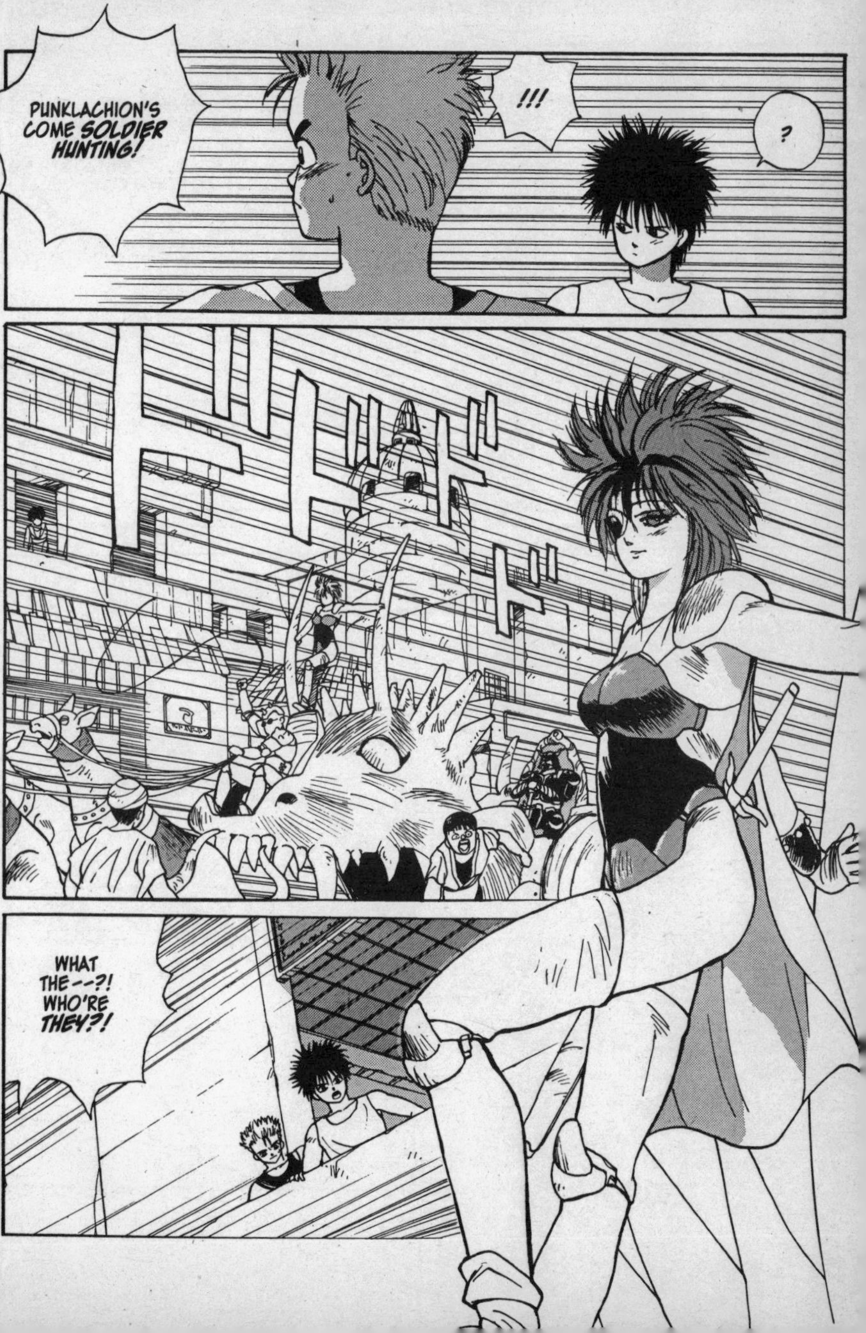
PUNKLACHION'S COME SOLDIER HUNTING!
!!!
?
ドドドド
WHAT THE--?! WHO'RE THEY?!

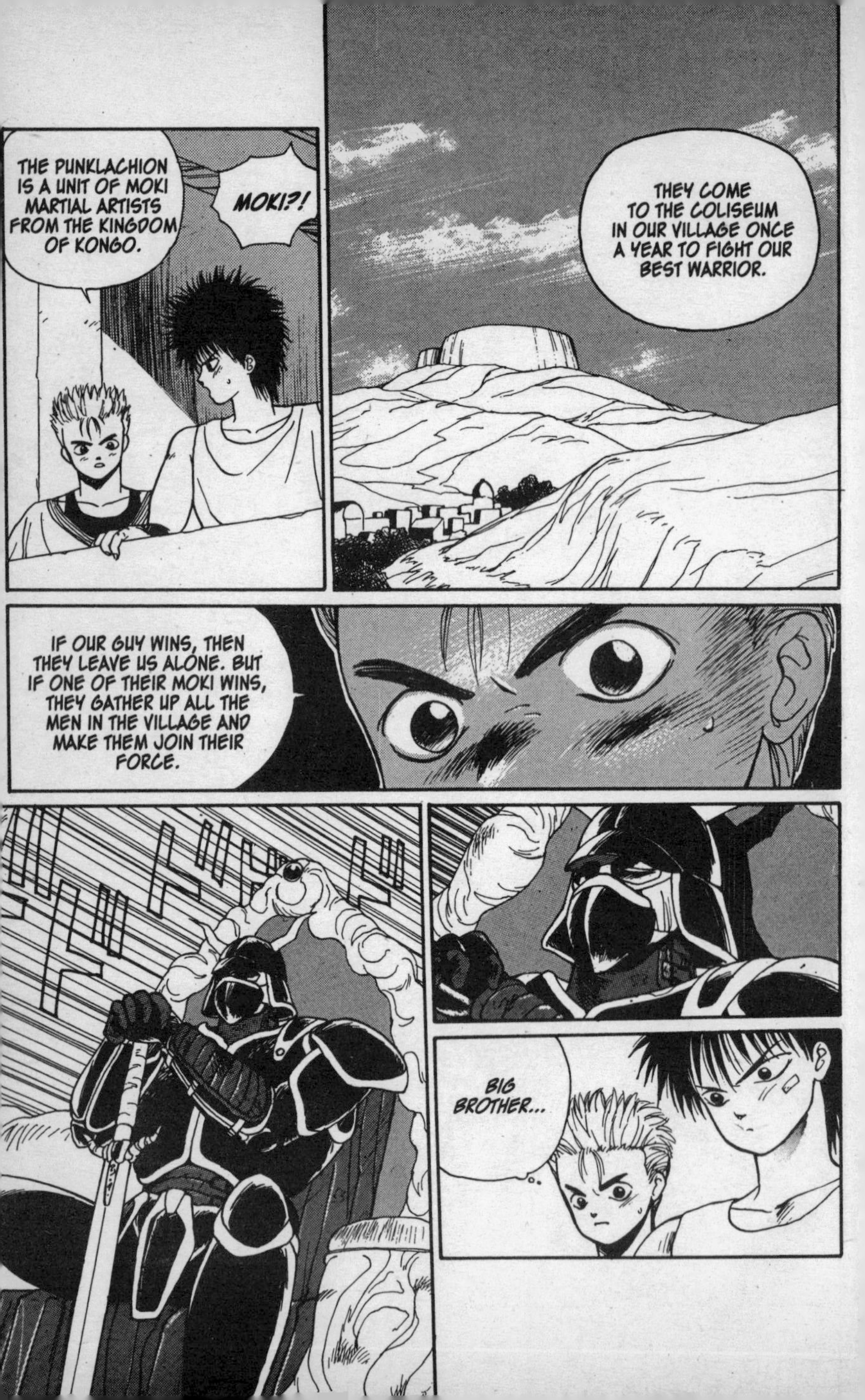
THE PUNKLACHION IS A UNIT OF MOKI MARTIAL ARTISTS FROM THE KINGDOM OF KONGO.
MOKI?!
THEY COME TO THE COLISEUM IN OUR VILLAGE ONCE A YEAR TO FIGHT OUR BEST WARRIOR.
IF OUR GUY WINS, THEN THEY LEAVE US ALONE. BUT IF ONE OF THEIR MOKI WINS, THEY GATHER UP ALL THE MEN IN THE VILLAGE AND MAKE THEM JOIN THEIR FORCE.
BIG BROTHER...

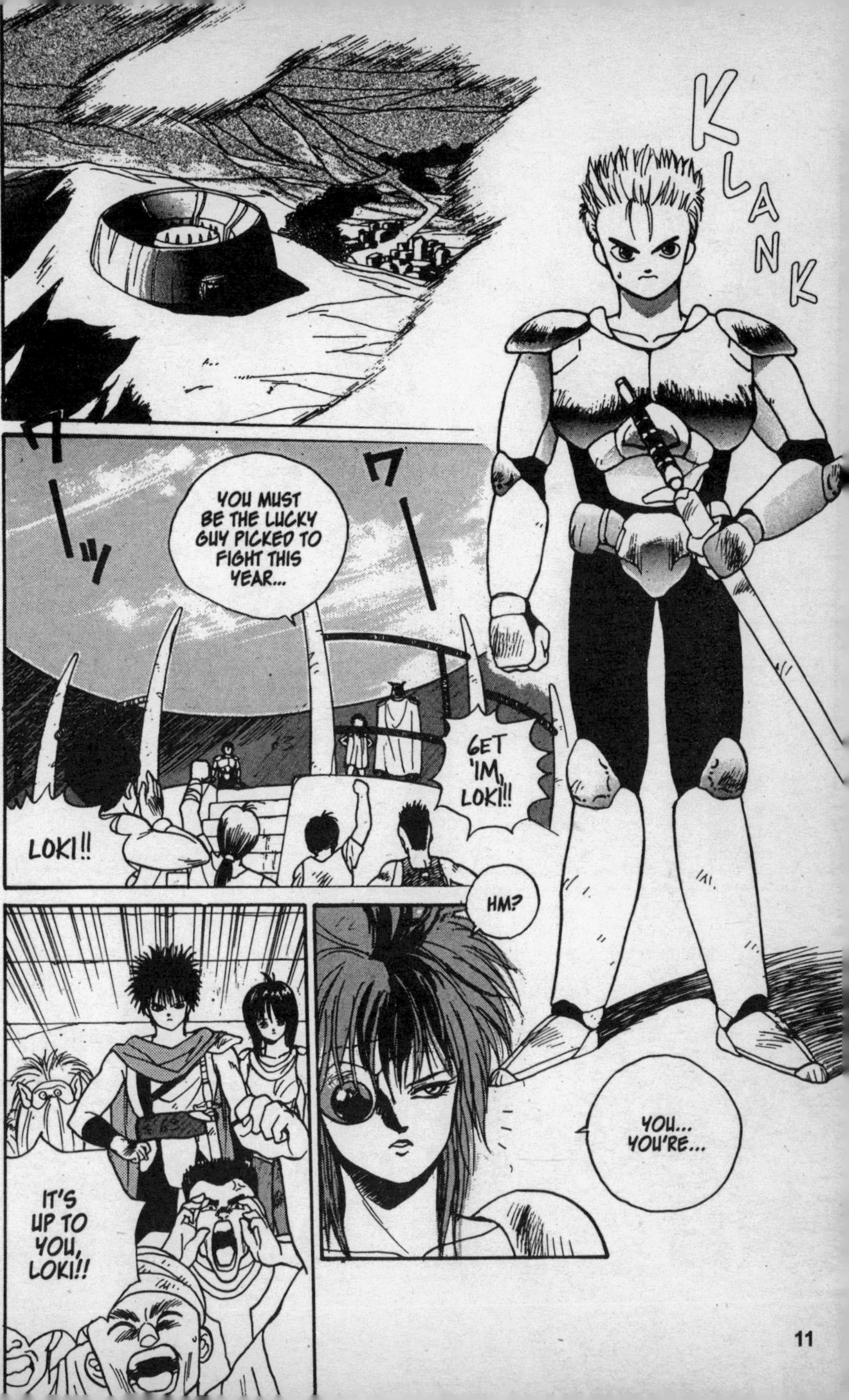
ワーッ
ワー
YOU MUST BE THE LUCKY GUY PICKED TO FIGHT THIS YEAR...
GET 'IM, LOKI!!
LOKI!!
IT'S UP TO YOU, LOKI!!
HM?
KLANK
YOU... YOU'RE...

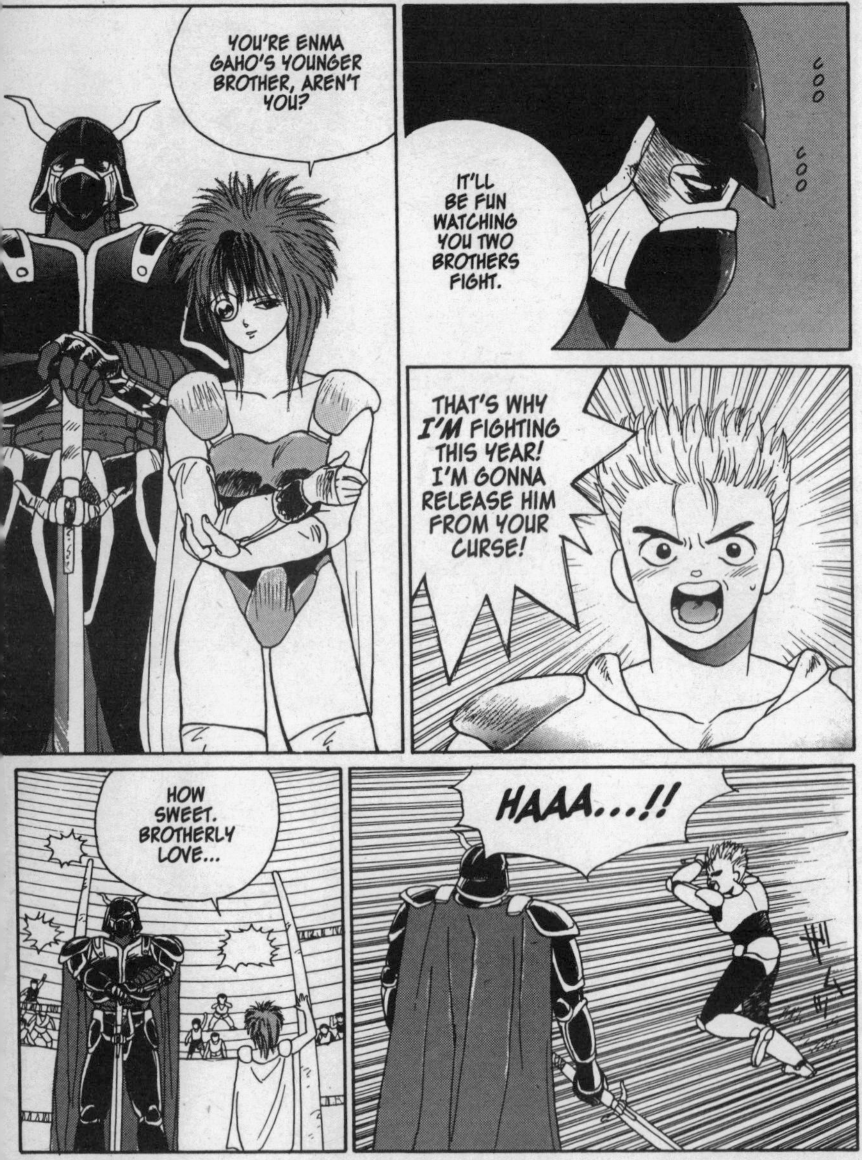
YOU'RE ENMA GAHO'S YOUNGER BROTHER, AREN'T YOU?
COO
COO
IT'LL BE FUN WATCHING YOU TWO BROTHERS FIGHT.
THAT'S WHY *I'M* FIGHTING THIS YEAR! I'M GONNA RELEASE HIM FROM YOUR CURSE!
HOW SWEET. BROTHERLY LOVE...
HAAA...!!

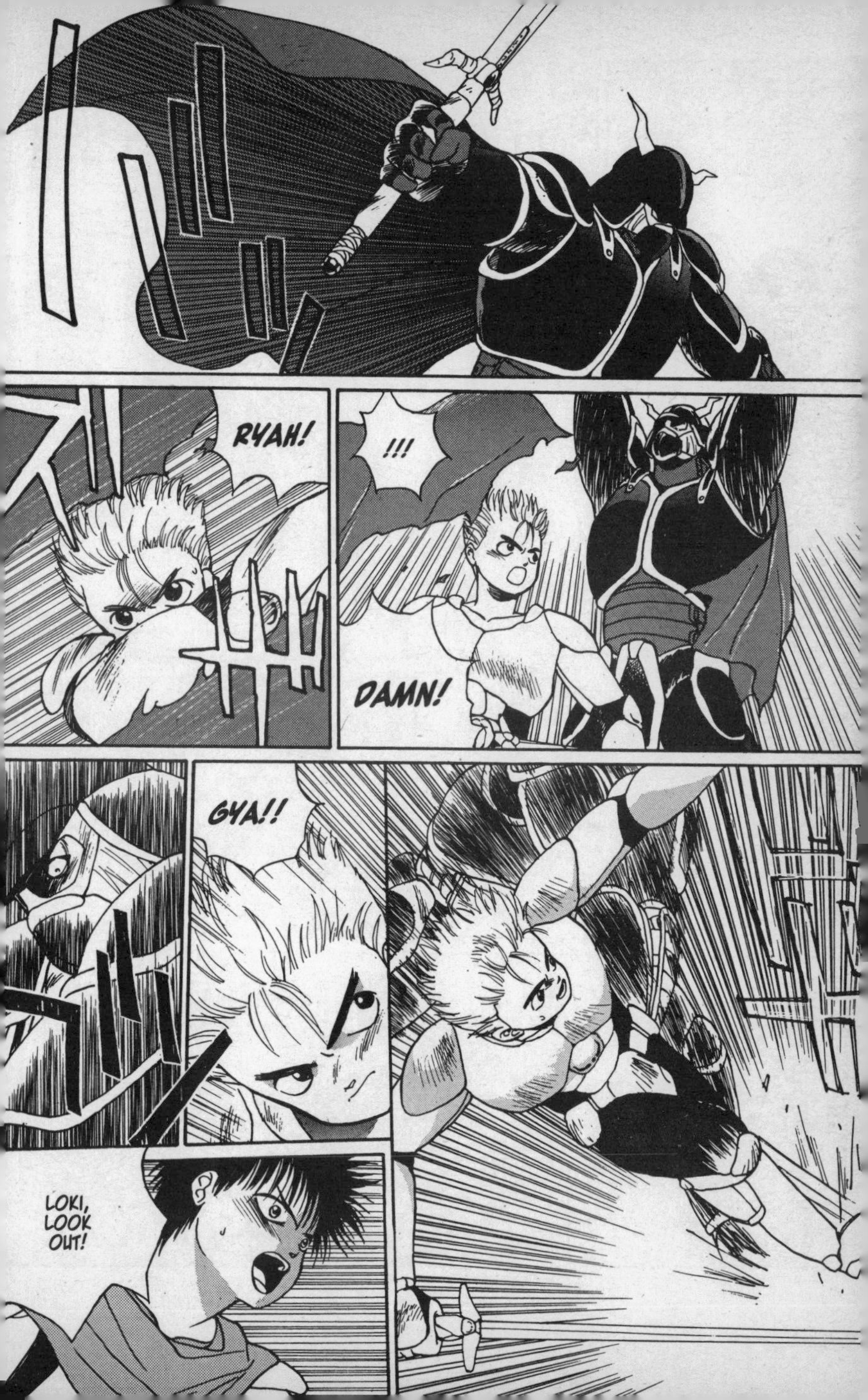
RYAH!
!!!
DAMN!
GYA!!
LOKI, LOOK OUT!

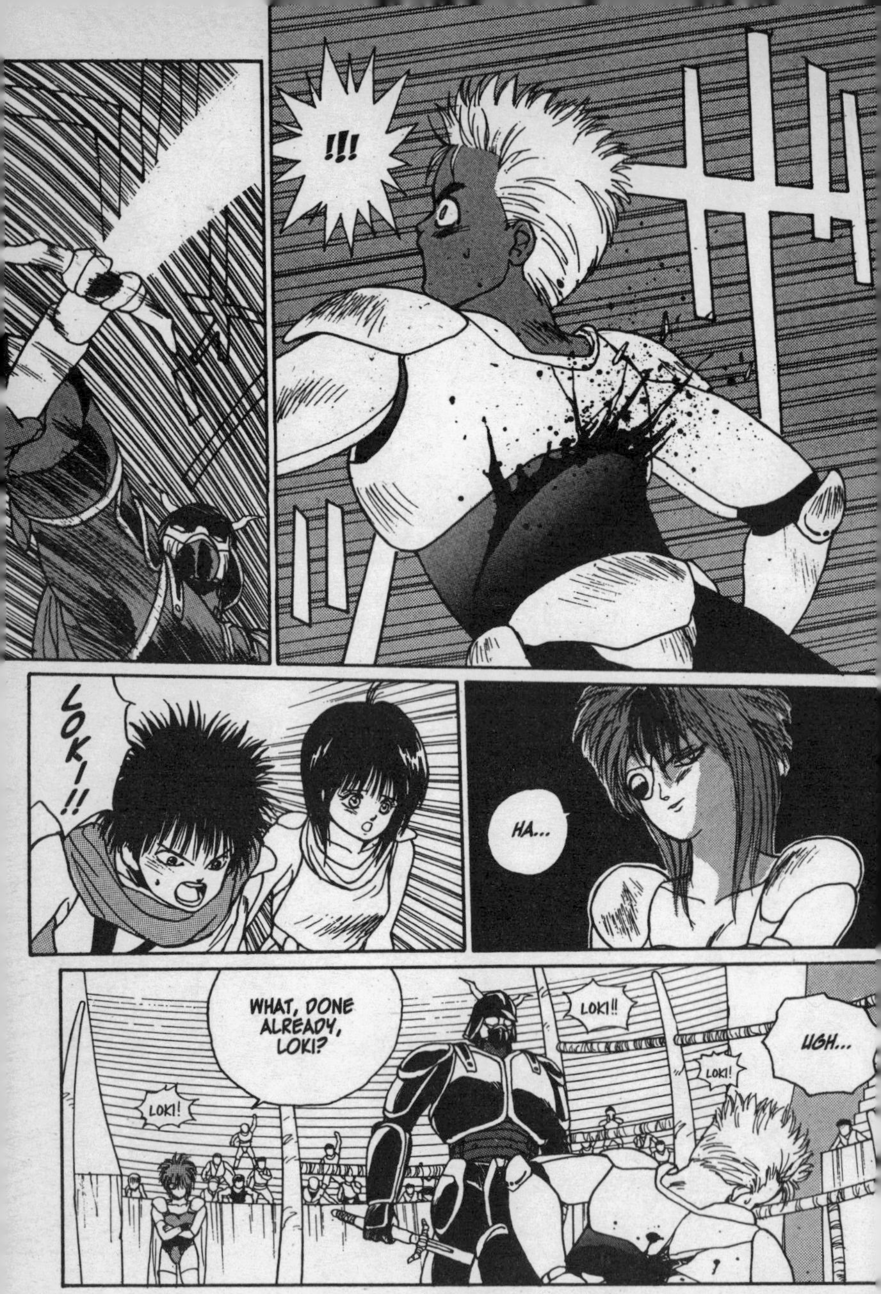

!!!
LOKI!!
HA...
WHAT, DONE ALREADY, LOKI?
LOKI!
LOKI!!
LOKI!
UGH...

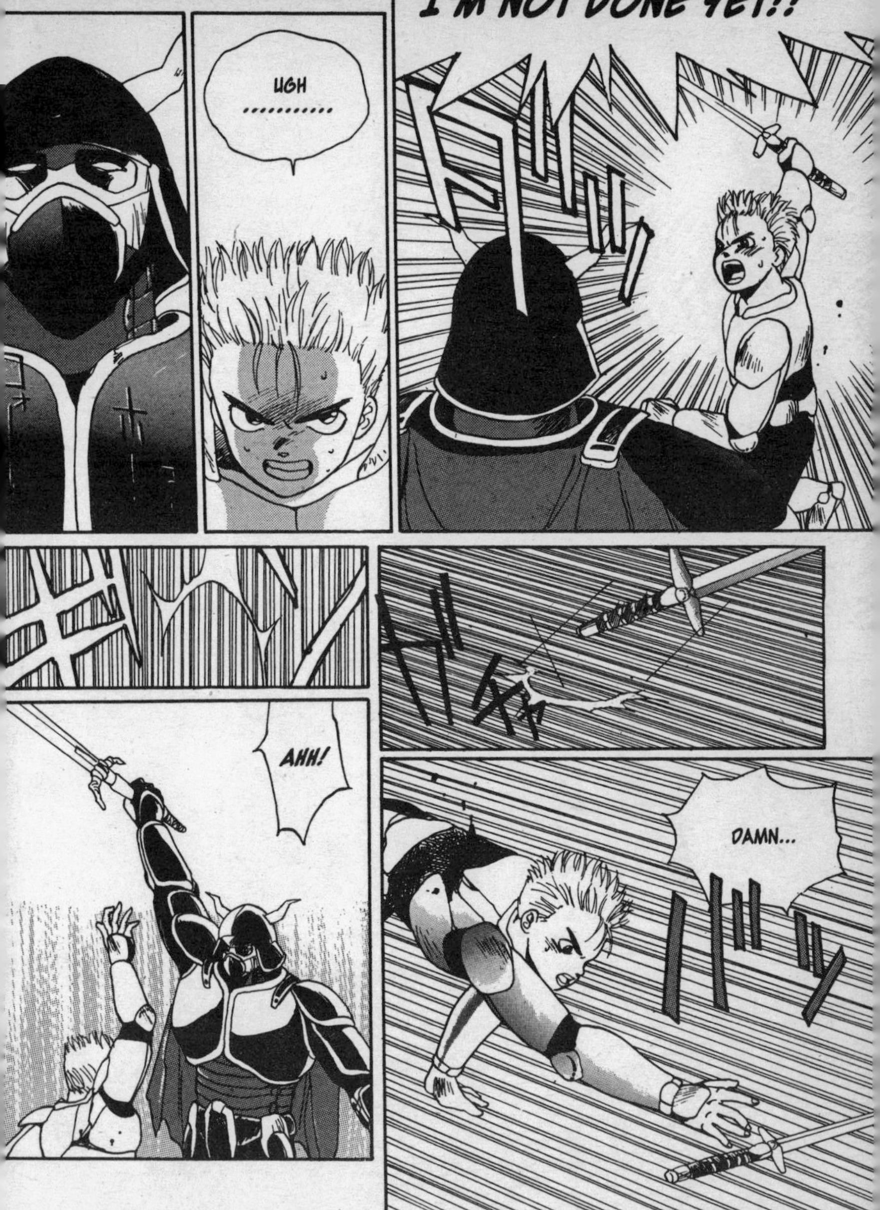
UGH ....
I'M NOT DONE YET!!
AHH!
DAMN...

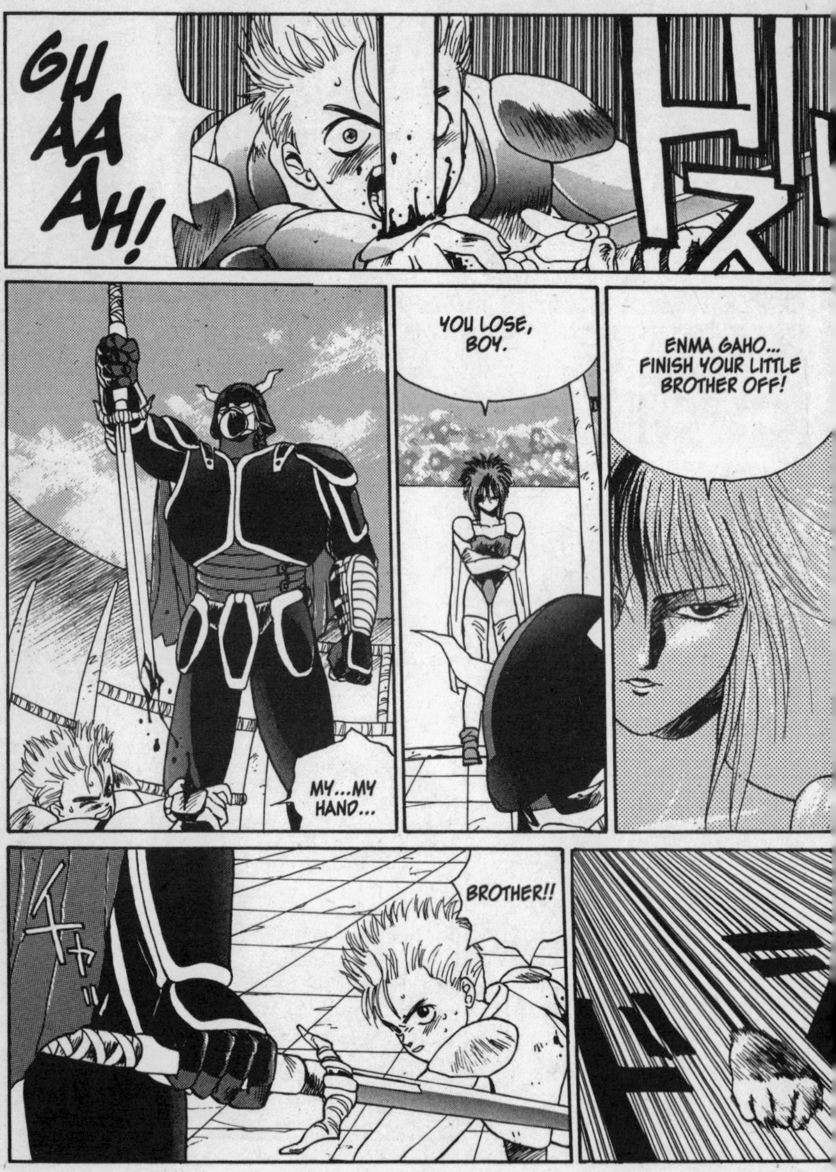
GUAAAH!
MY...MY HAND...
YOU LOSE, BOY.
ENMA GAHO... FINISH YOUR LITTLE BROTHER OFF!
BROTHER!!

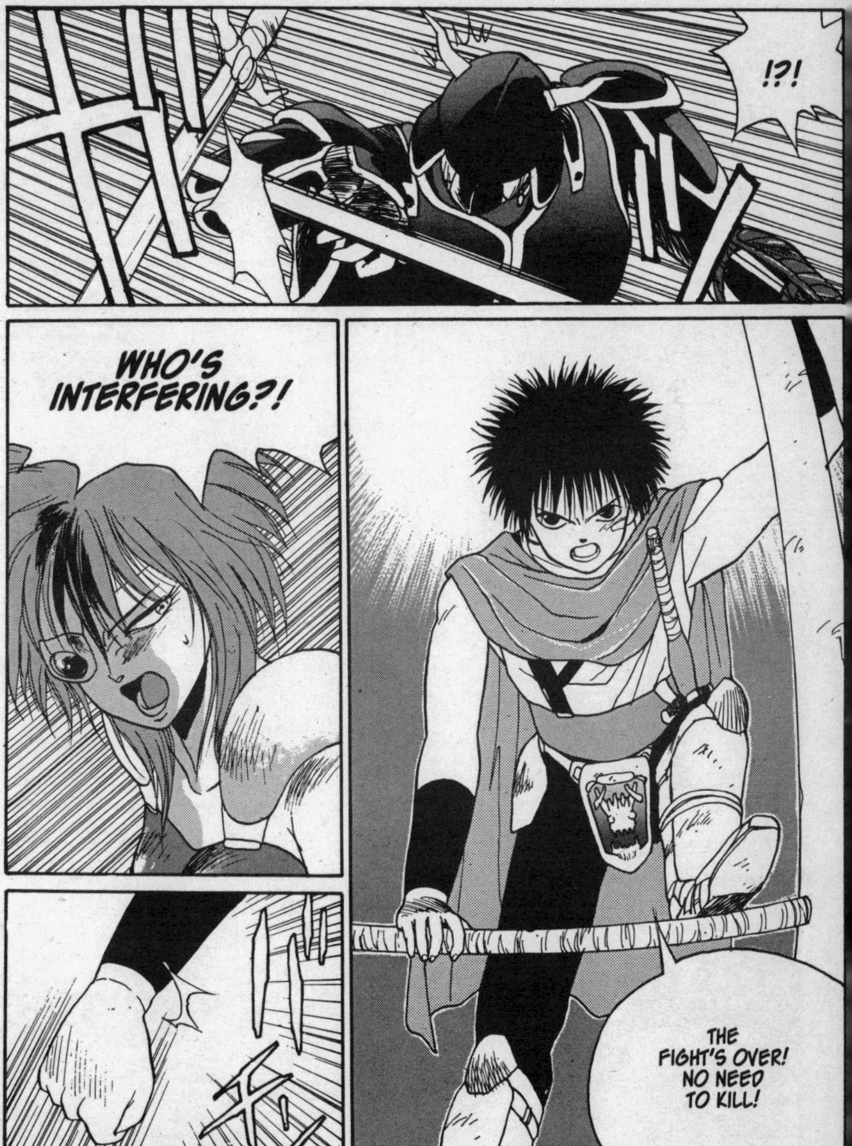
!?!
WHO'S INTERFERING?!
THE FIGHT'S OVER! NO NEED TO KILL!

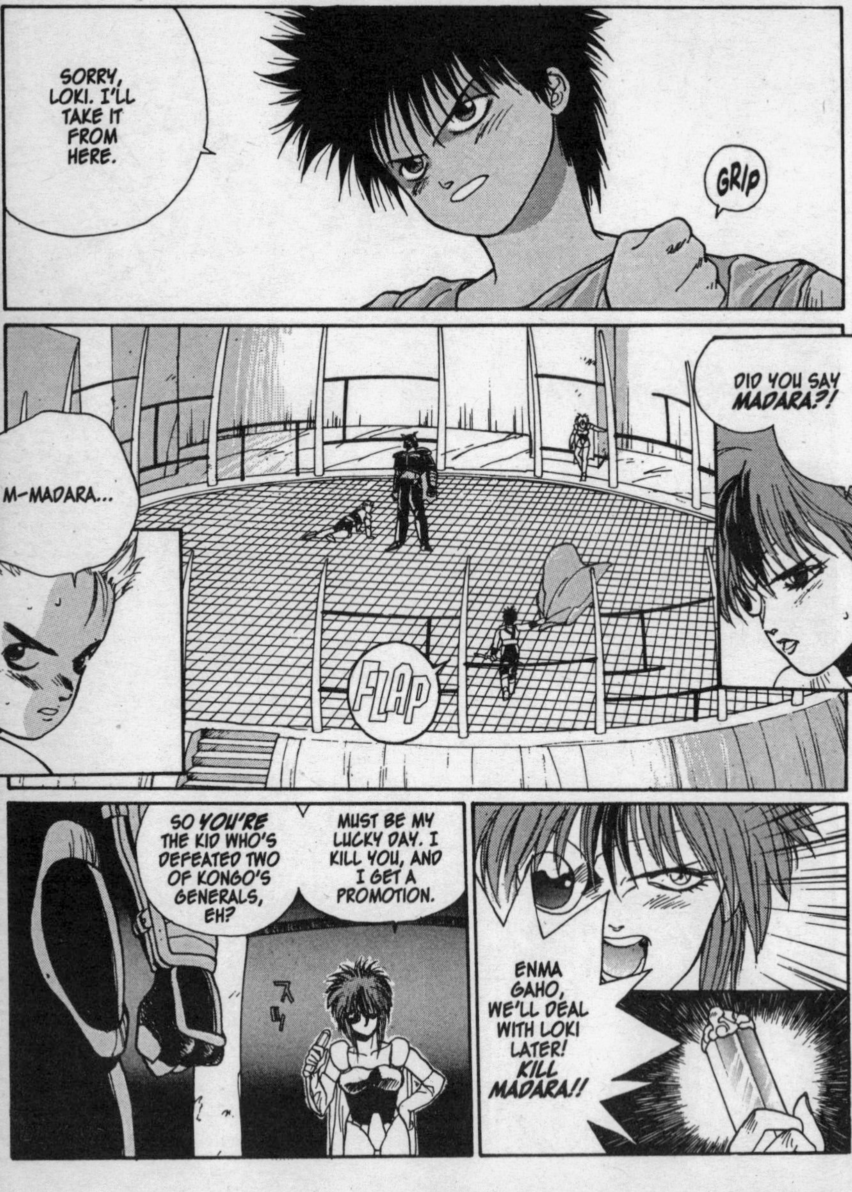

SORRY, LOKI. I'LL TAKE IT FROM HERE.
GRIP
M-MADARA...
FLAP
DID YOU SAY *MADARA?!*
SO *YOU'RE* THE KID WHO'S DEFEATED TWO OF KONGO'S GENERALS, EH?
MUST BE MY LUCKY DAY. I KILL YOU, AND I GET A PROMOTION.
ENMA GAHO, WE'LL DEAL WITH LOKI LATER! *KILL MADARA!!*

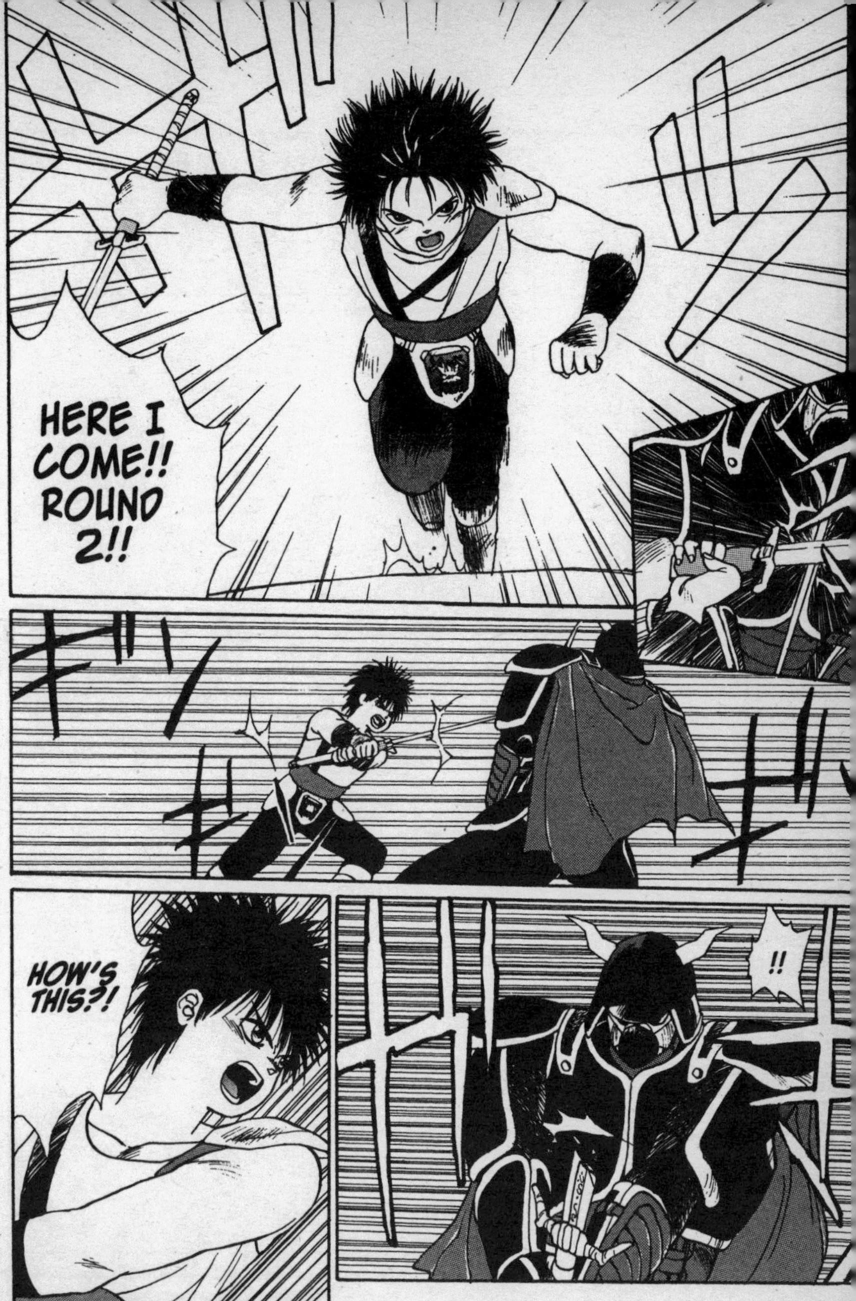
HERE I COME!! ROUND 2!!
HOW'S THIS?!
!!

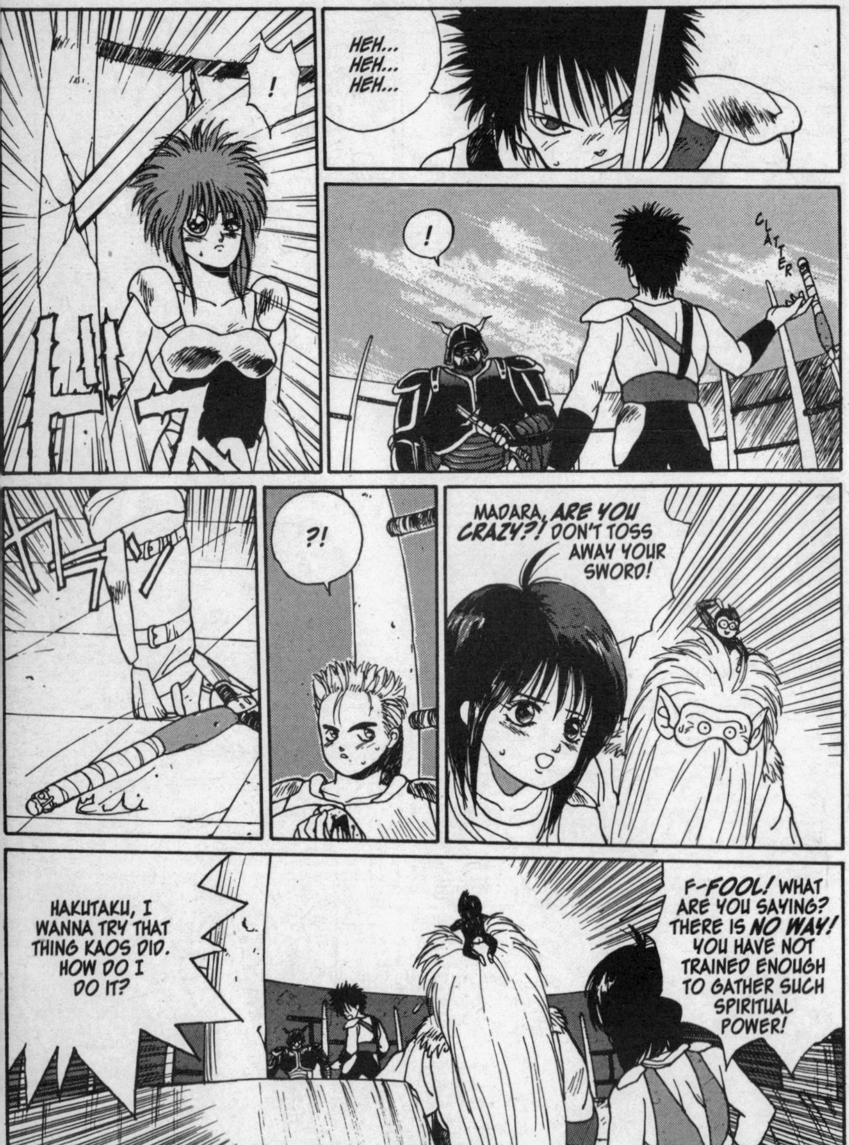
!
HEH... HEH... HEH...
!
CLATTER
?!
MADARA, ARE YOU CRAZY?! DON'T TOSS AWAY YOUR SWORD!
HAKUTAKU, I WANNA TRY THAT THING KAOS DID. HOW DO I DO IT?
F-FOOL! WHAT ARE YOU SAYING? THERE IS NO WAY! YOU HAVE NOT TRAINED ENOUGH TO GATHER SUCH SPIRITUAL POWER!

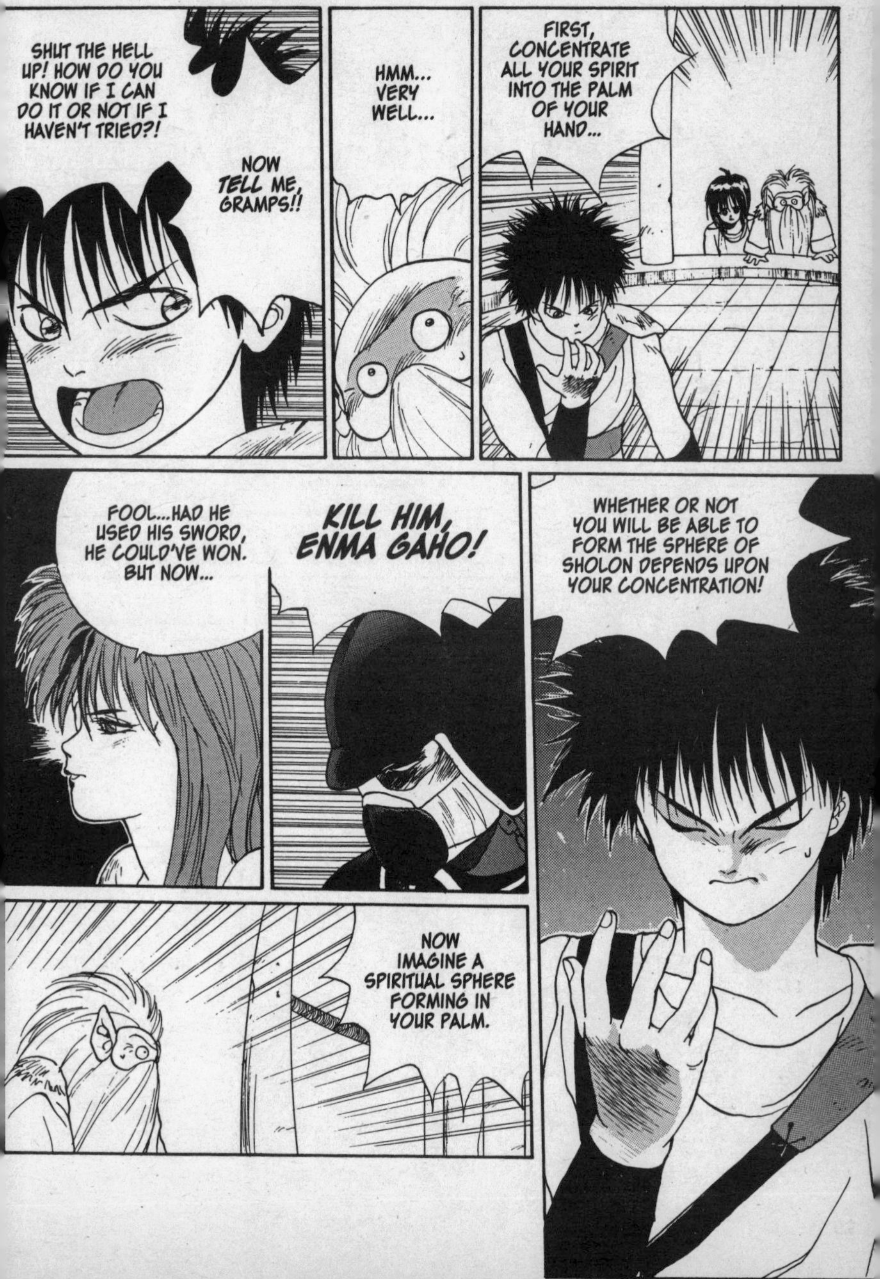
SHUT THE HELL UP! HOW DO YOU KNOW IF I CAN DO IT OR NOT IF I HAVEN'T TRIED?!
NOW TELL ME, GRAMPS!!
HMM... VERY WELL...
FIRST, CONCENTRATE ALL YOUR SPIRIT INTO THE PALM OF YOUR HAND...
FOOL...HAD HE USED HIS SWORD, HE COULD'VE WON. BUT NOW...
KILL HIM, ENMA GAHO!
NOW IMAGINE A SPIRITUAL SPHERE FORMING IN YOUR PALM.
WHETHER OR NOT YOU WILL BE ABLE TO FORM THE SPHERE OF SHOLON DEPENDS UPON YOUR CONCENTRATION!

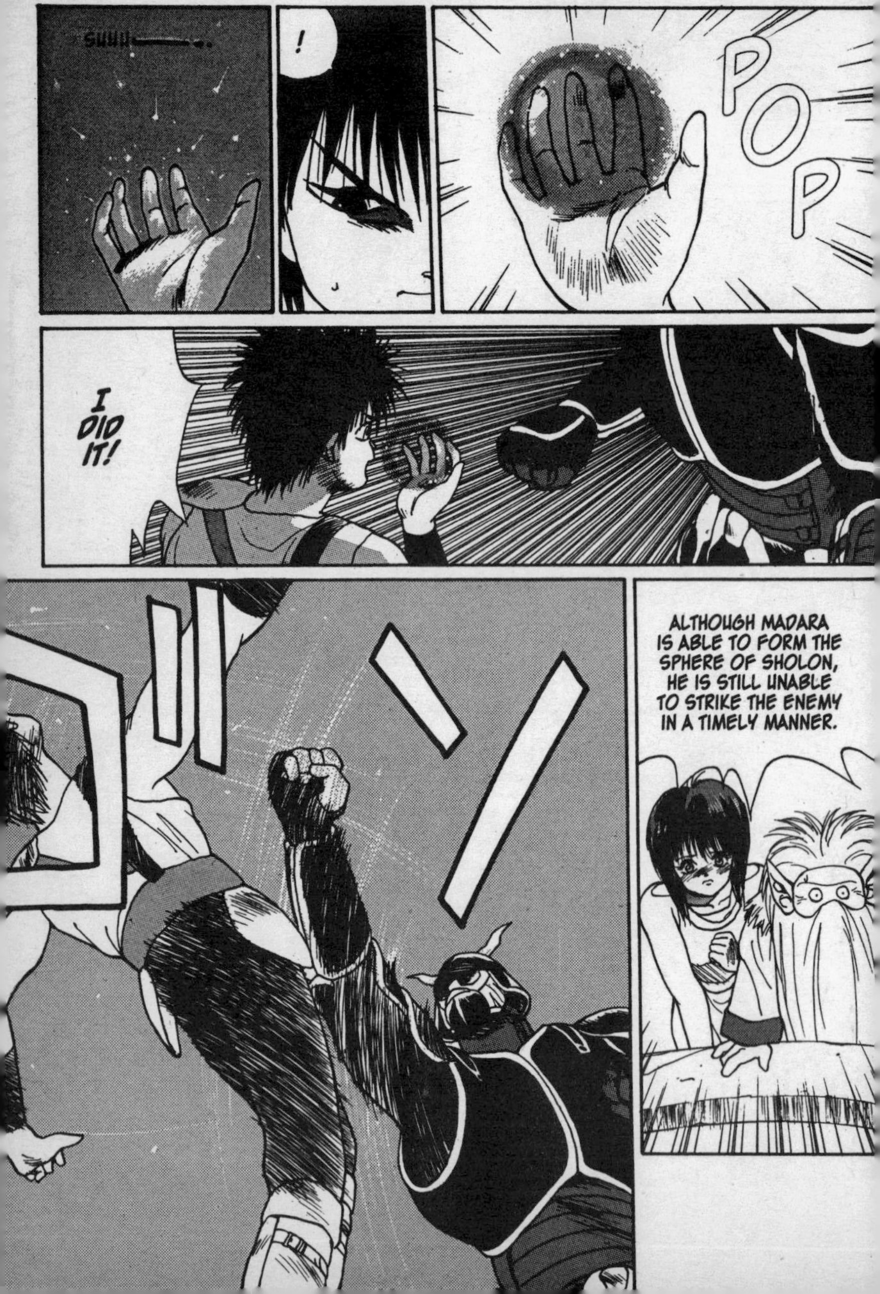
SHUHH———…
!
POP
I DID IT!
ALTHOUGH MADARA IS ABLE TO FORM THE SPHERE OF SHOLON, HE IS STILL UNABLE TO STRIKE THE ENEMY IN A TIMELY MANNER.

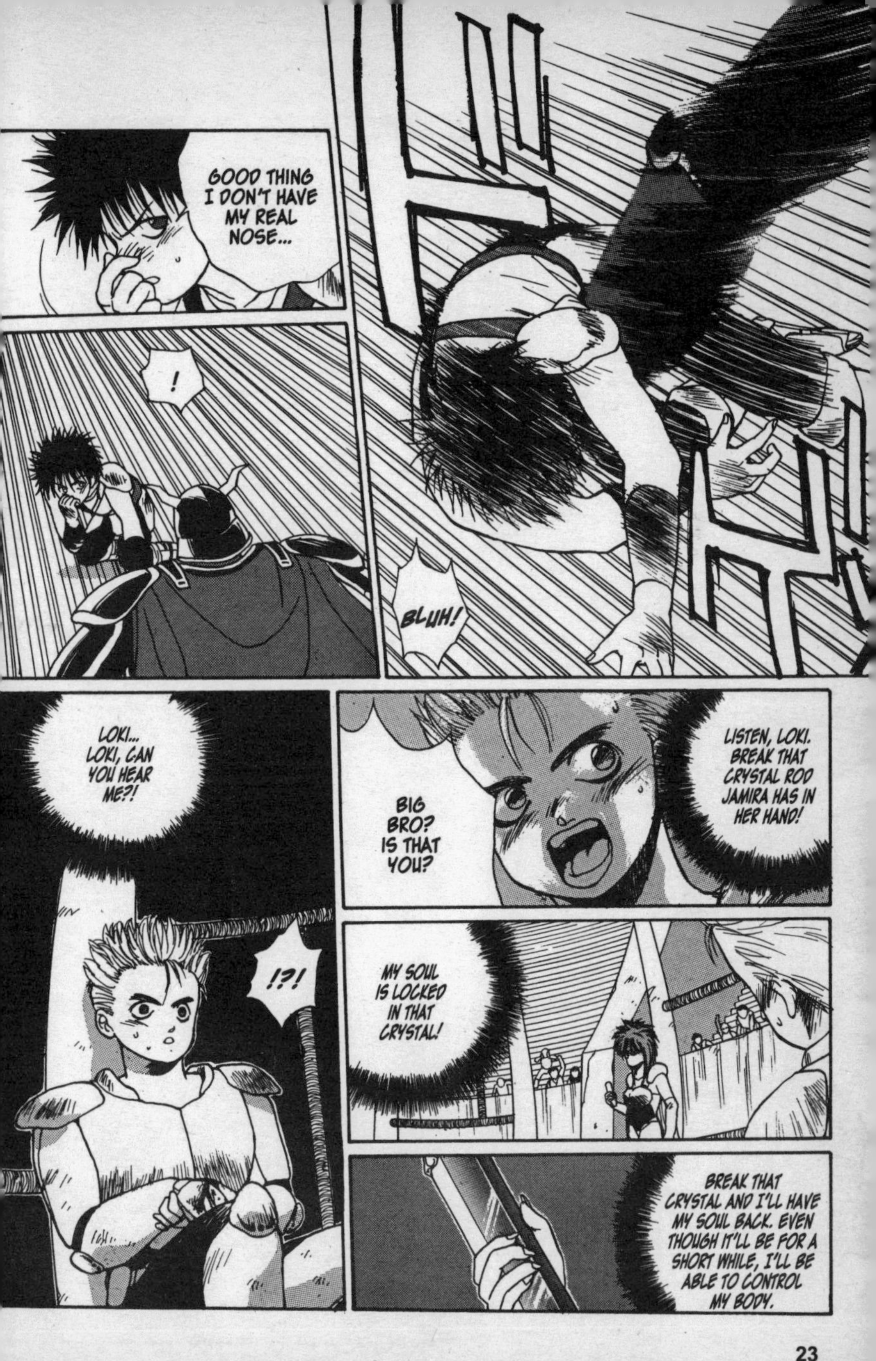
GOOD THING I DON'T HAVE MY REAL NOSE...
!
BLUH!
LOKI... LOKI, CAN YOU HEAR ME?!
!?!
BIG BRO? IS THAT YOU?
LISTEN, LOKI. BREAK THAT CRYSTAL ROD JAMIRA HAS IN HER HAND!
MY SOUL IS LOCKED IN THAT CRYSTAL!
BREAK THAT CRYSTAL AND I'LL HAVE MY SOUL BACK. EVEN THOUGH IT'LL BE FOR A SHORT WHILE, I'LL BE ABLE TO CONTROL MY BODY.

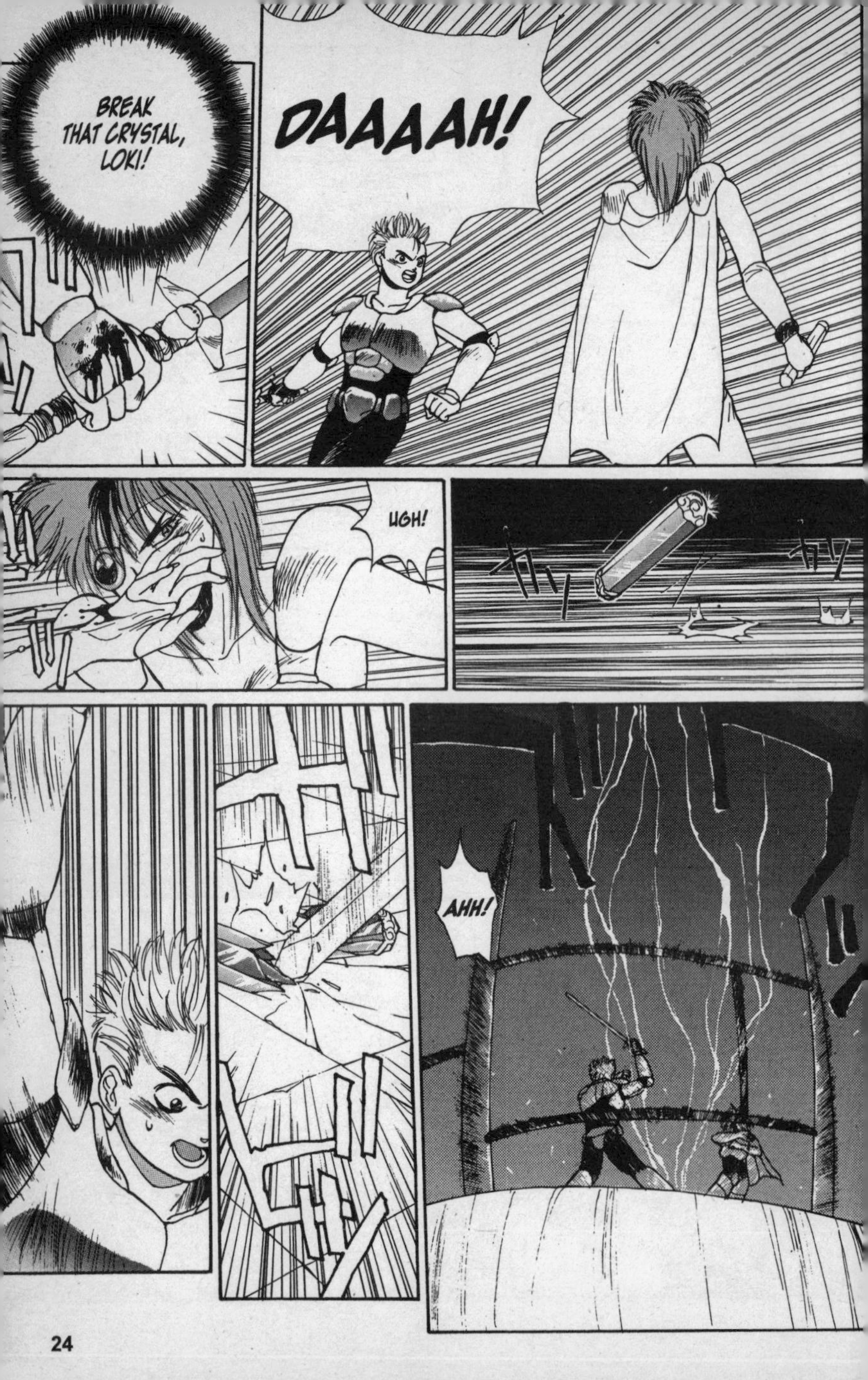
BREAK THAT CRYSTAL, LOKI!
DAAAAH!
UGH!
AHH!

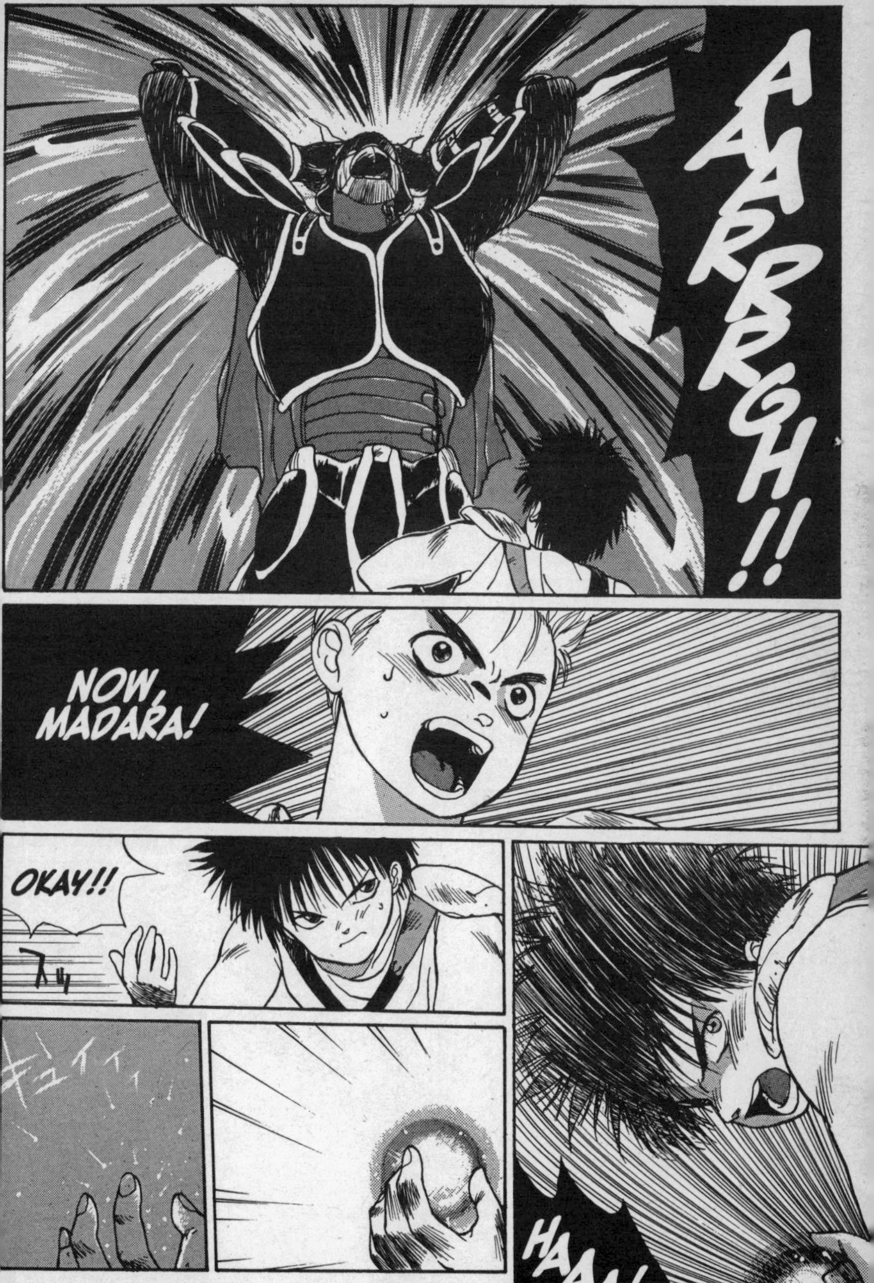
AARRRGH!!
NOW, MADARA!
OKAY!!
スッ
キュイイ
HAAAA!

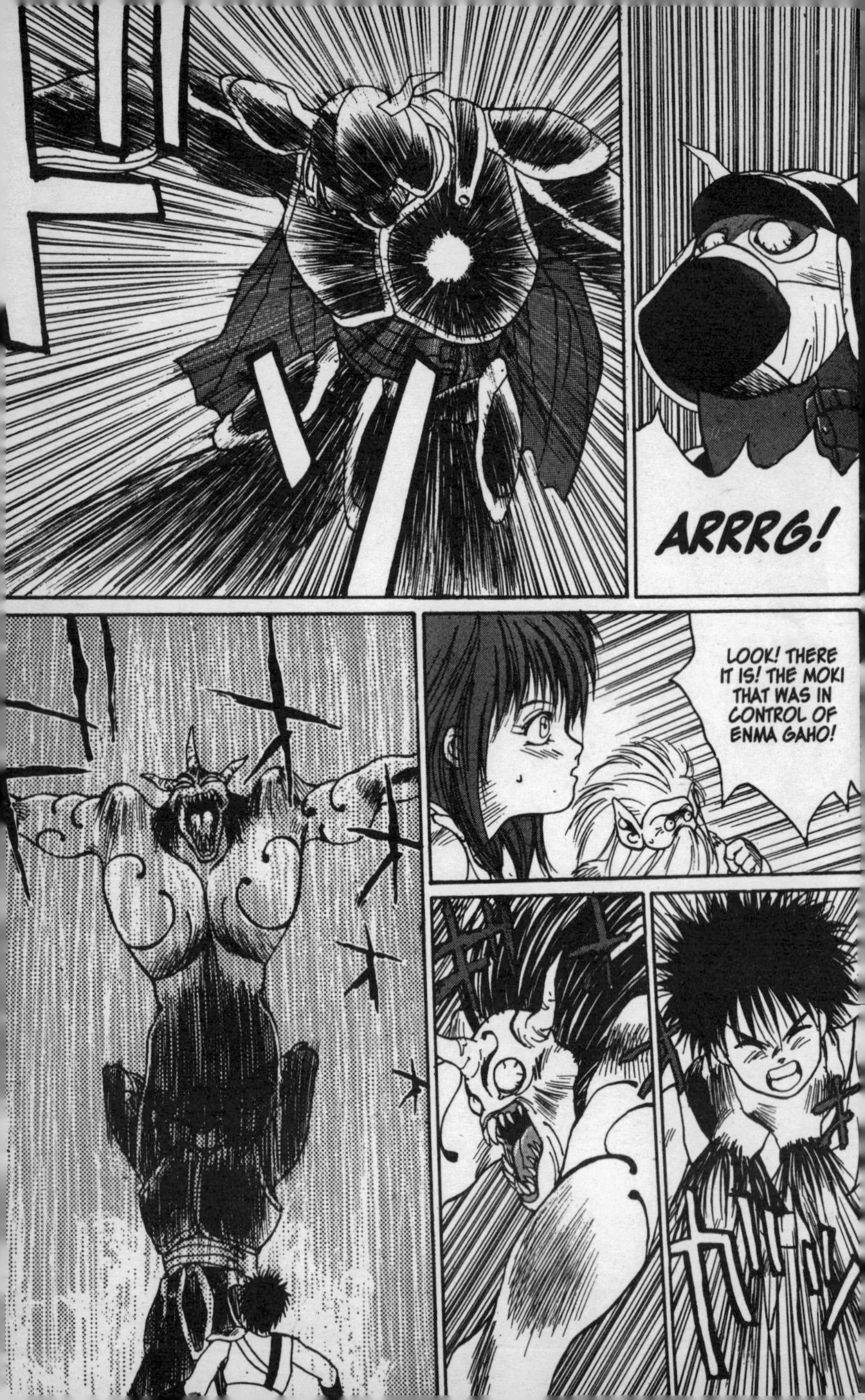
ARRRG!
LOOK! THERE IT IS! THE MOKI THAT WAS IN CONTROL OF ENMA GAHO!

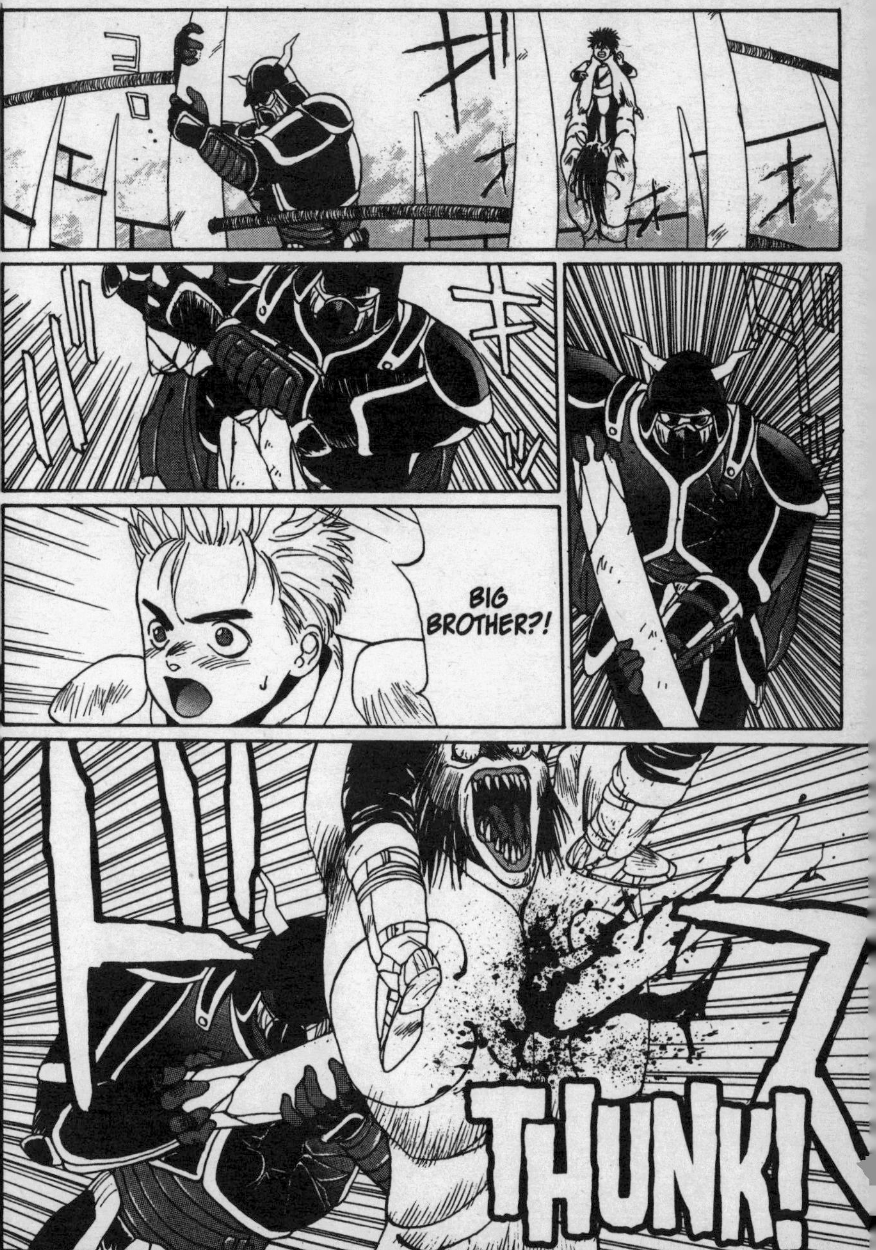
BIG BROTHER?!
THUNK!

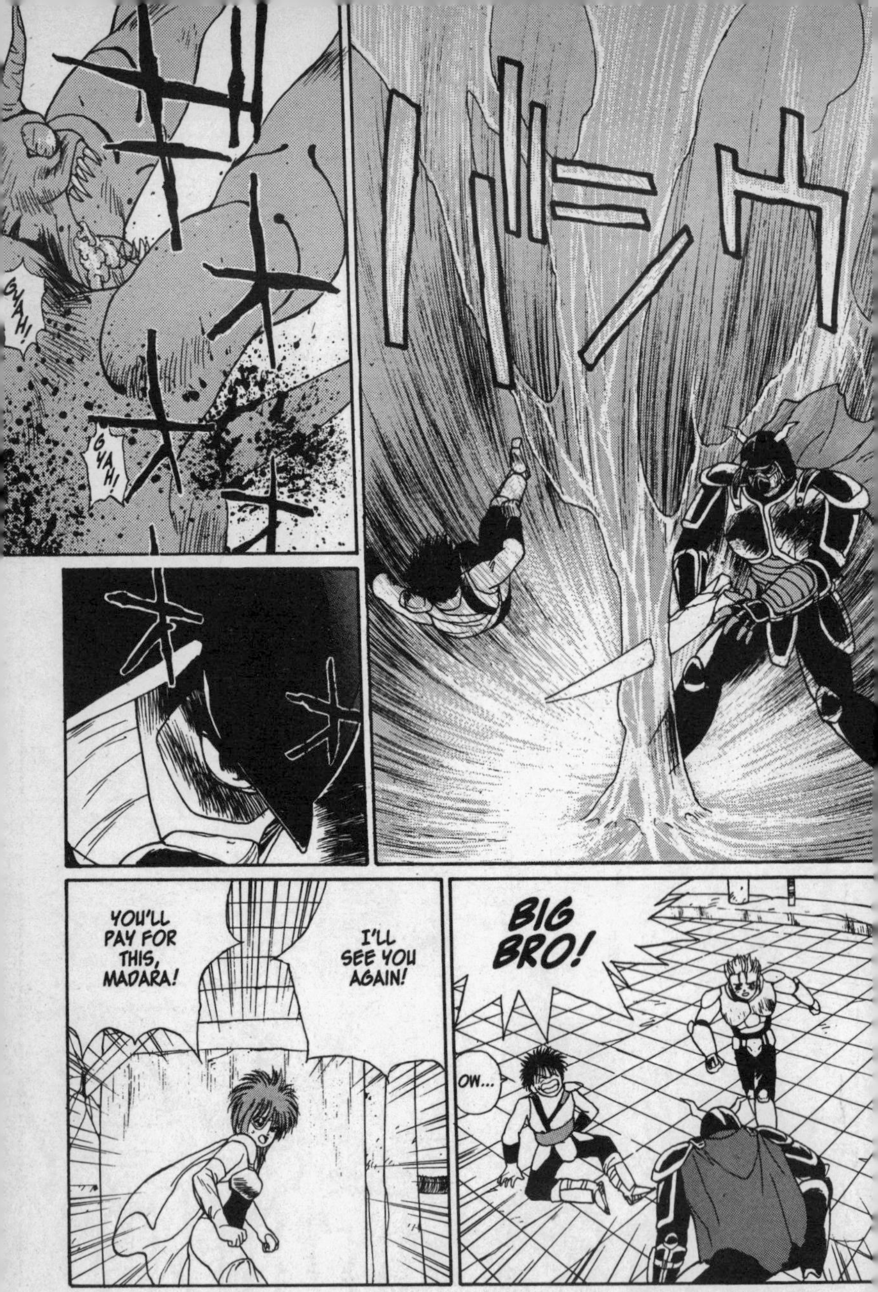
GYAH!
GYAH!
YOU'LL PAY FOR THIS, MADARA!
I'LL SEE YOU AGAIN!
BIG BRO!
OW...

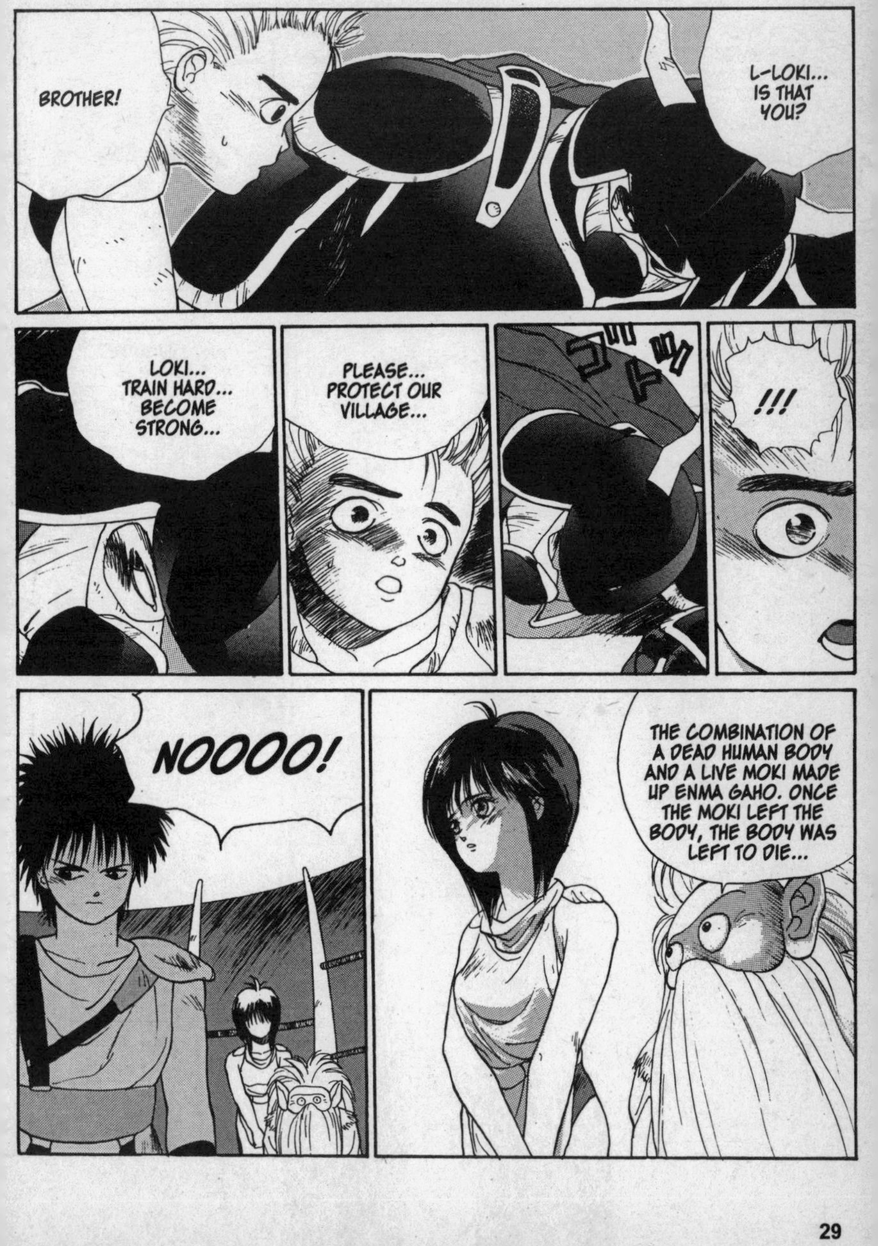
BROTHER!
L-LOKI... IS THAT YOU?
LOKI... TRAIN HARD... BECOME STRONG...
PLEASE... PROTECT OUR VILLAGE...
ゴトッ
!!!
NOOOO!
THE COMBINATION OF A DEAD HUMAN BODY AND A LIVE MOKI MADE UP ENMA GAHO. ONCE THE MOKI LEFT THE BODY, THE BODY WAS LEFT TO DIE...

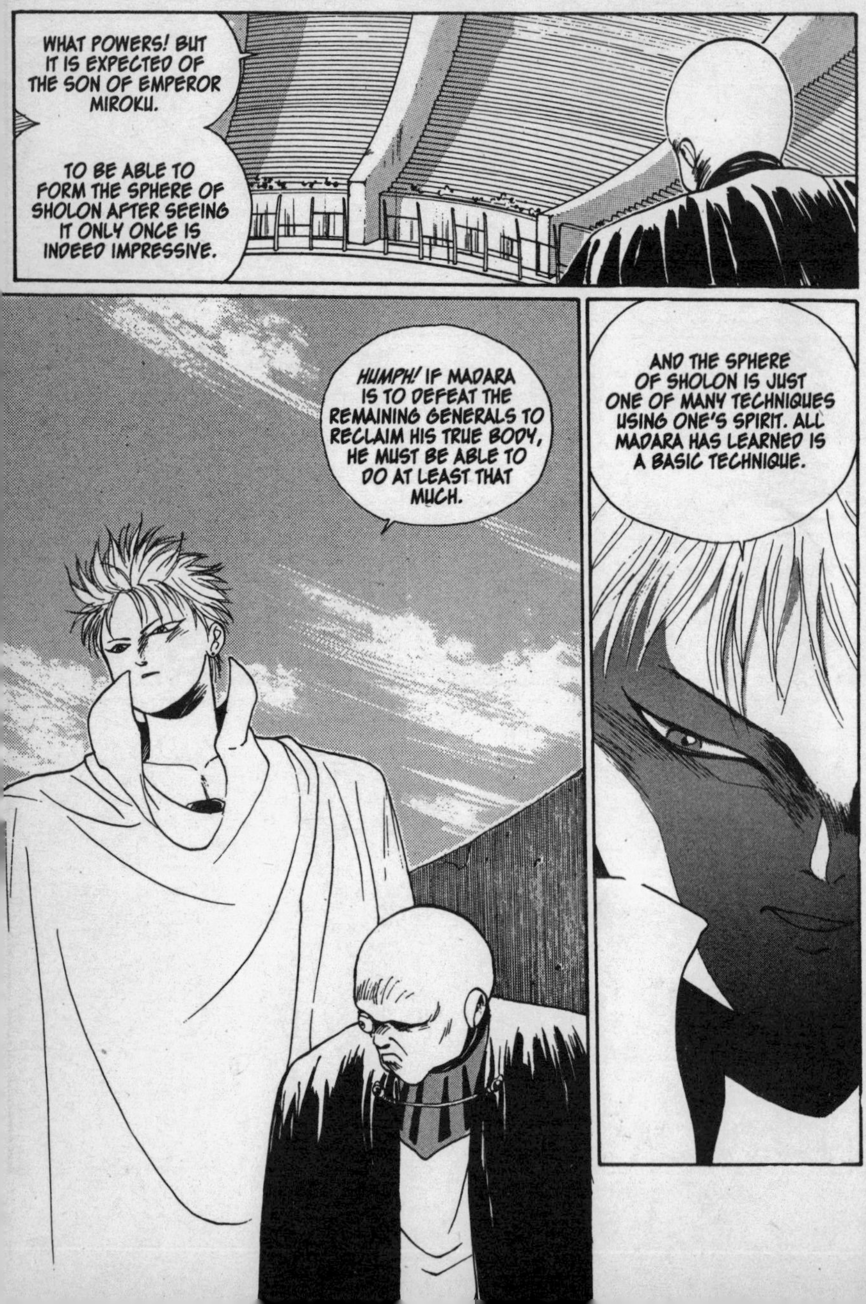
WHAT POWERS! BUT IT IS EXPECTED OF THE SON OF EMPEROR MIROKU.
TO BE ABLE TO FORM THE SPHERE OF SHOLON AFTER SEEING IT ONLY ONCE IS INDEED IMPRESSIVE.
HUMPH! IF MADARA IS TO DEFEAT THE REMAINING GENERALS TO RECLAIM HIS TRUE BODY, HE MUST BE ABLE TO DO AT LEAST THAT MUCH.
AND THE SPHERE OF SHOLON IS JUST ONE OF MANY TECHNIQUES USING ONE'S SPIRIT. ALL MADARA HAS LEARNED IS A BASIC TECHNIQUE.

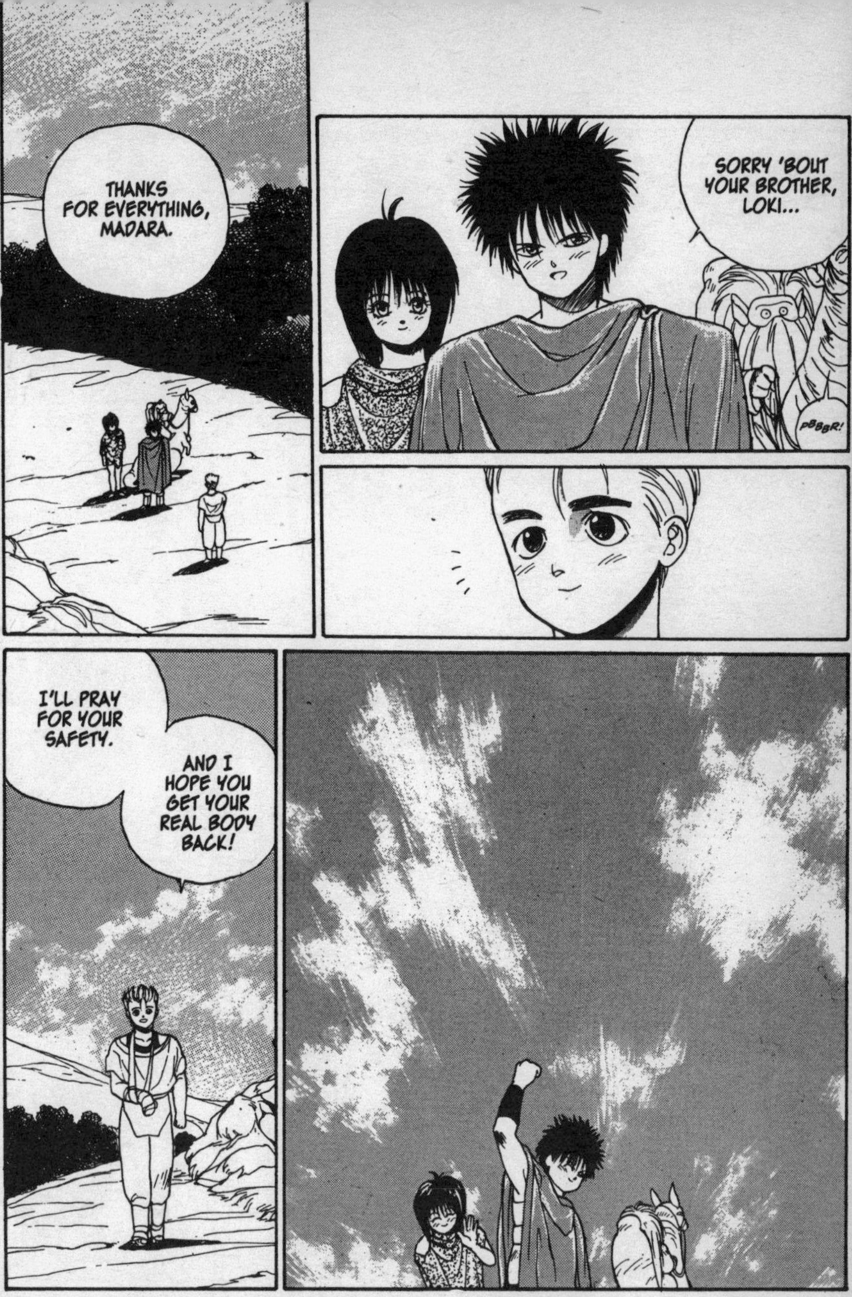
THANKS FOR EVERYTHING, MADARA.
SORRY 'BOUT YOUR BROTHER, LOKI...
PBBBR!
I'LL PRAY FOR YOUR SAFETY.
AND I HOPE YOU GET YOUR REAL BODY BACK!

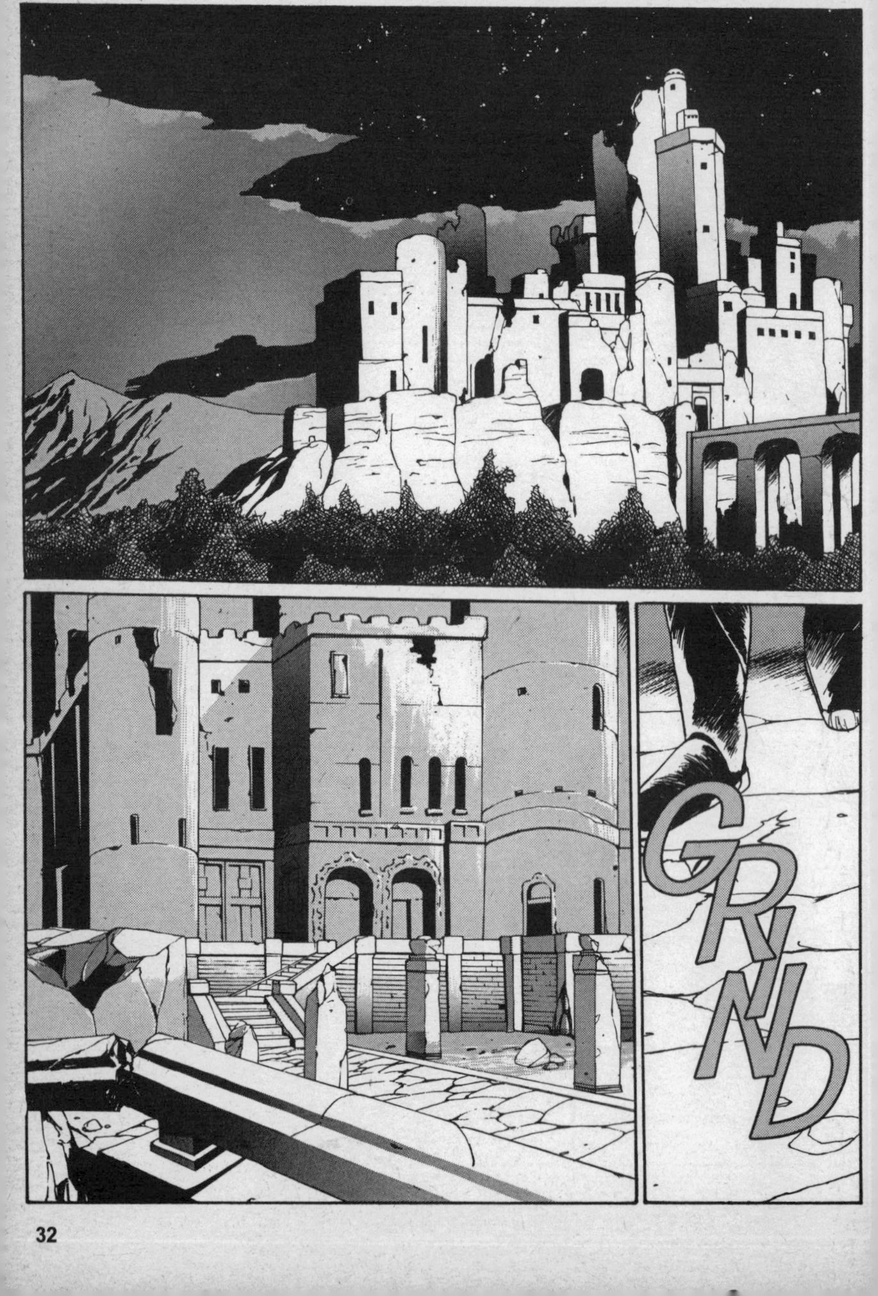
GRIND

第三章 相克譚

Chapter 3: **The Tale of the Rivalry**

"In the Home of the Sleeping Gods, he who
opens the gates to the Holy Land of Agartha shall
surpass the deities, the demons and mankind to
become the true ruler of all."

– A Foretelling of the Divine Ikoze

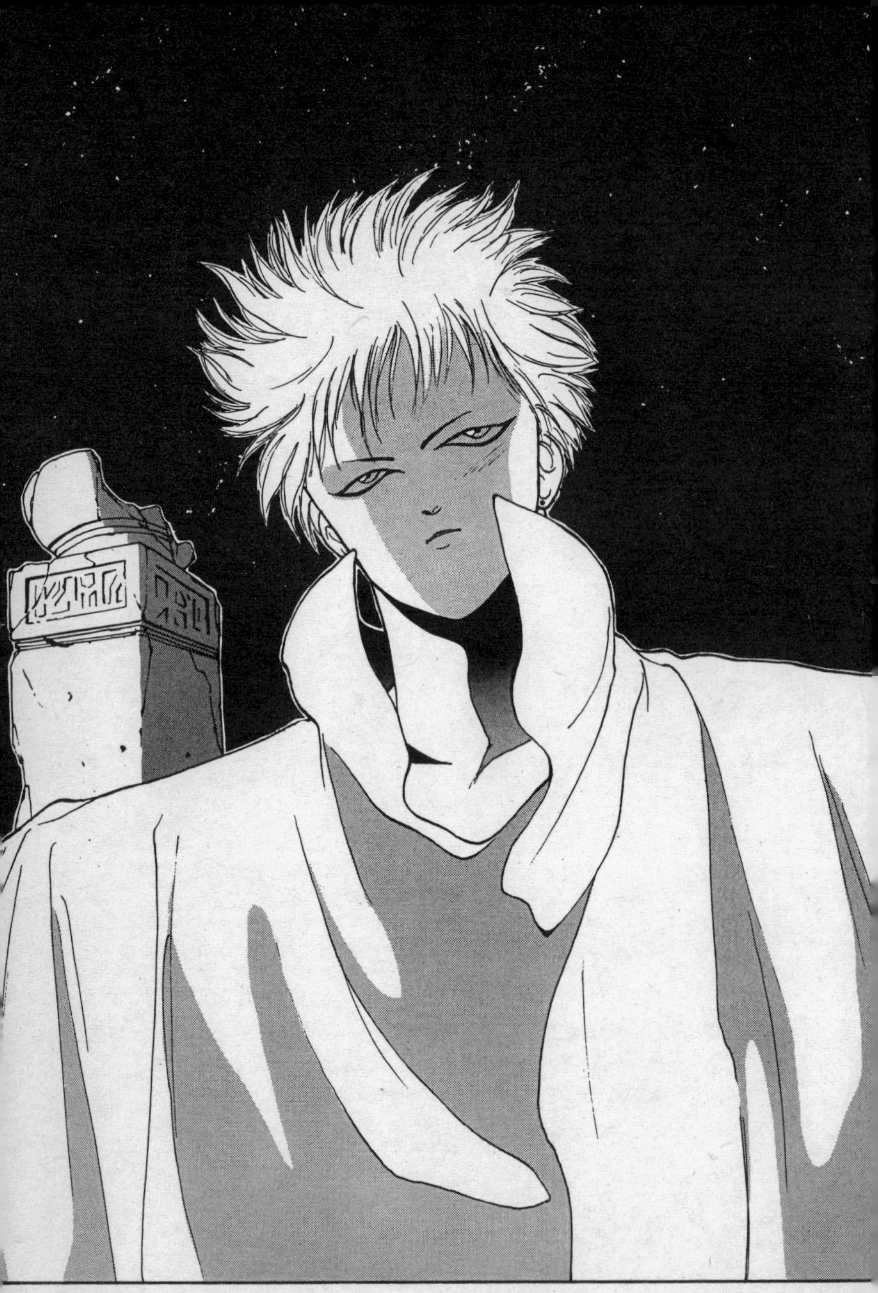

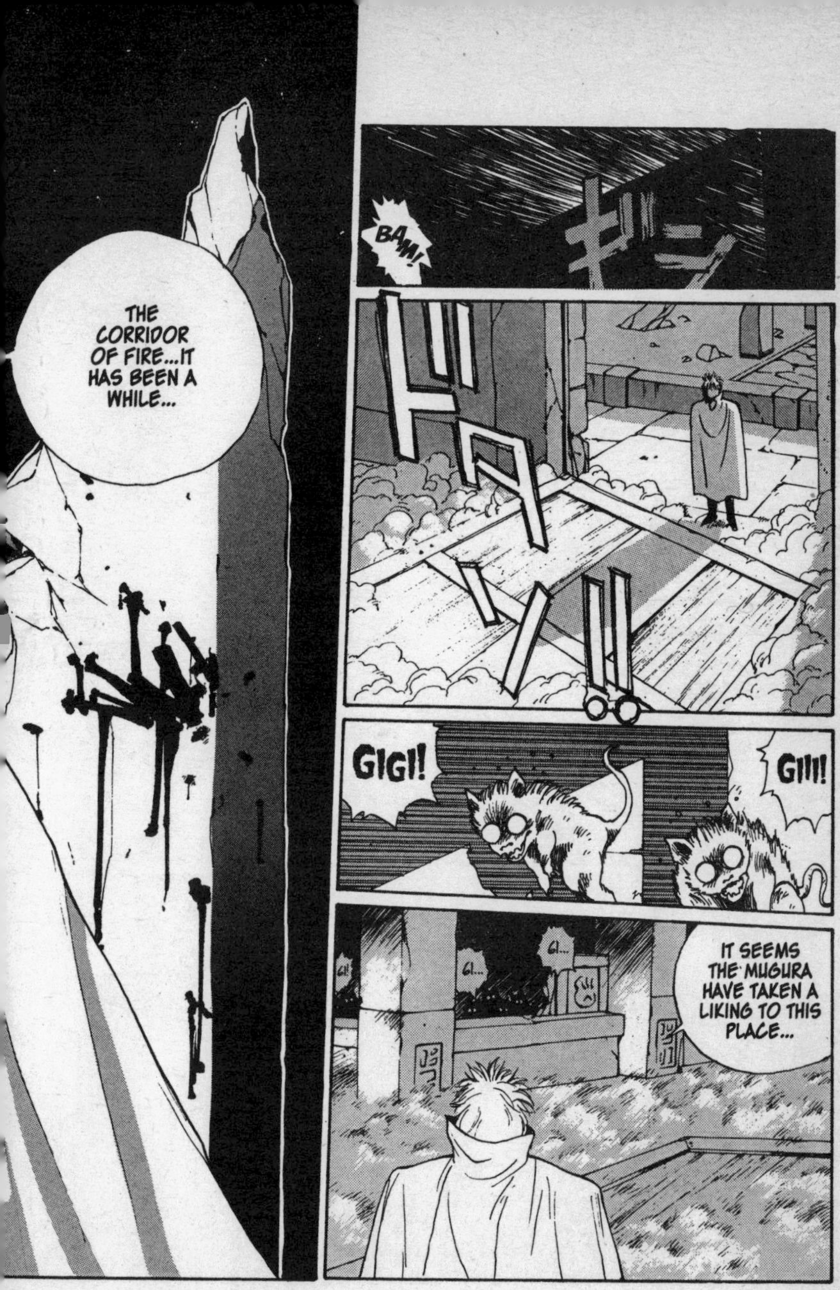
THE CORRIDOR OF FIRE...IT HAS BEEN A WHILE...
BAM!
GIGI!
GIIII!
GI!
GI...
GI...
IT SEEMS THE MUGURA HAVE TAKEN A LIKING TO THIS PLACE...

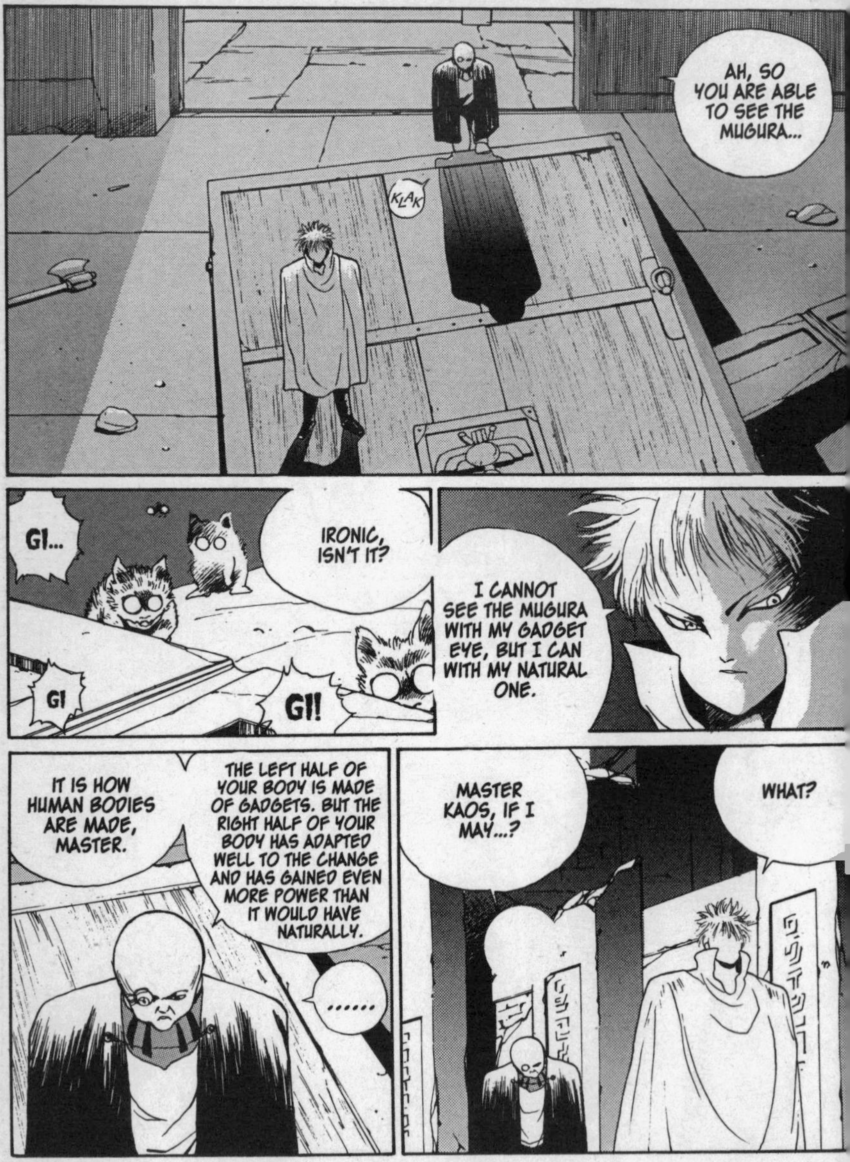

KLAK
AH, SO YOU ARE ABLE TO SEE THE MUGURA...
GI...
GI
GI!
IRONIC, ISN'T IT?
I CANNOT SEE THE MUGURA WITH MY GADGET EYE, BUT I CAN WITH MY NATURAL ONE.
IT IS HOW HUMAN BODIES ARE MADE, MASTER.
THE LEFT HALF OF YOUR BODY IS MADE OF GADGETS. BUT THE RIGHT HALF OF YOUR BODY HAS ADAPTED WELL TO THE CHANGE AND HAS GAINED EVEN MORE POWER THAN IT WOULD HAVE NATURALLY.
......
MASTER KAOS, IF I MAY...?
WHAT?

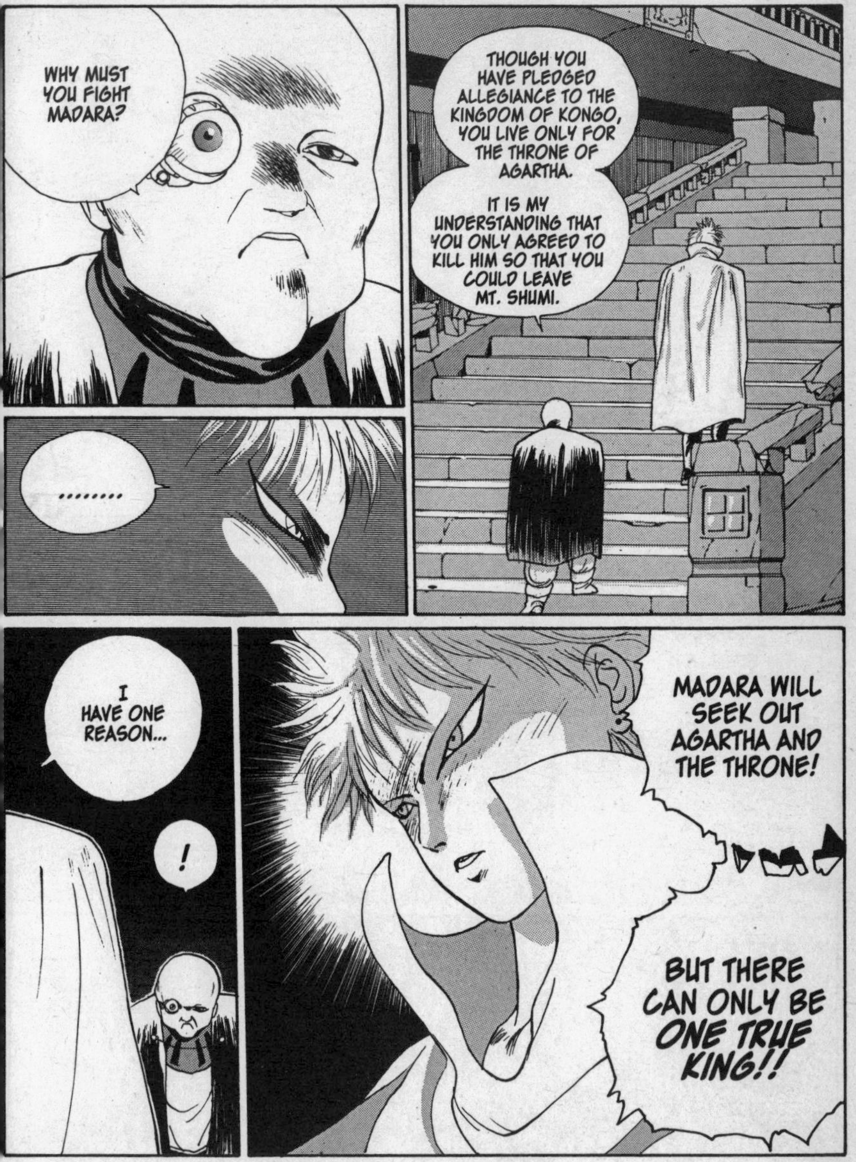
WHY MUST YOU FIGHT MADARA?
....
THOUGH YOU HAVE PLEDGED ALLEGIANCE TO THE KINGDOM OF KONGO, YOU LIVE ONLY FOR THE THRONE OF AGARTHA.
IT IS MY UNDERSTANDING THAT YOU ONLY AGREED TO KILL HIM SO THAT YOU COULD LEAVE MT. SHUMI.
I HAVE ONE REASON...
!
MADARA WILL SEEK OUT AGARTHA AND THE THRONE!
BUT THERE CAN ONLY BE ONE TRUE KING!!

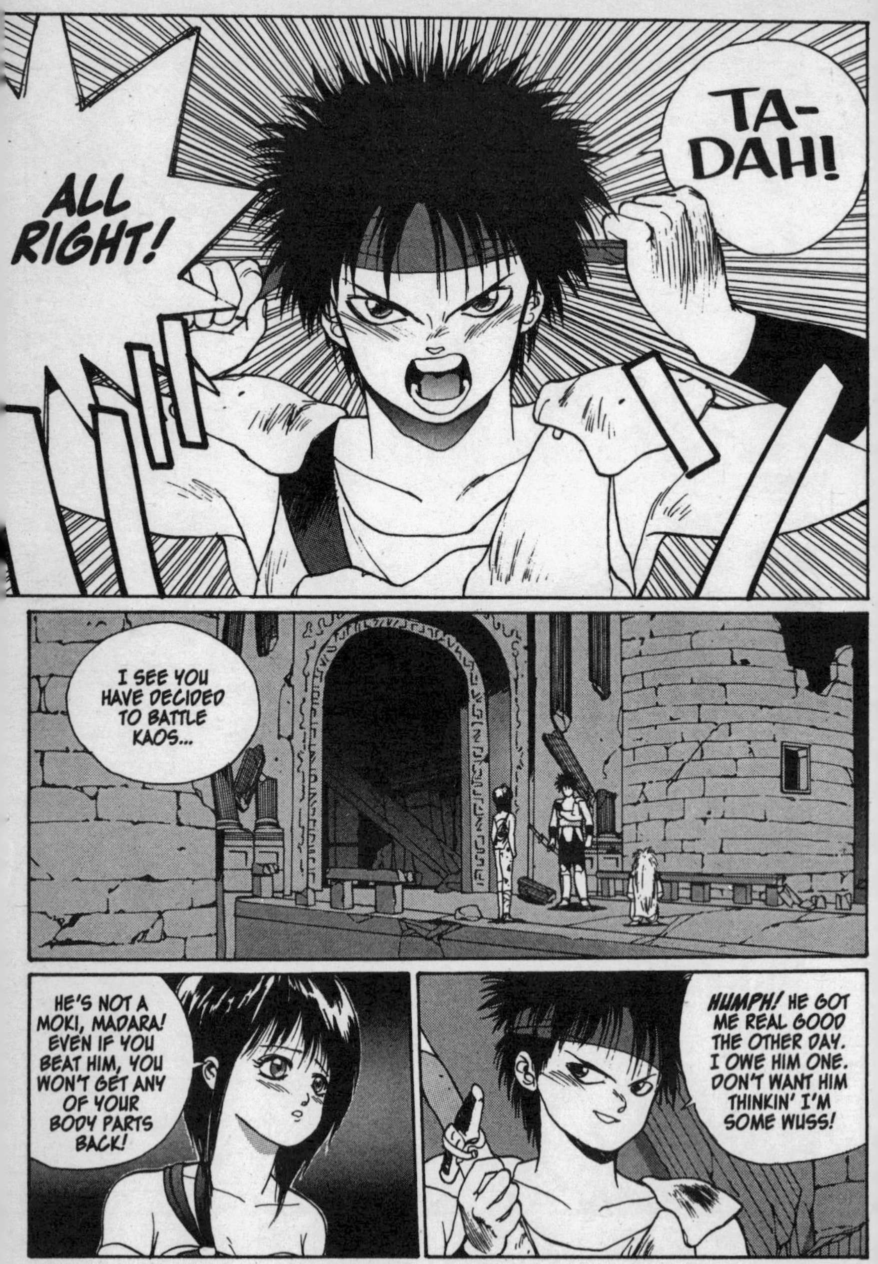
ALL RIGHT!
TA-DAH!
I SEE YOU HAVE DECIDED TO BATTLE KAOS...
HE'S NOT A MOKI, MADARA! EVEN IF YOU BEAT HIM, YOU WON'T GET ANY OF YOUR BODY PARTS BACK!
HUMPH! HE GOT ME REAL GOOD THE OTHER DAY. I OWE HIM ONE. DON'T WANT HIM THINKIN' I'M SOME WUSS!

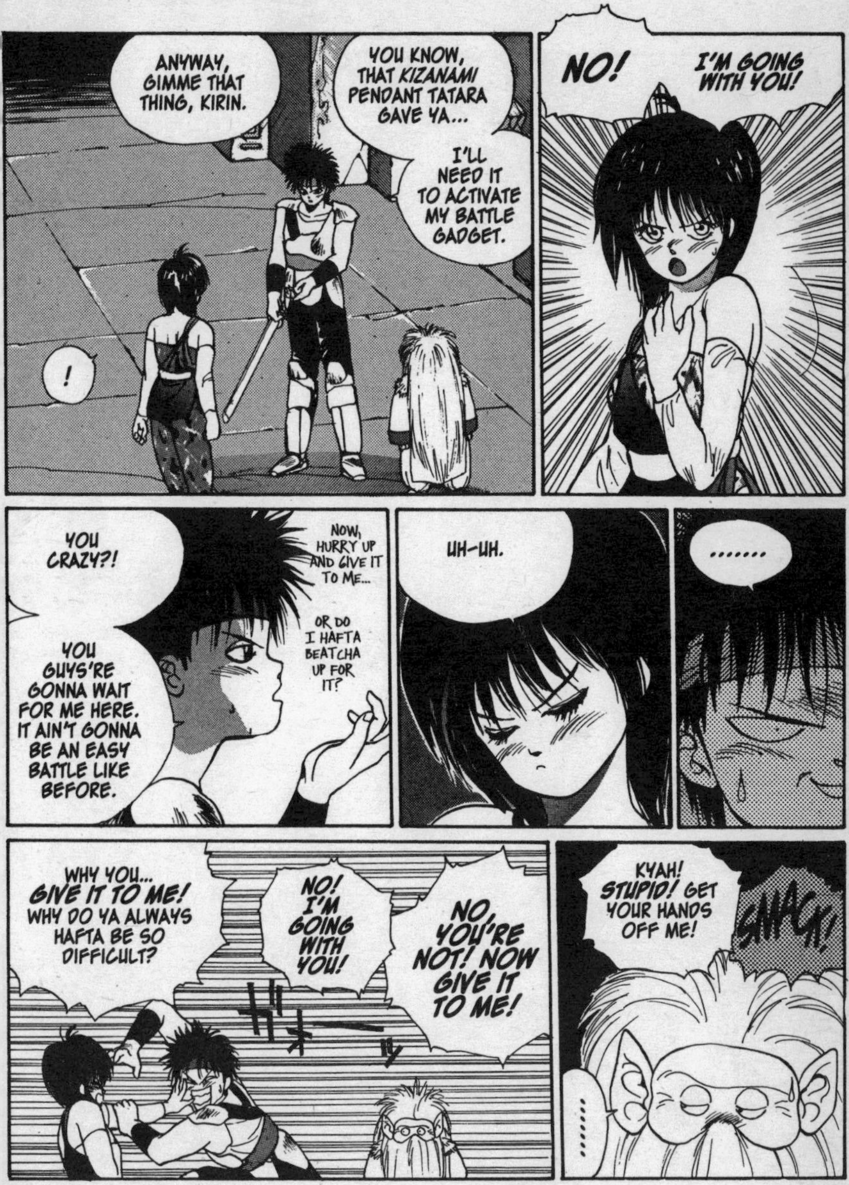

ANYWAY, GIMME THAT THING, KIRIN.
YOU KNOW, THAT KIZANAMI PENDANT TATARA GAVE YA...
I'LL NEED IT TO ACTIVATE MY BATTLE GADGET.
!
NO!
I'M GOING WITH YOU!
YOU CRAZY?!
YOU GUYS'RE GONNA WAIT FOR ME HERE. IT AIN'T GONNA BE AN EASY BATTLE LIKE BEFORE.
NOW, HURRY UP AND GIVE IT TO ME...
OR DO I HAFTA BEATCHA UP FOR IT?
UH-UH.
....
WHY YOU... GIVE IT TO ME! WHY DO YA ALWAYS HAFTA BE SO DIFFICULT?
NO! I'M GOING WITH YOU!
NO, YOU'RE NOT! NOW GIVE IT TO ME!
KYAH! STUPID! GET YOUR HANDS OFF ME!
SMACK!
......

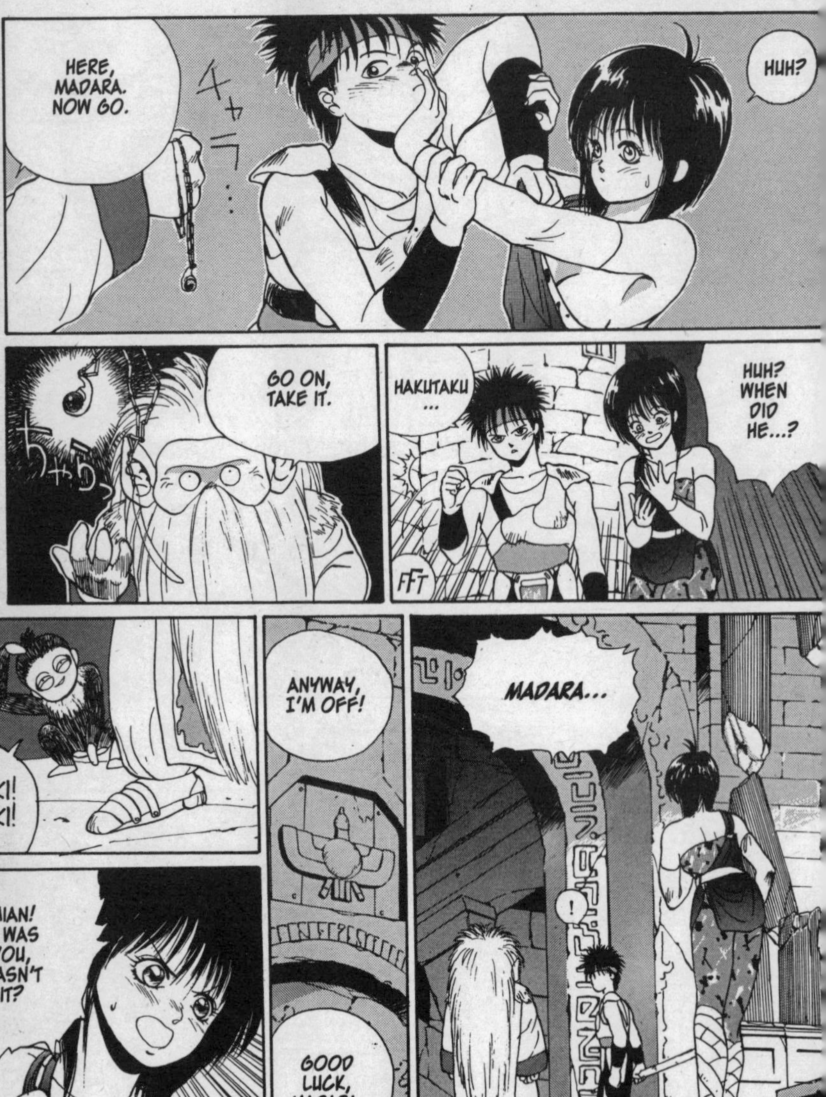
HERE, MADARA. NOW GO.
キャラ…
HUH?
ちゃりっ
GO ON, TAKE IT.
HAKUTAKU ...
HUH? WHEN DID HE...?
FFT
KIKI! KIKI!
MIAN! IT WAS YOU, WASN'T IT?
ANYWAY, I'M OFF!
GOOD LUCK, MADARA...
MADARA...
!

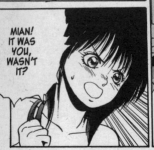

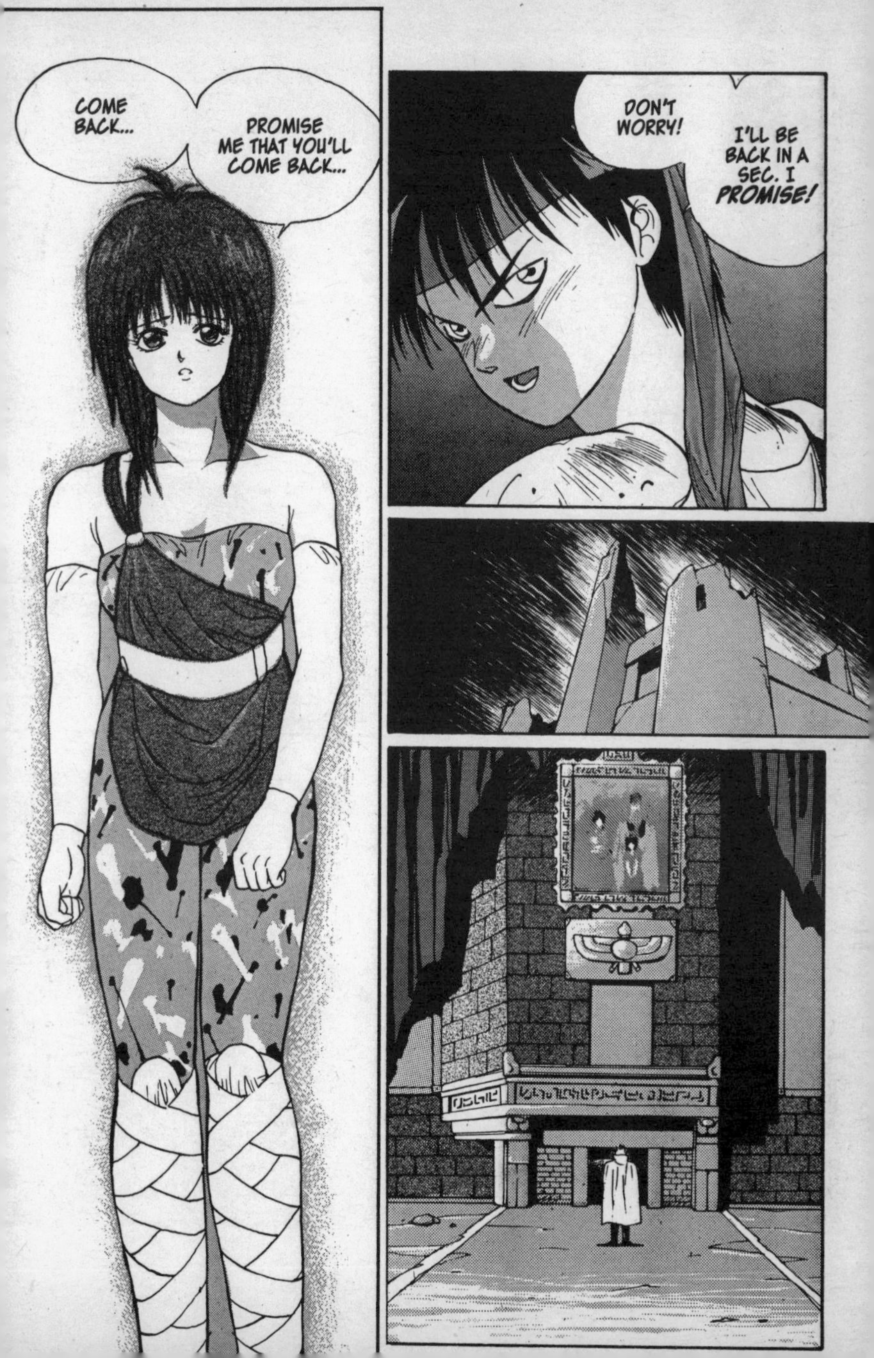
COME BACK...
PROMISE ME THAT YOU'LL COME BACK...
DON'T WORRY!
I'LL BE BACK IN A SEC. I PROMISE!

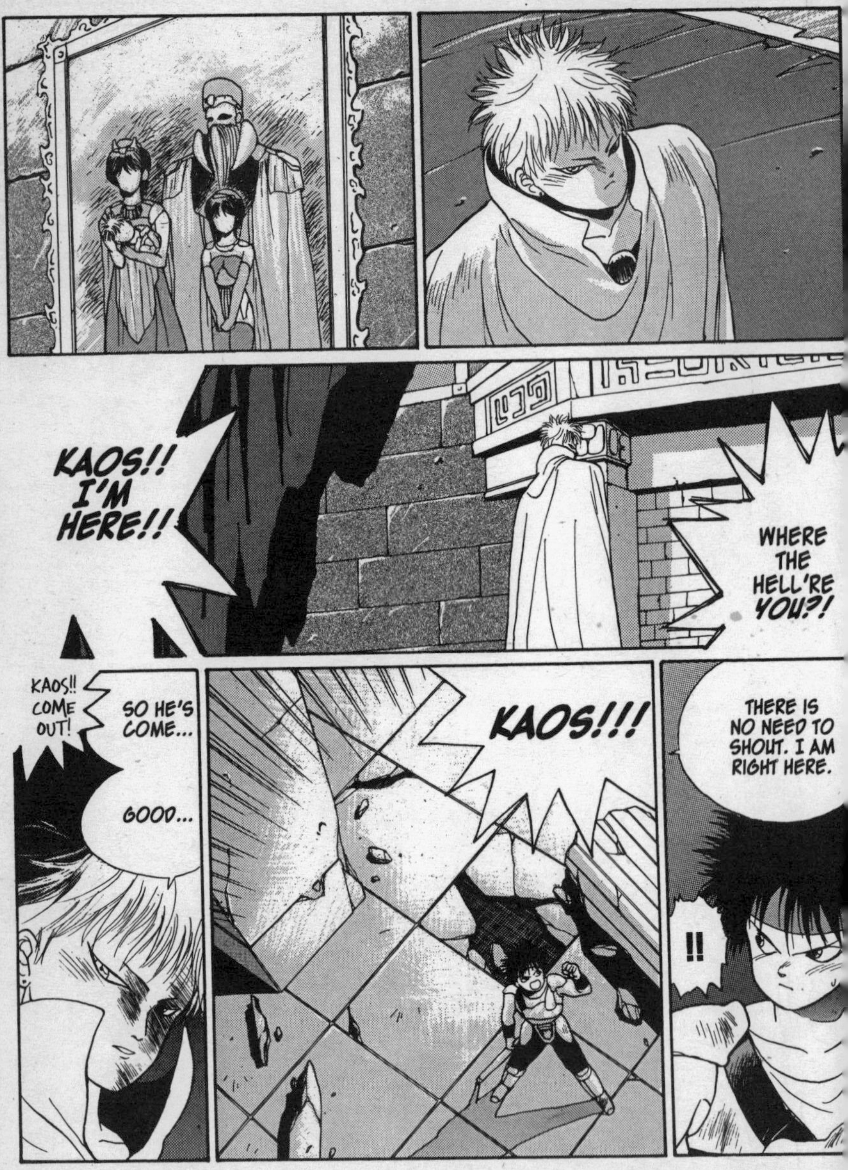

KAOS!! I'M HERE!!
WHERE THE HELL'RE YOU?!
KAOS!! COME OUT!
SO HE'S COME...
GOOD...
KAOS!!!
THERE IS NO NEED TO SHOUT. I AM RIGHT HERE.
!!

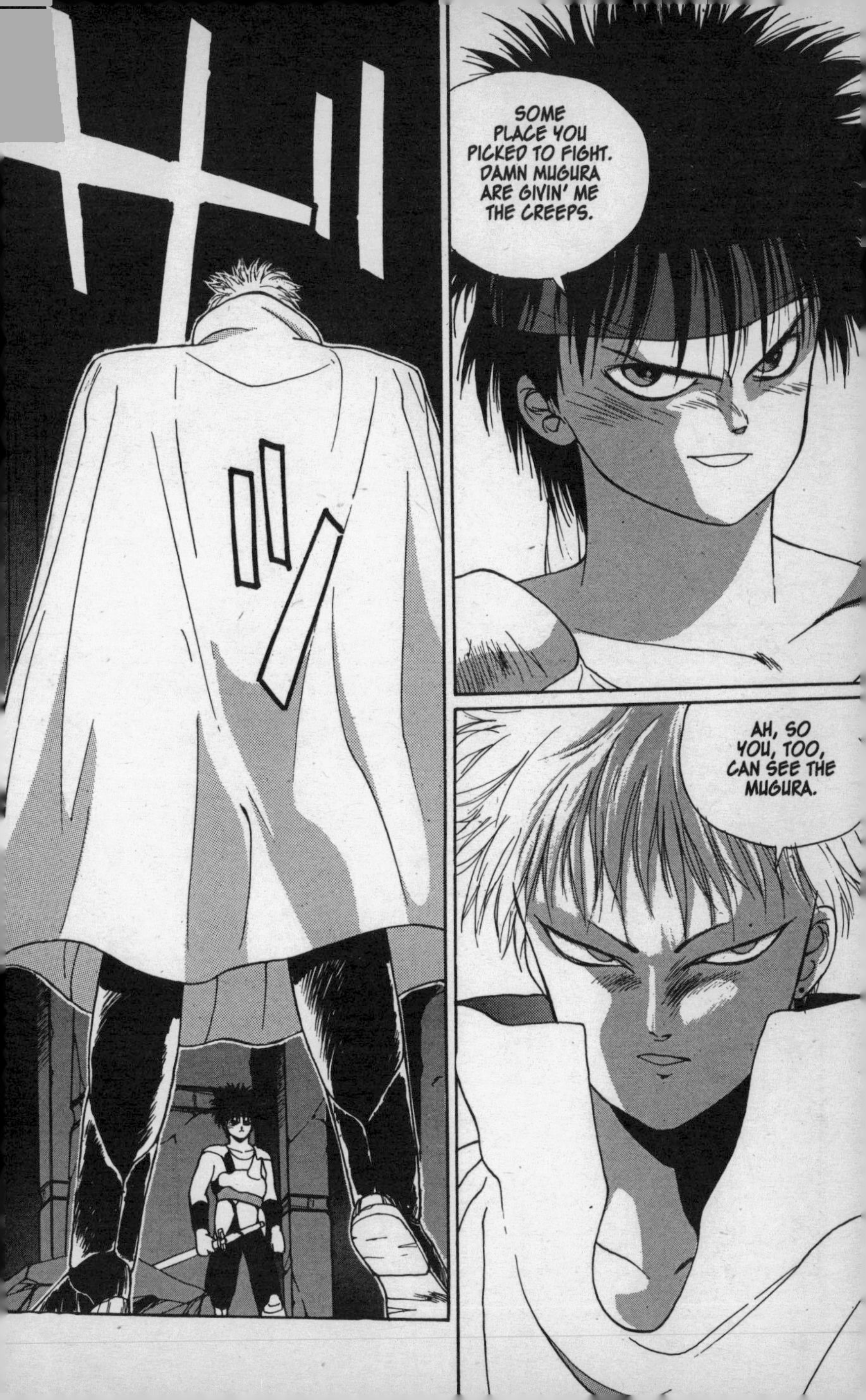
SOME PLACE YOU PICKED TO FIGHT. DAMN MUGURA ARE GIVIN' ME THE CREEPS.
AH, SO YOU, TOO, CAN SEE THE MUGURA.

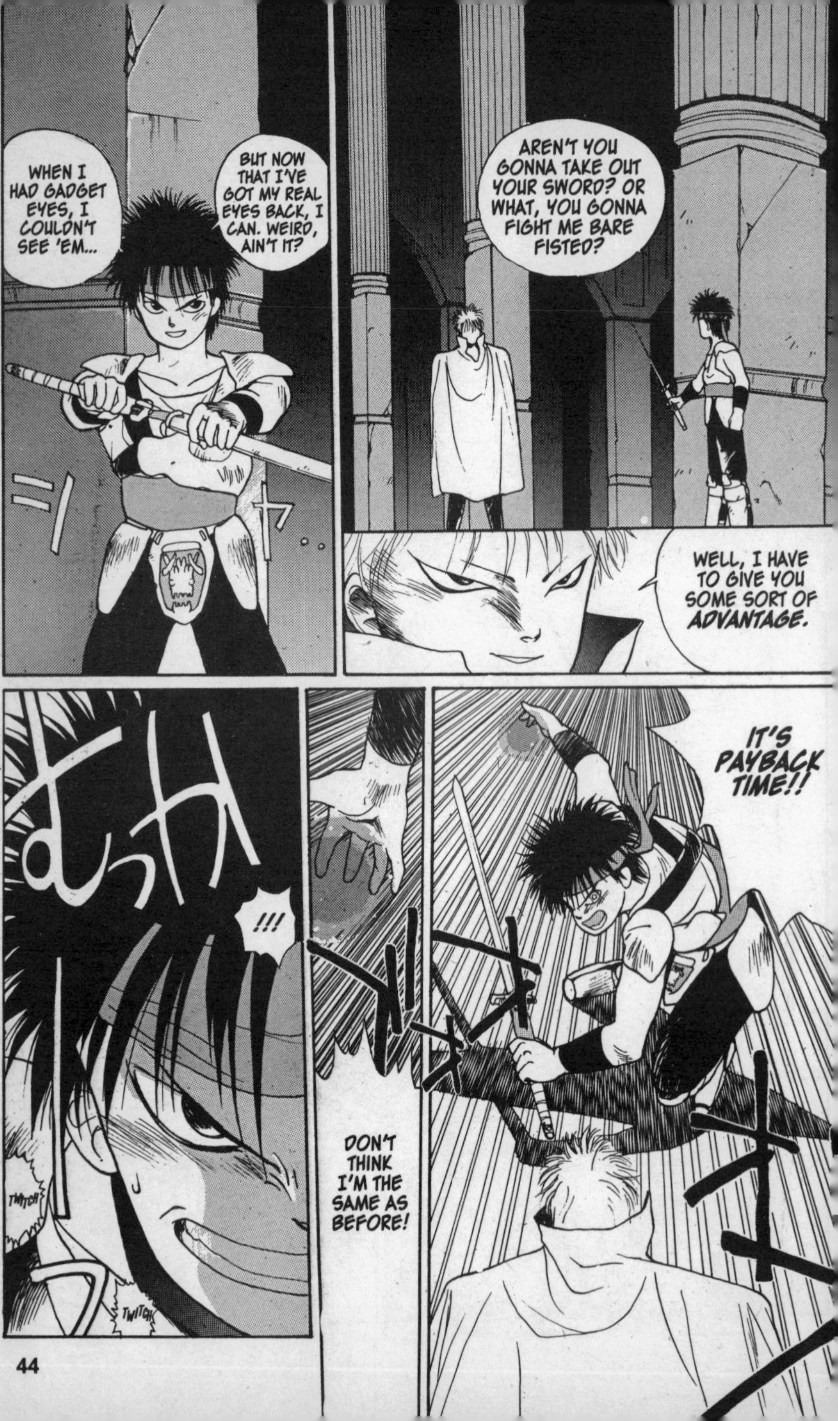

WHEN I HAD GADGET EYES, I COULDN'T SEE 'EM...
BUT NOW THAT I'VE GOT MY REAL EYES BACK, I CAN. WEIRD, AIN'T IT?
AREN'T YOU GONNA TAKE OUT YOUR SWORD? OR WHAT, YOU GONNA FIGHT ME BARE FISTED?
WELL, I HAVE TO GIVE YOU SOME SORT OF ADVANTAGE.
!!!
TWITCH
TWITCH
IT'S PAYBACK TIME!!
DON'T THINK I'M THE SAME AS BEFORE!

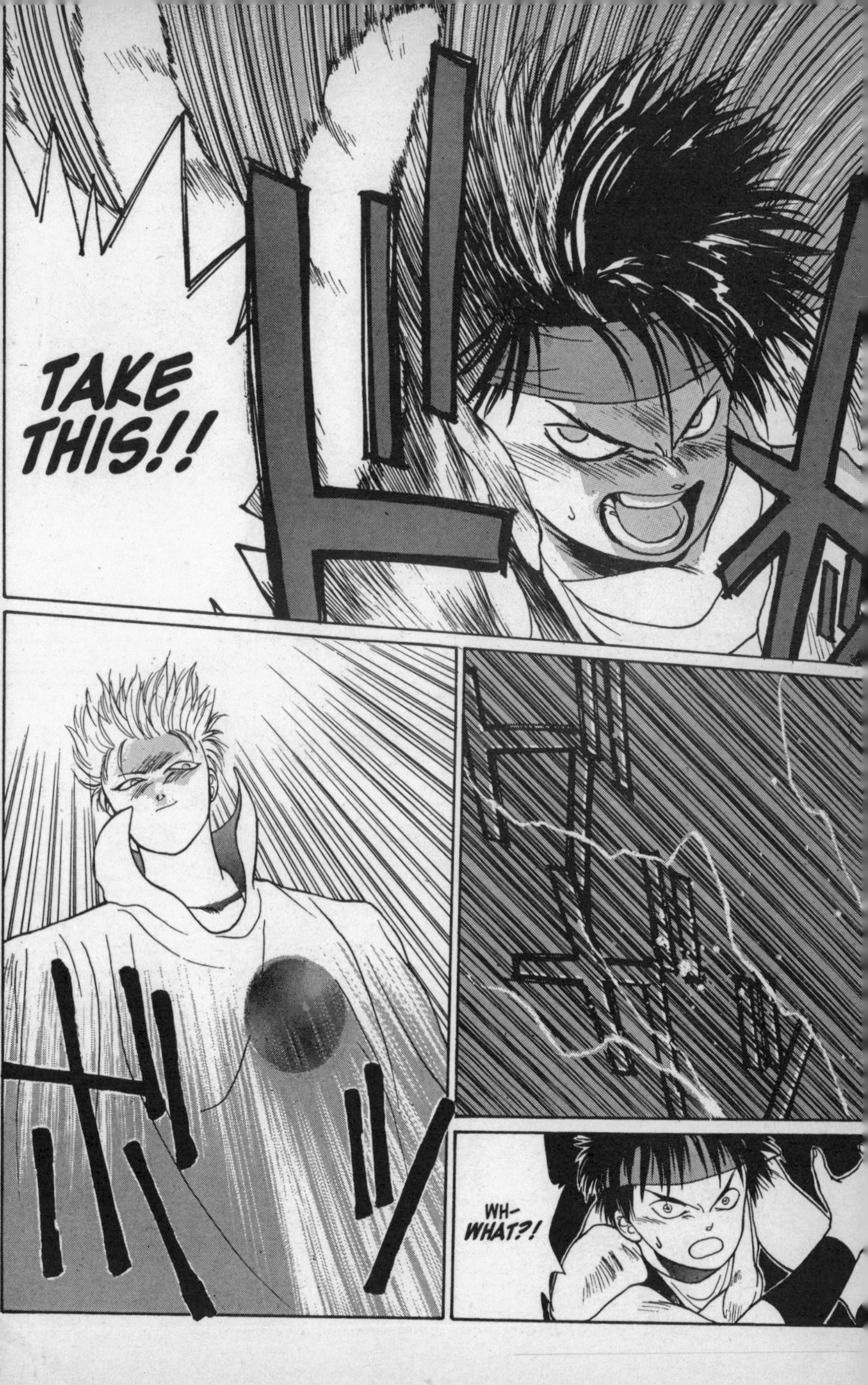
TAKE THIS!!
WH-
WHAT?!

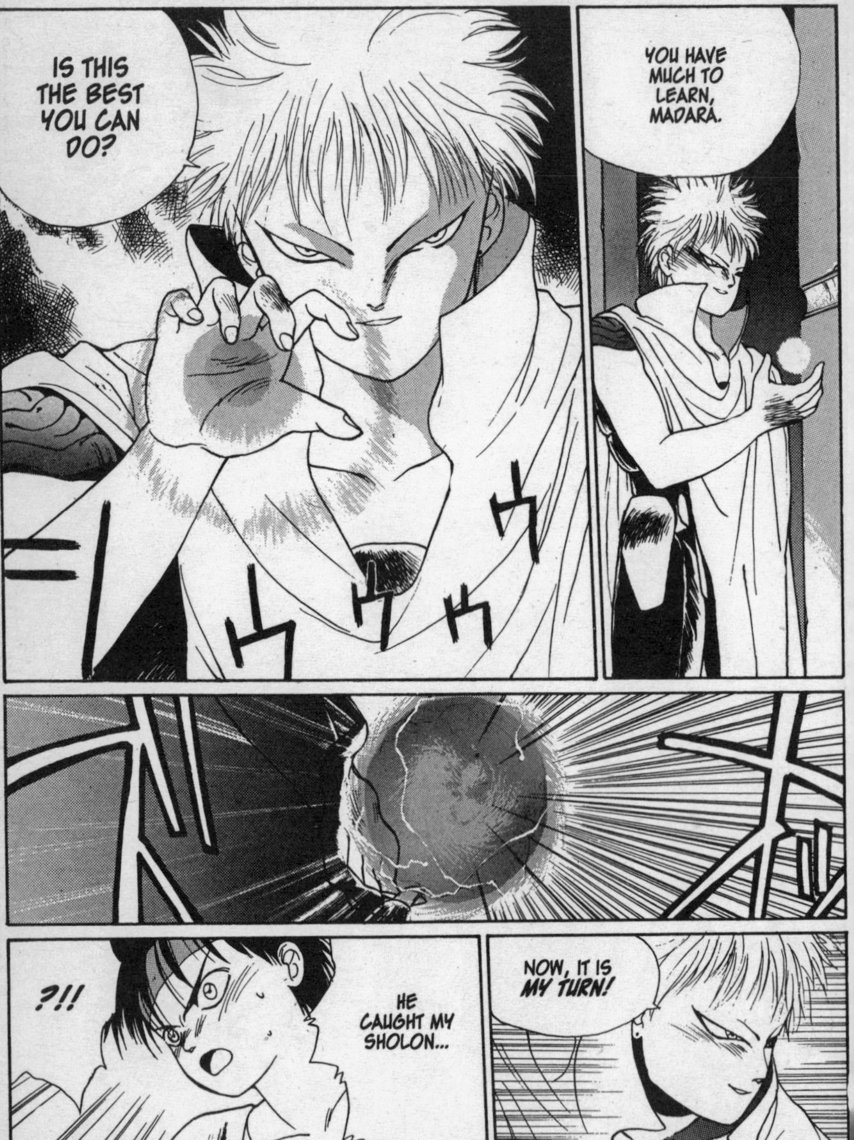
IS THIS THE BEST YOU CAN DO?
YOU HAVE MUCH TO LEARN, MADARA.
?!!
HE CAUGHT MY SHOLON...
NOW, IT IS MY TURN!

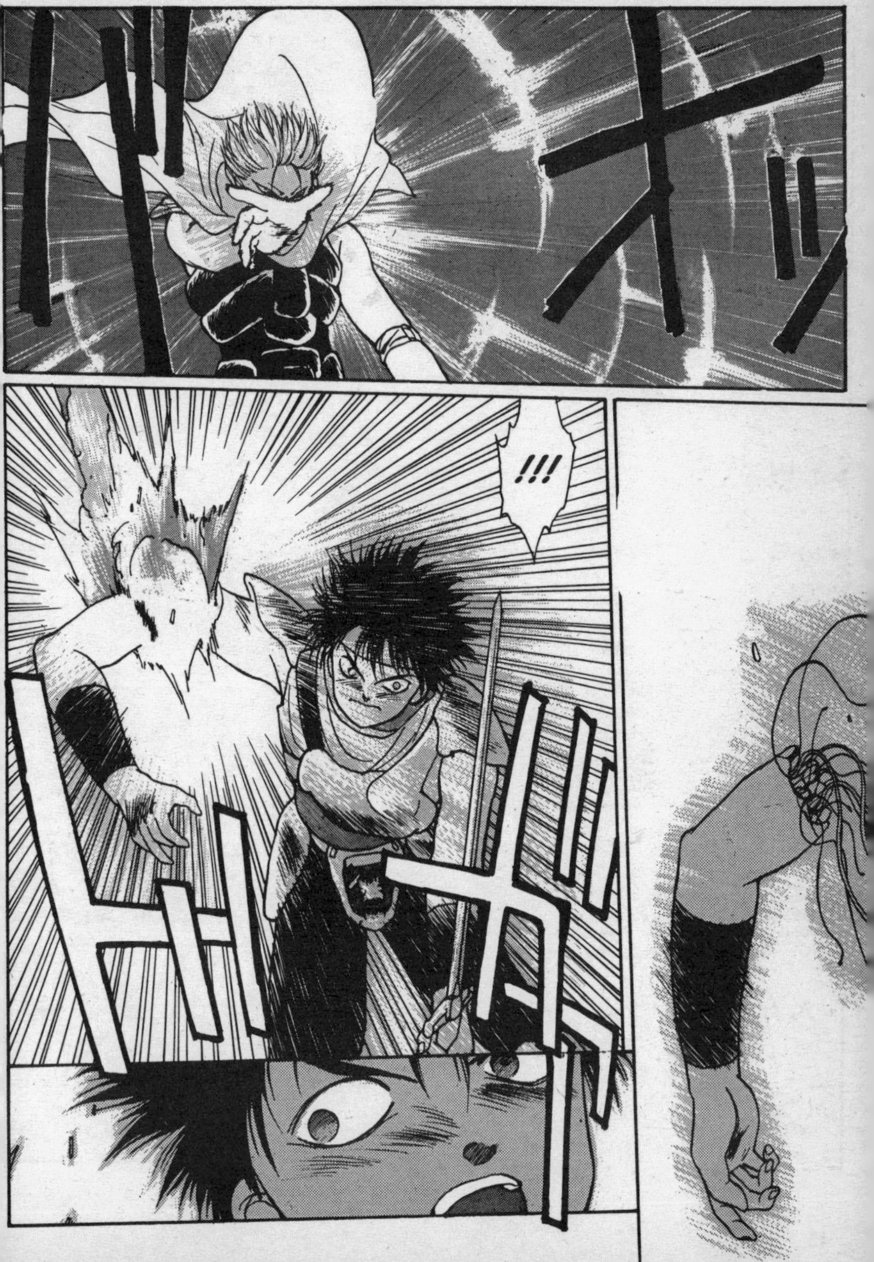
!!!

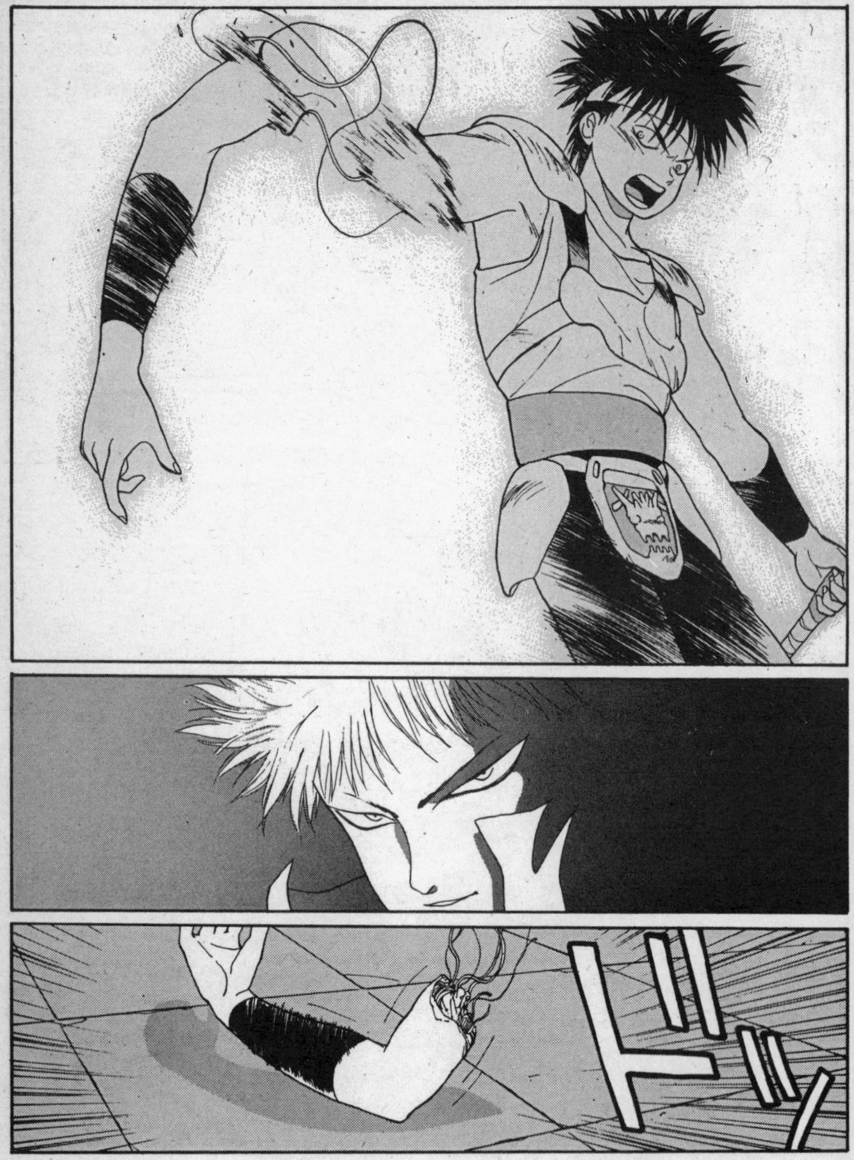
ドッ

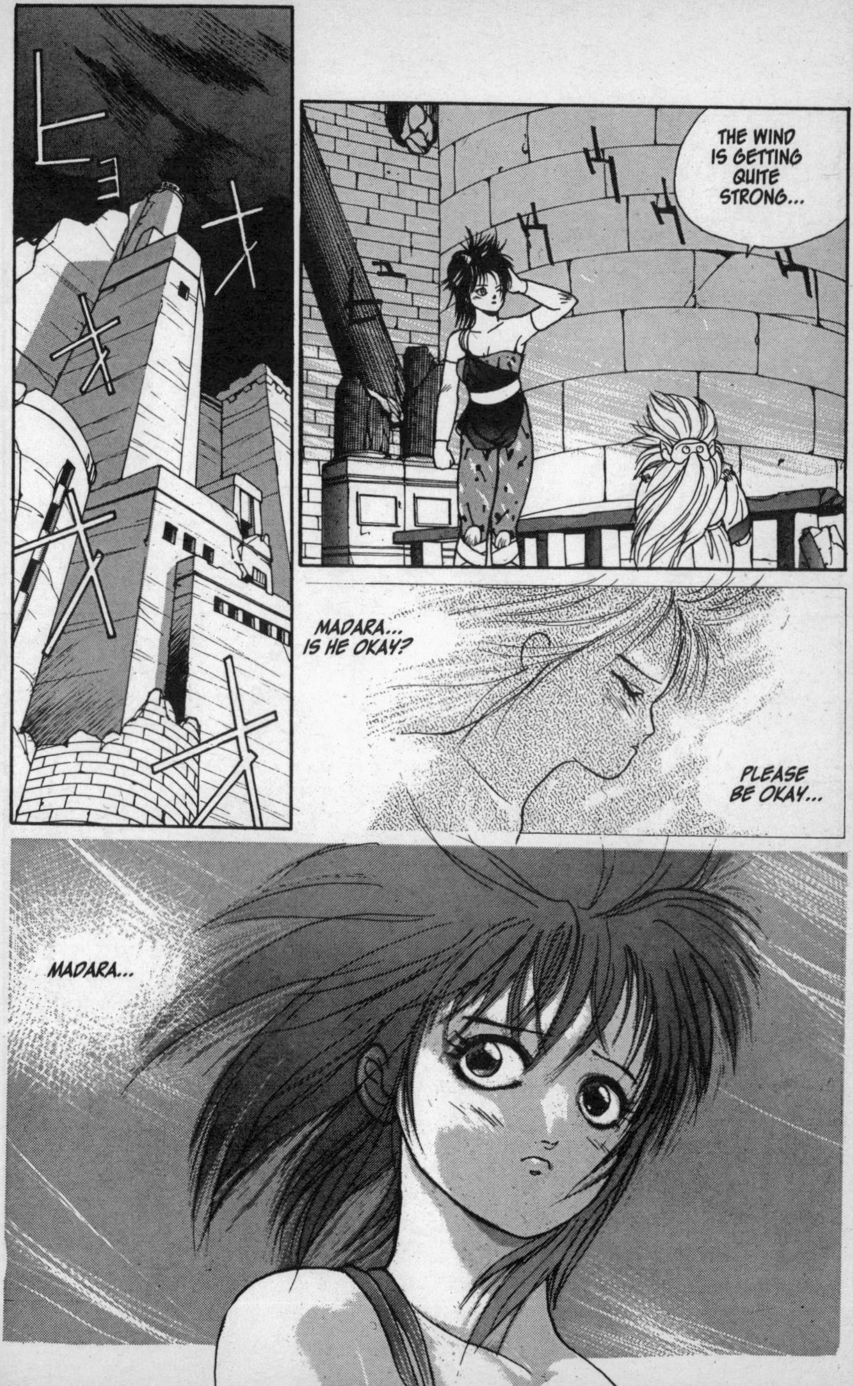
THE WIND IS GETTING QUITE STRONG...
MADARA... IS HE OKAY?
PLEASE BE OKAY...
MADARA...

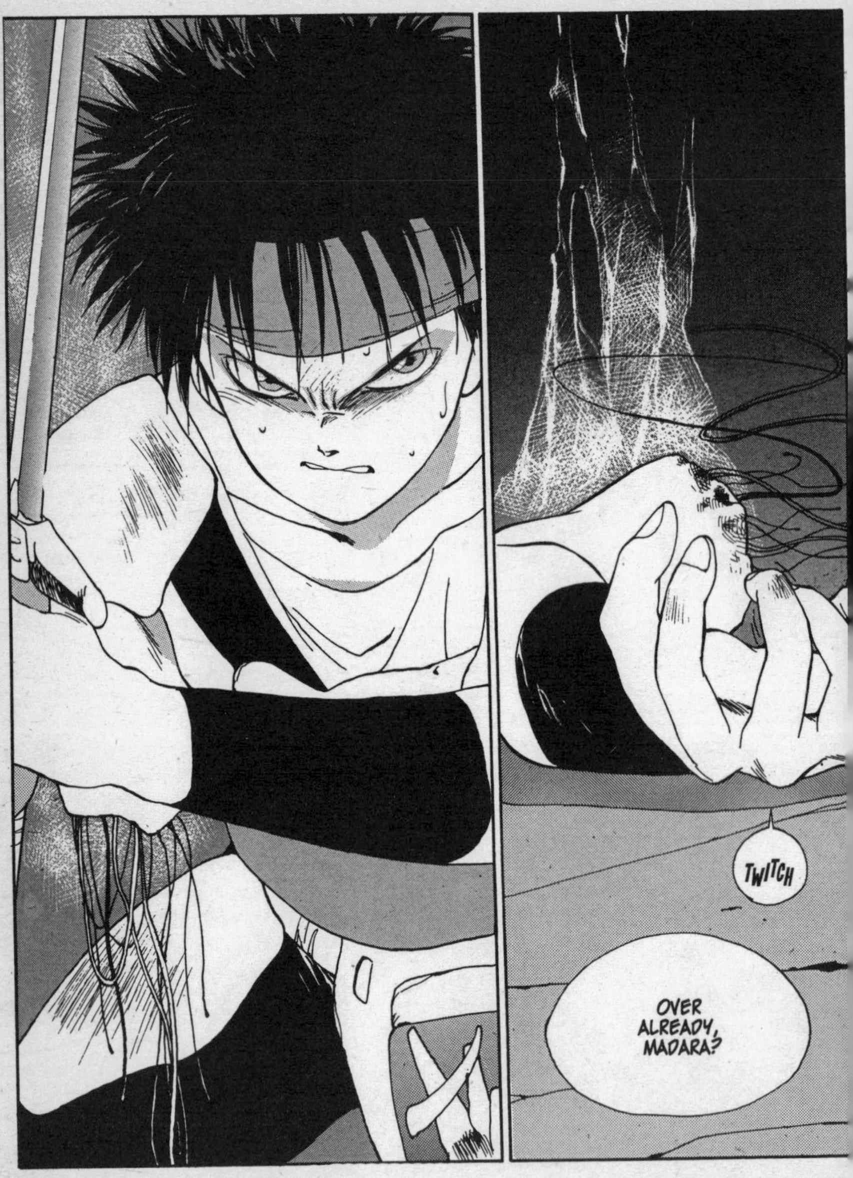
TWITCH
OVER ALREADY, MADARA?

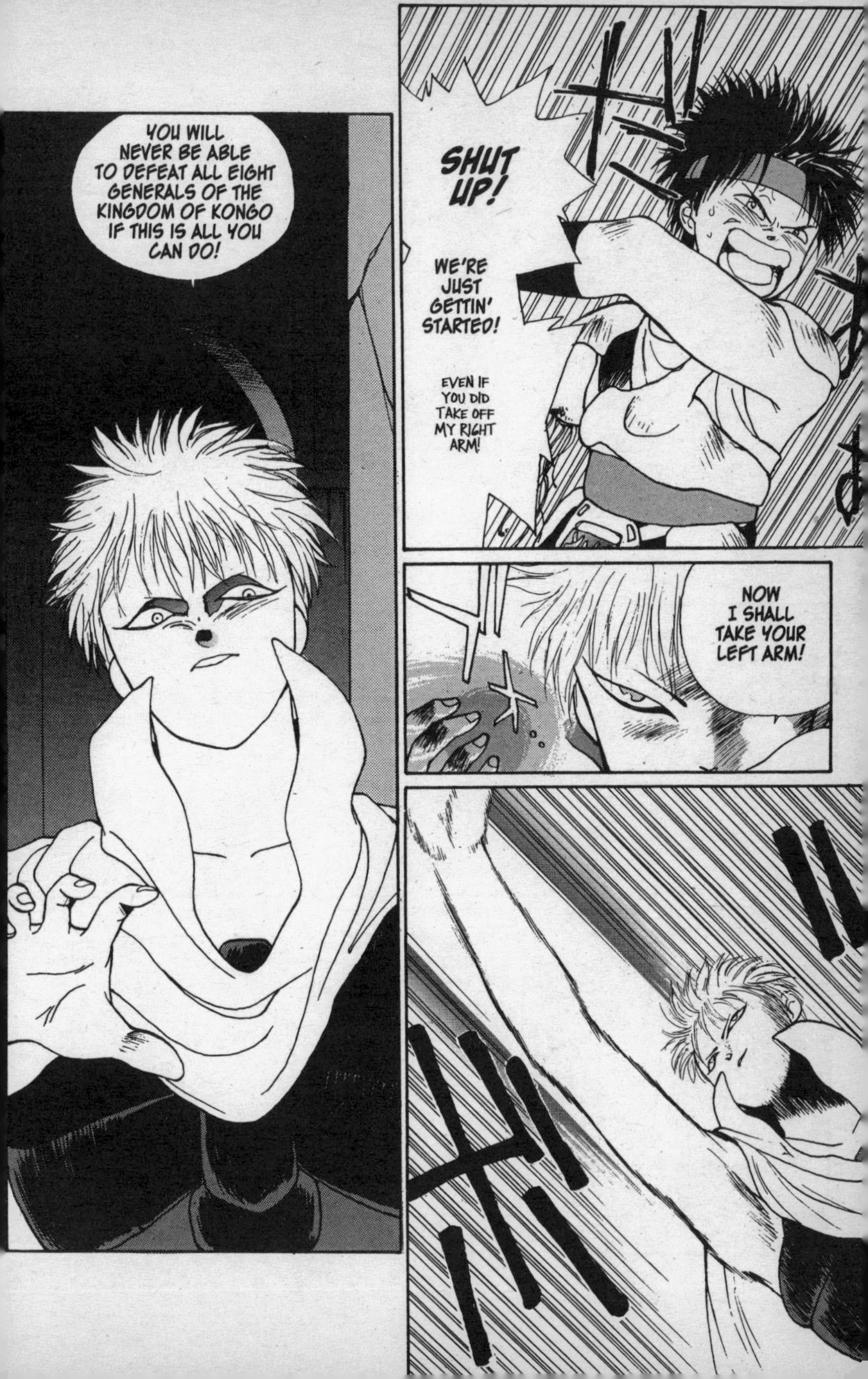
YOU WILL NEVER BE ABLE TO DEFEAT ALL EIGHT GENERALS OF THE KINGDOM OF KONGO IF THIS IS ALL YOU CAN DO!
SHUT UP!
WE'RE JUST GETTIN' STARTED!
EVEN IF YOU DID TAKE OFF MY RIGHT ARM!
NOW I SHALL TAKE YOUR LEFT ARM!

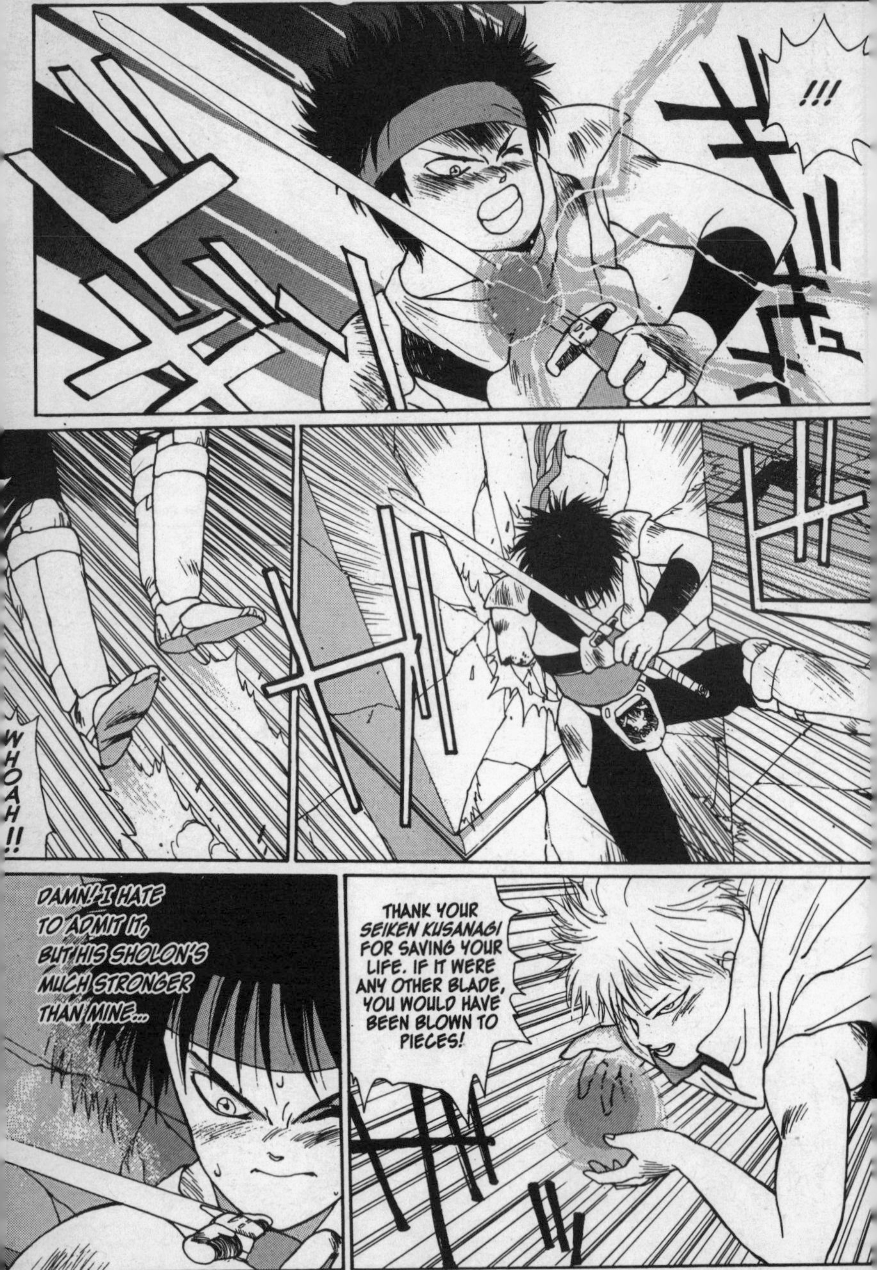
!!!
WHOAH!!
DAMN! I HATE TO ADMIT IT, BUT HIS SHOLON'S MUCH STRONGER THAN MINE...
THANK YOUR SEIKEN KUSANAGI FOR SAVING YOUR LIFE. IF IT WERE ANY OTHER BLADE, YOU WOULD HAVE BEEN BLOWN TO PIECES!

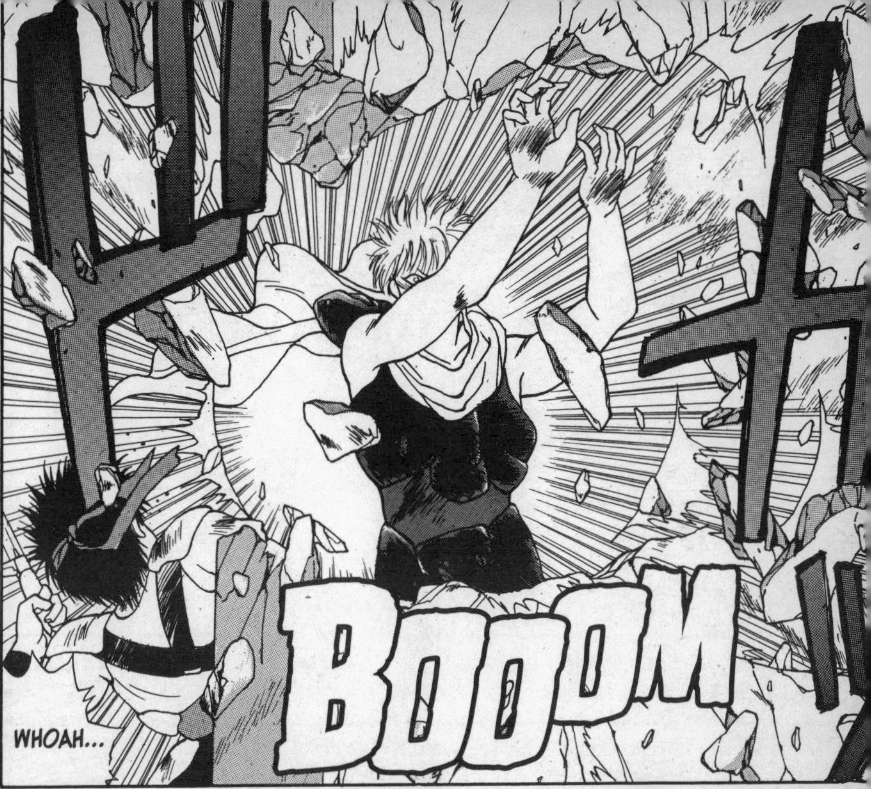
WHOAH...
BOOOM

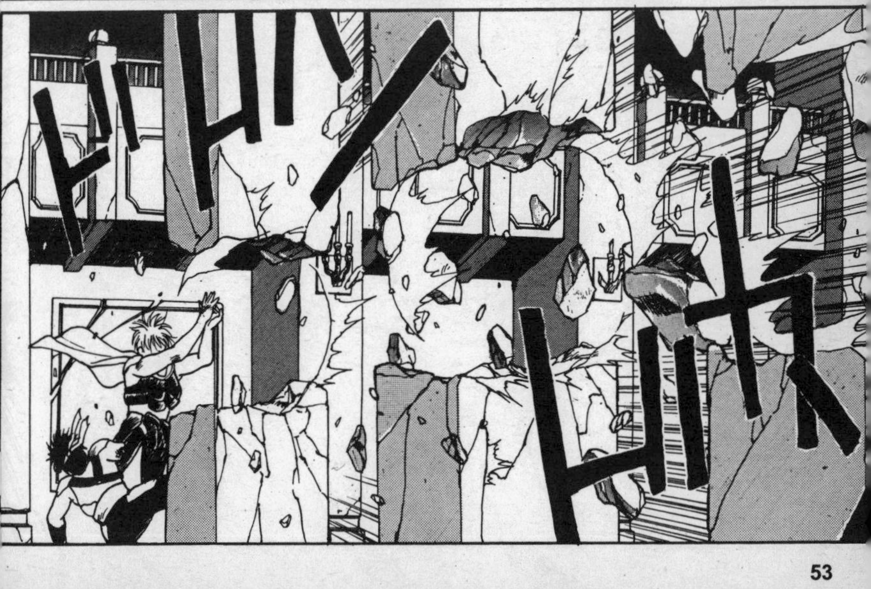

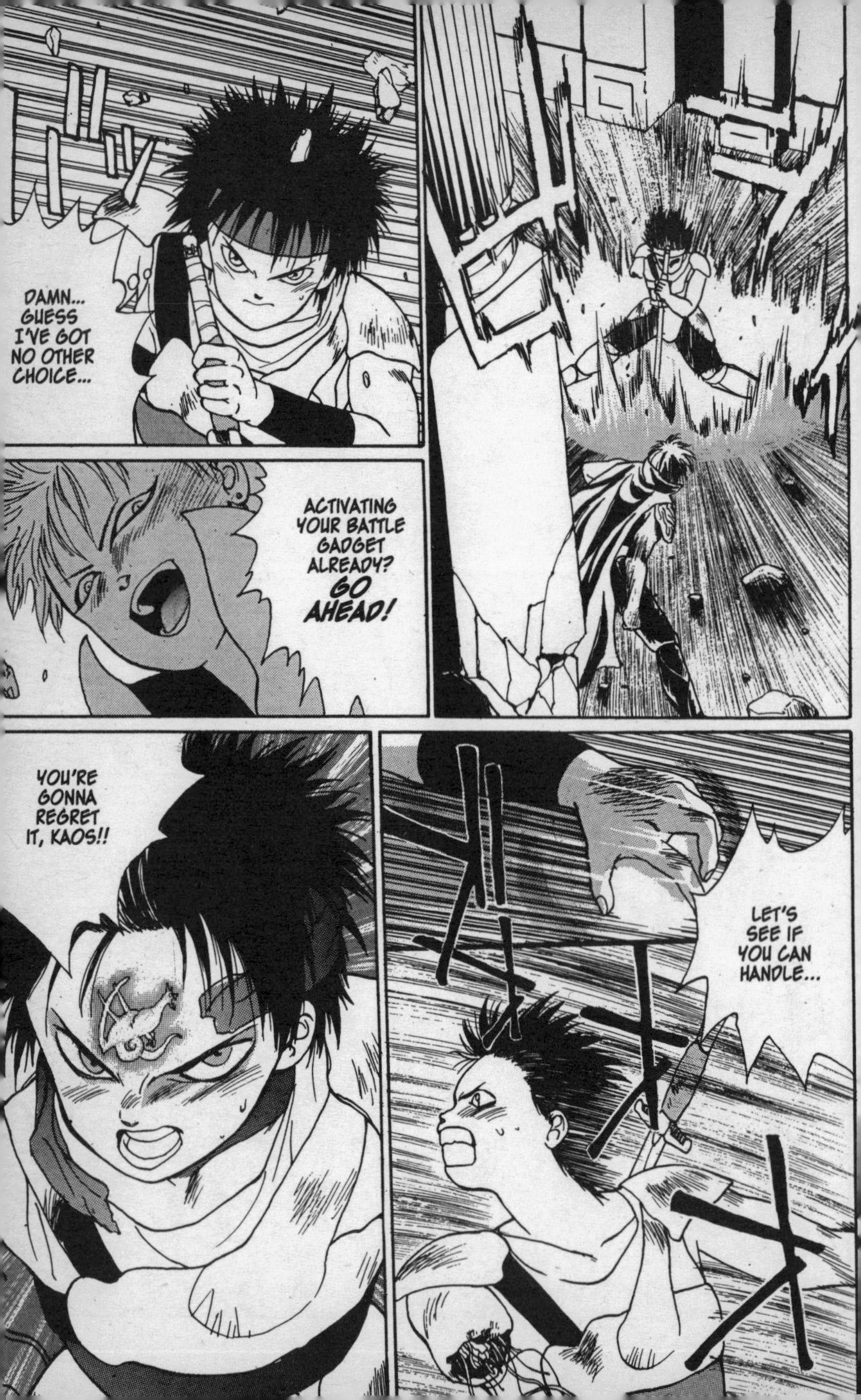
DAMN... GUESS I'VE GOT NO OTHER CHOICE...
ACTIVATING YOUR BATTLE GADGET ALREADY? GO AHEAD!
YOU'RE GONNA REGRET IT, KAOS!!
LET'S SEE IF YOU CAN HANDLE...

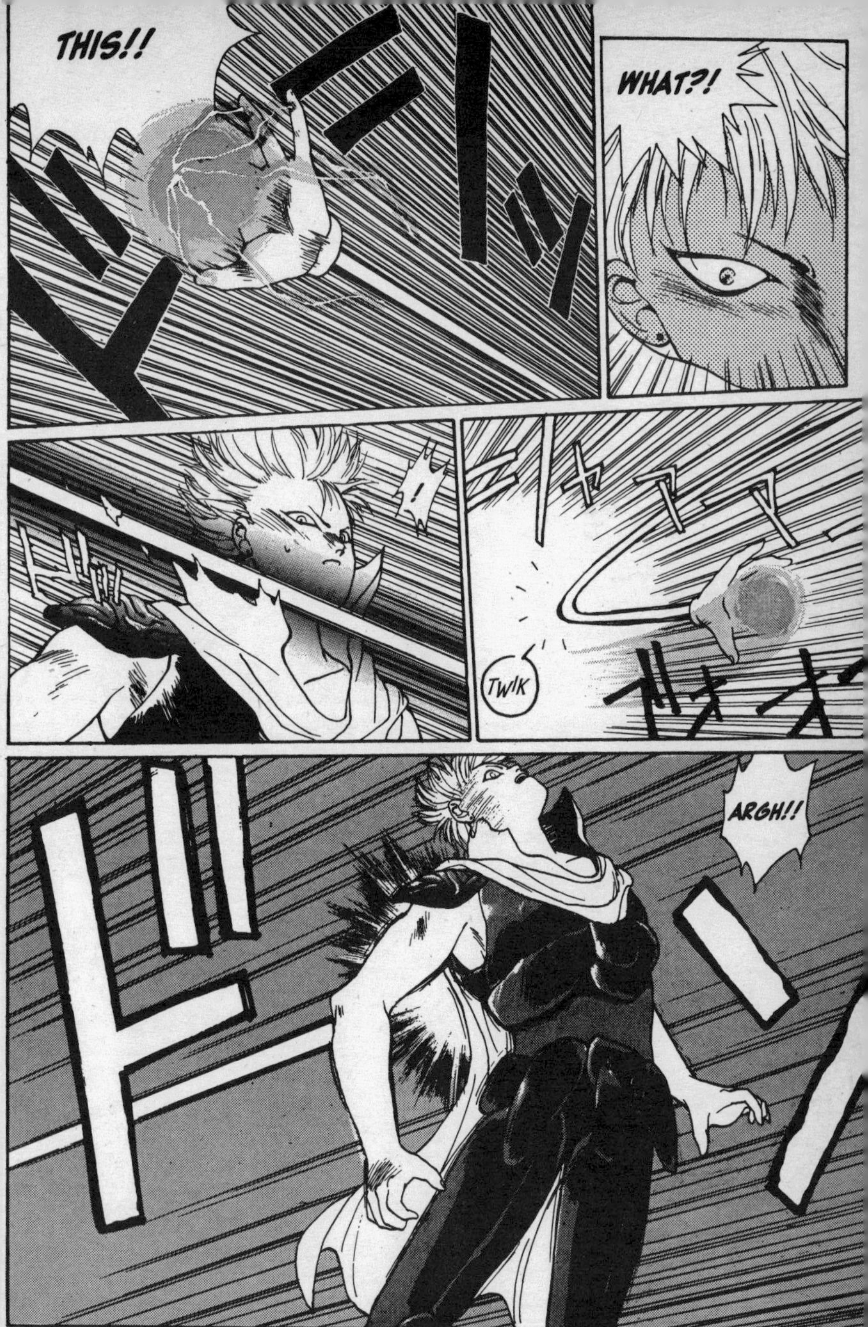
THIS!!
WHAT?!
!
TWIK
ARGH!!

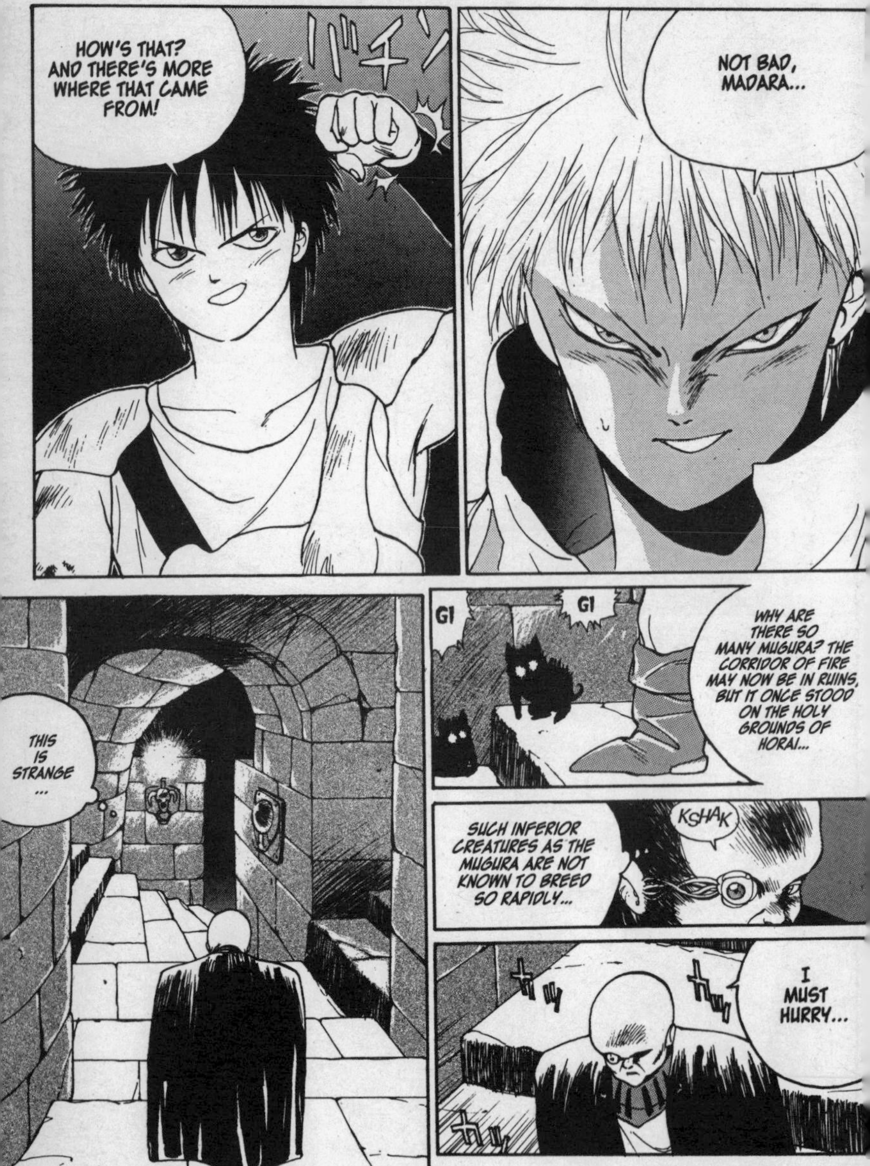
HOW'S THAT? AND THERE'S MORE WHERE THAT CAME FROM!
NOT BAD, MADARA...
THIS IS STRANGE ...
GI
GI
WHY ARE THERE SO MANY MUGURA? THE CORRIDOR OF FIRE MAY NOW BE IN RUINS, BUT IT ONCE STOOD ON THE HOLY GROUNDS OF HORAI...
SUCH INFERIOR CREATURES AS THE MUGURA ARE NOT KNOWN TO BREED SO RAPIDLY...
KSHAK
I MUST HURRY...

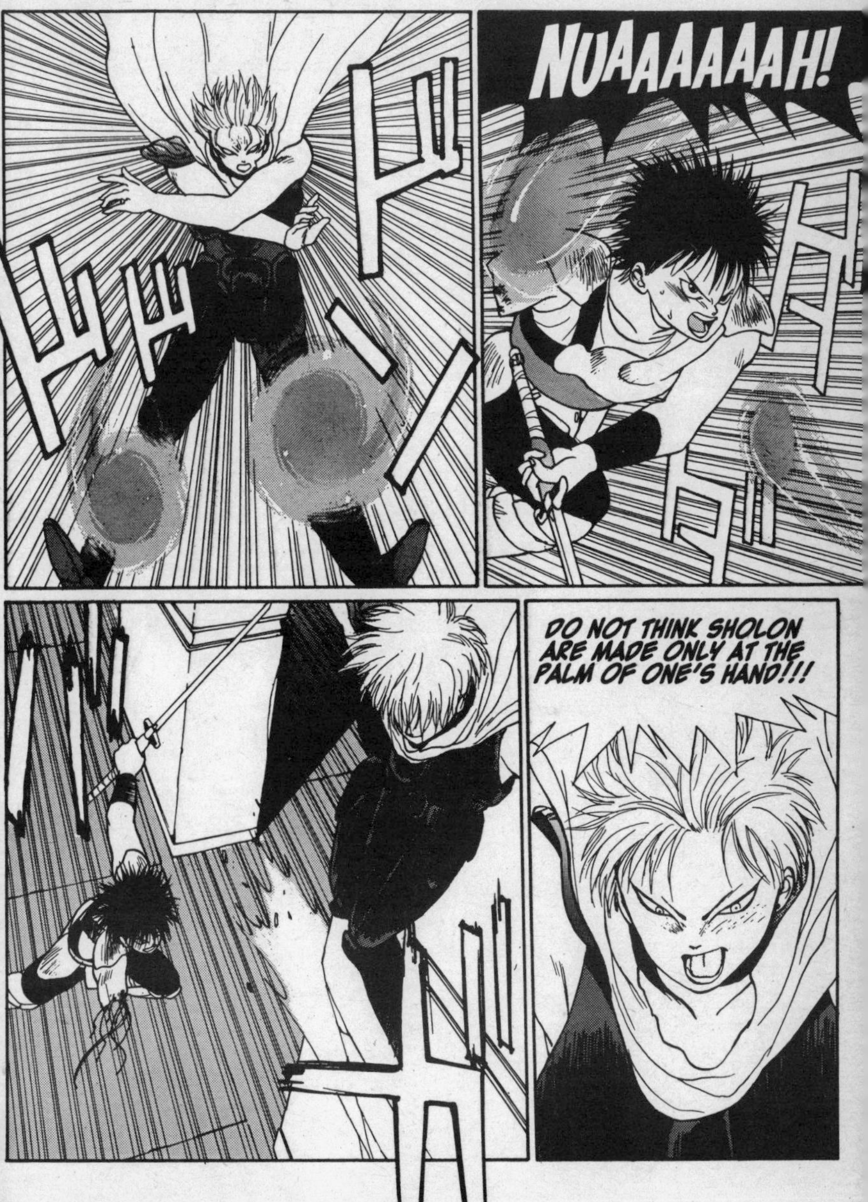
NUAAAAAAAH!
DO NOT THINK SHOLON ARE MADE ONLY AT THE PALM OF ONE'S HAND!!!

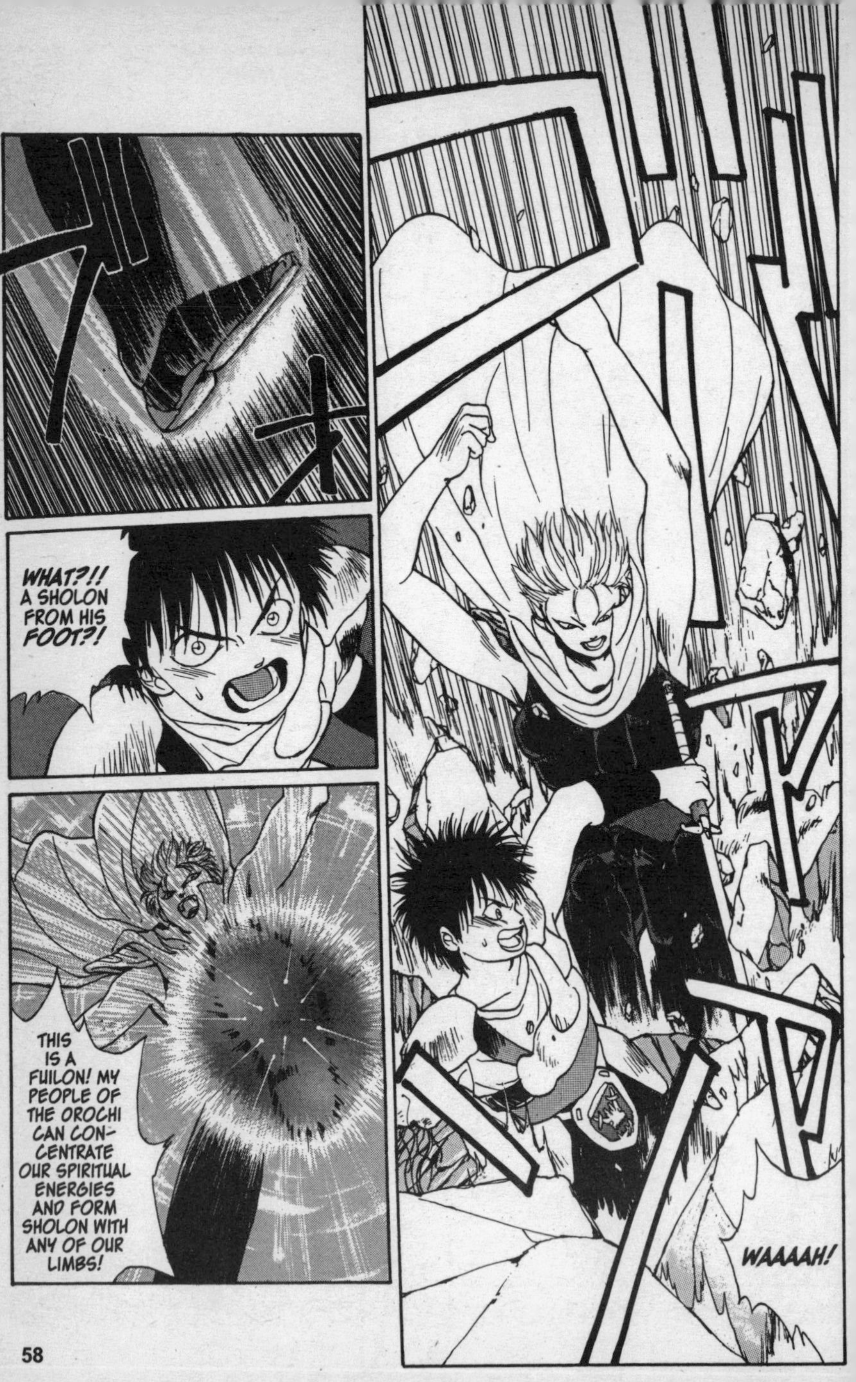
WHAT?!! A SHOLON FROM HIS FOOT?!
THIS IS A FUILON! MY PEOPLE OF THE OROCHI CAN CON-CENTRATE OUR SPIRITUAL ENERGIES AND FORM SHOLON WITH ANY OF OUR LIMBS!
WAAAAH!

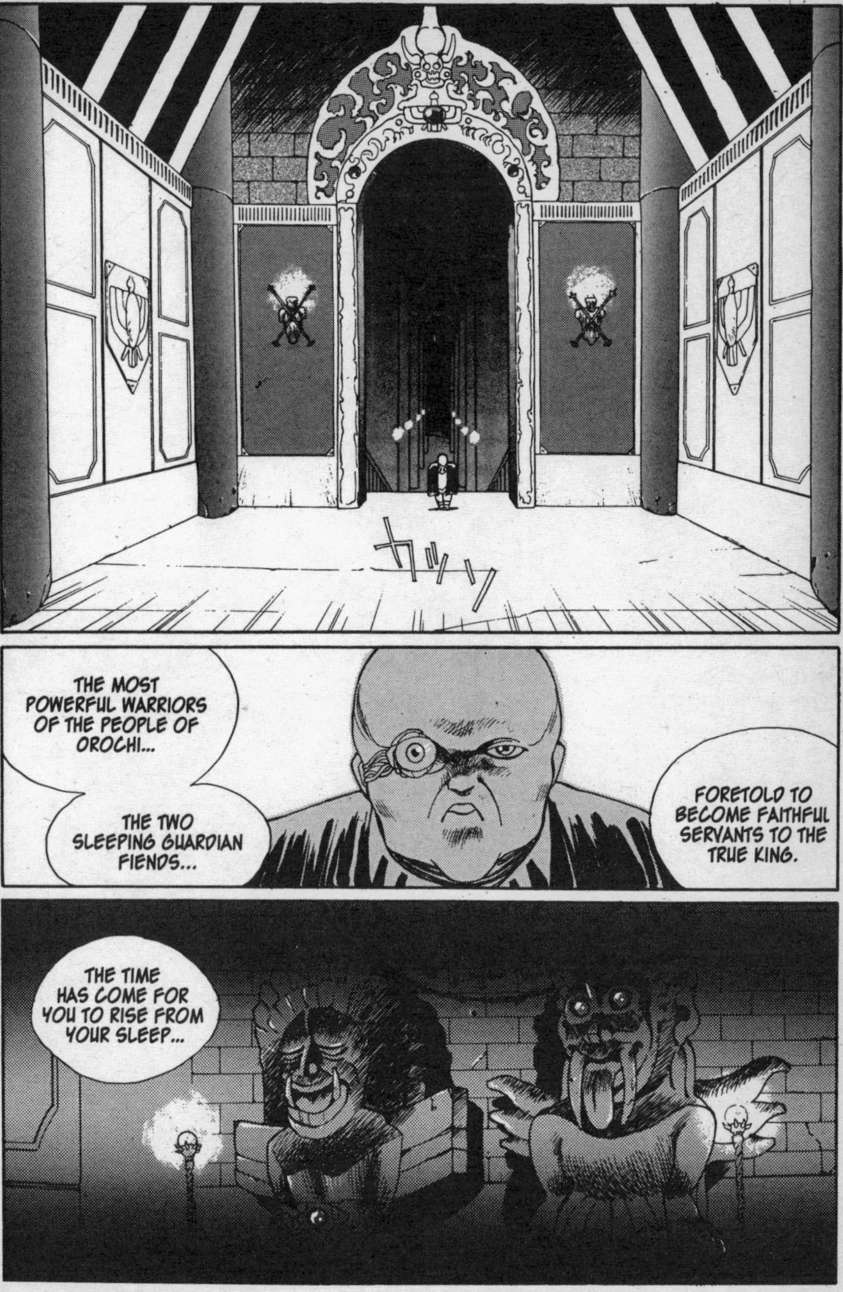
THE MOST POWERFUL WARRIORS OF THE PEOPLE OF OROCHI...
THE TWO SLEEPING GUARDIAN FIENDS...
FORETOLD TO BECOME FAITHFUL SERVANTS TO THE TRUE KING.
THE TIME HAS COME FOR YOU TO RISE FROM YOUR SLEEP...

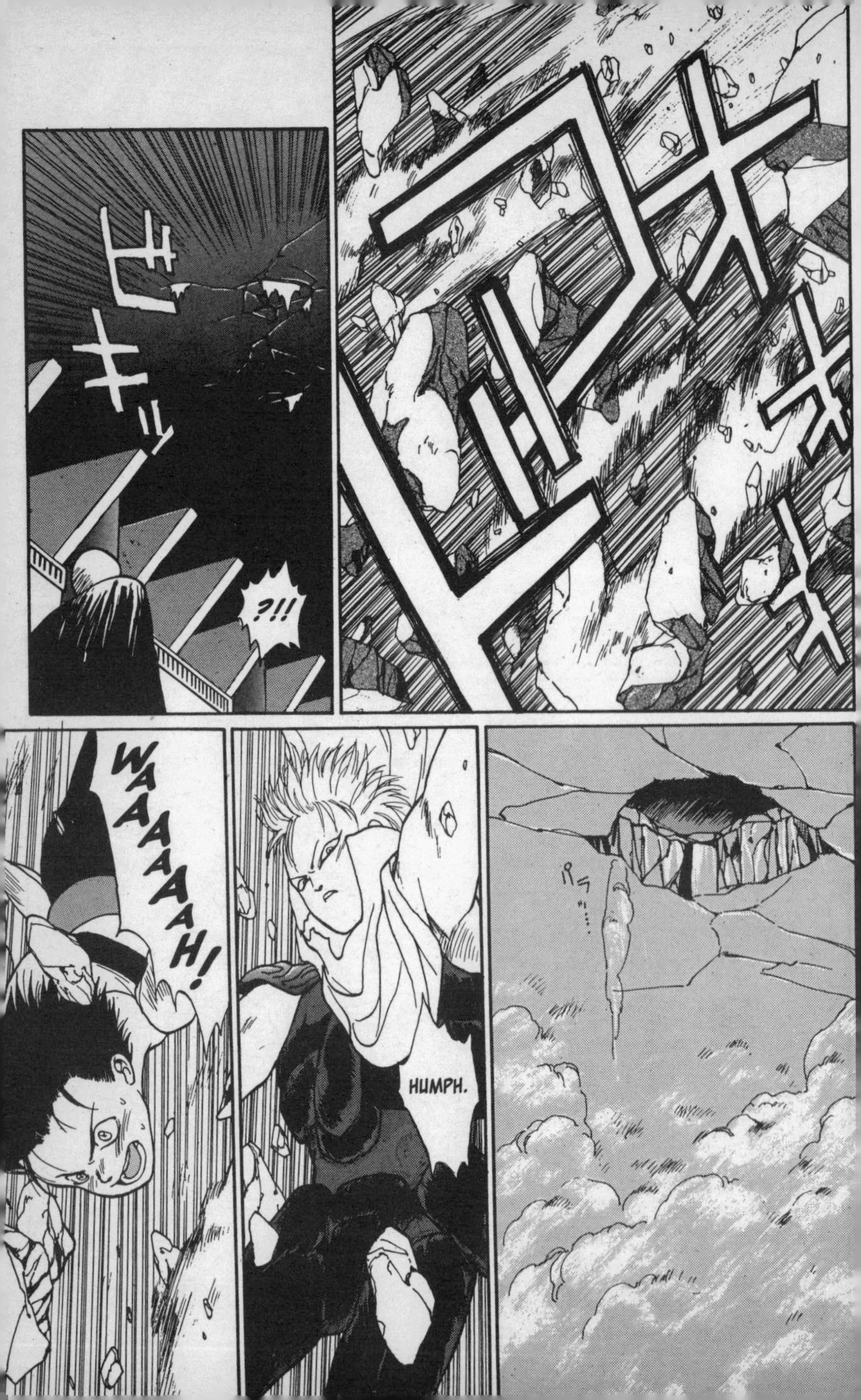
?!!
WAAAAAAH!
HUMPH.

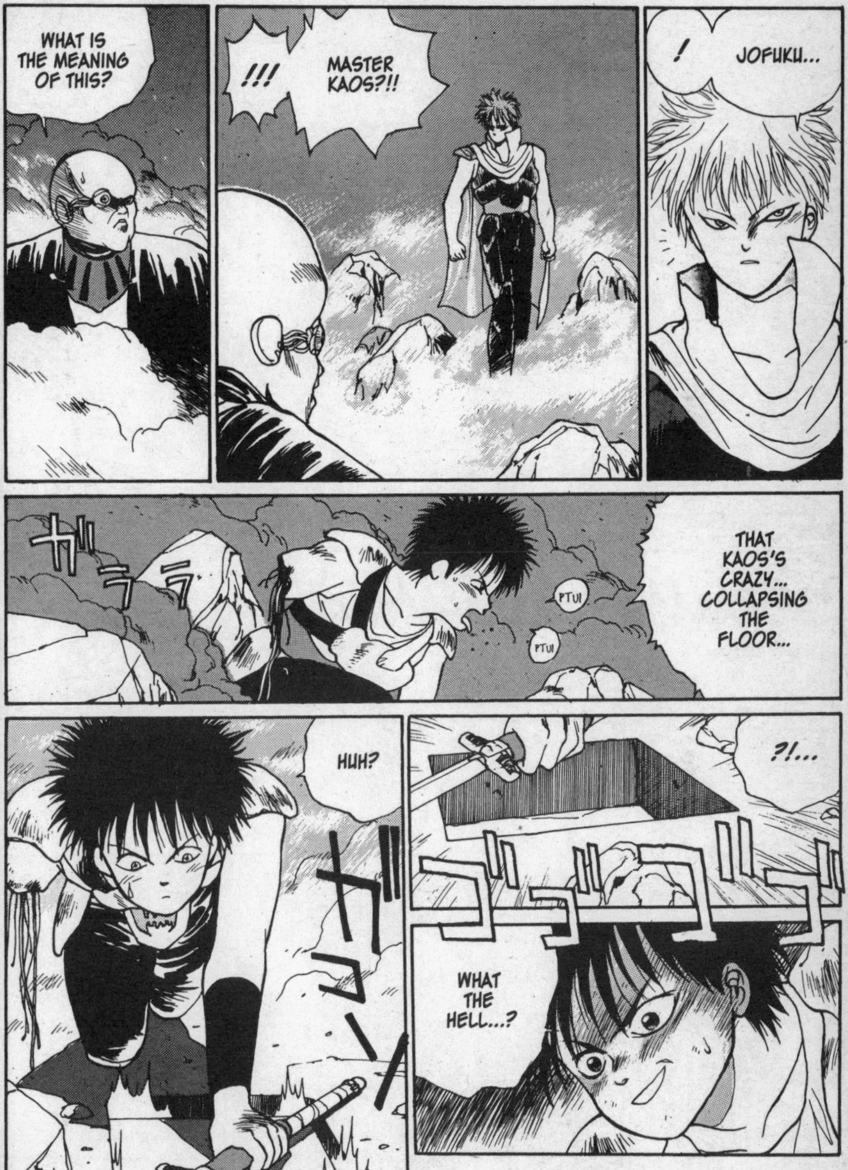
WHAT IS THE MEANING OF THIS?
!!!
MASTER KAOS?!!
!
JOFUKU...
PTUI
PTUI
THAT KAOS'S CRAZY... COLLAPSING THE FLOOR...
HUH?
?!...
WHAT THE HELL...?

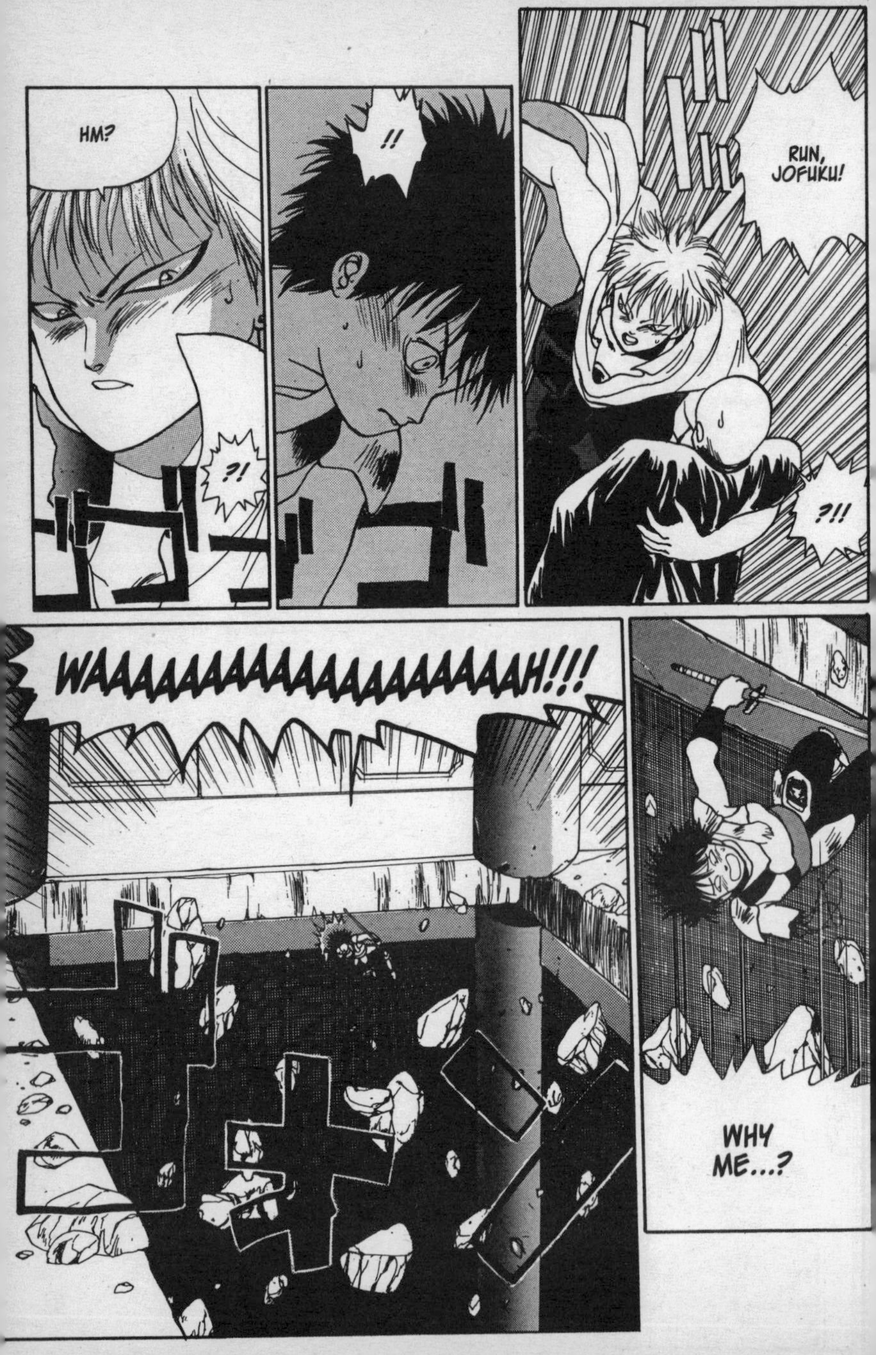
HM?
!!
RUN, JOFUKU!
?!
?!!
WAAAAAAAAAAAAAAAAAAAAH!!!
WHY ME...?

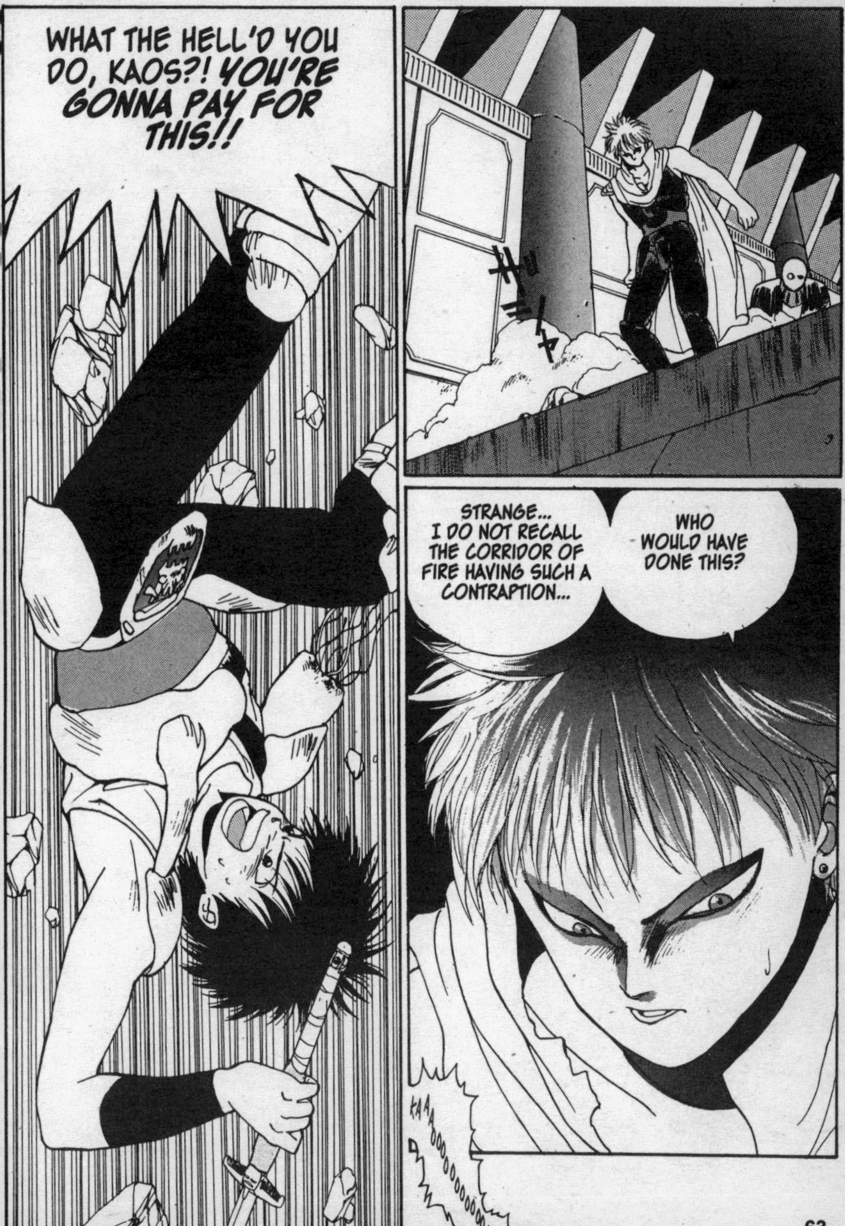

WHAT THE HELL'D YOU DO, KAOS?! YOU'RE GONNA PAY FOR THIS!!
STRANGE... I DO NOT RECALL THE CORRIDOR OF FIRE HAVING SUCH A CONTRAPTION...
WHO WOULD HAVE DONE THIS?
KAAAOOOOOOOOOOOOOOS!!

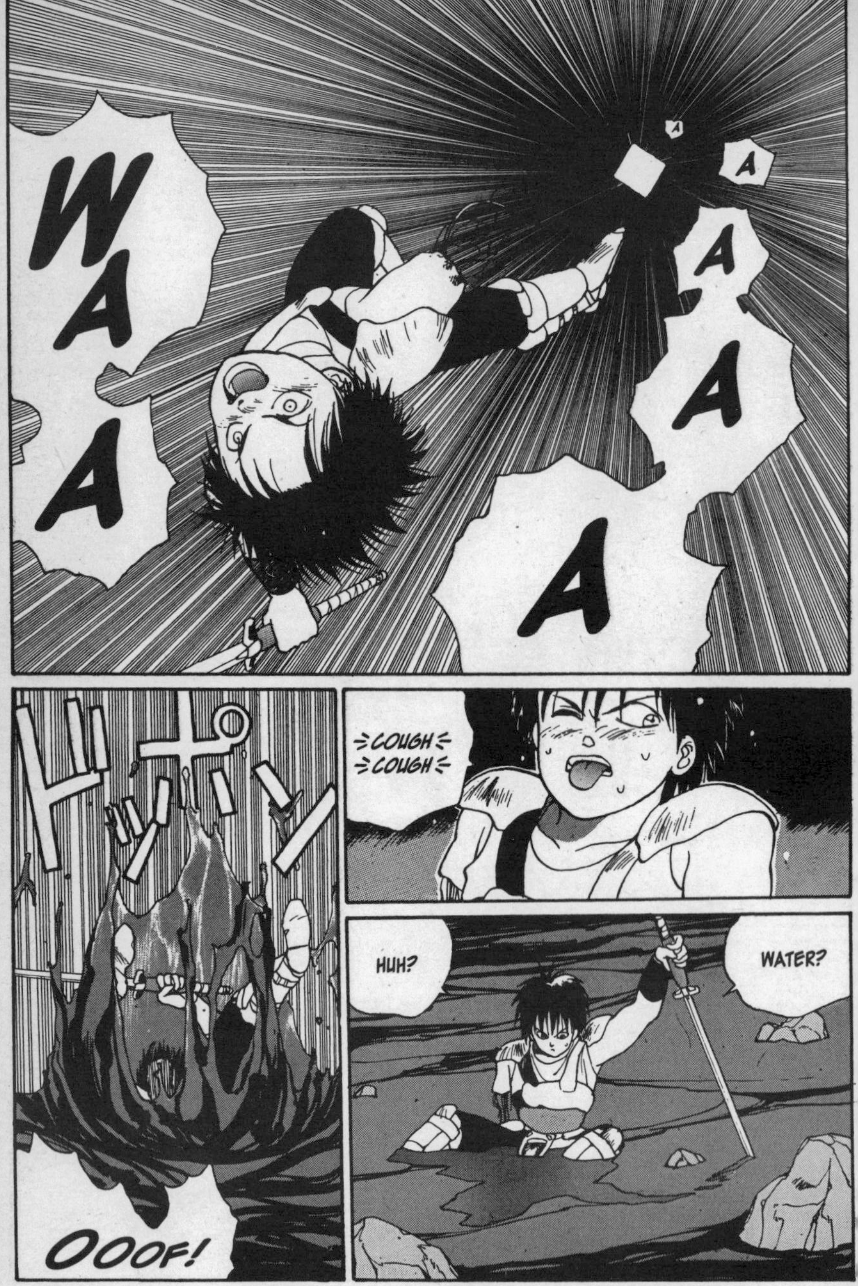

WAAAAAAAA
OOOF!
COUGH
COUGH
HUH?
WATER?

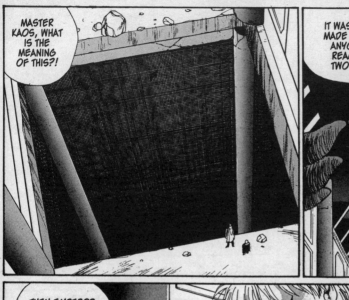

MASTER KAOS, WHAT IS THE MEANING OF THIS?!

IT WAS PROBABLY MADE TO PREVENT ANYONE FROM REACHING THE TWO STATUES...

THEN EMPEROR MIROKU MUST BE BEHIND THIS...

....

WHATEVER THE CASE, JOFUKU, PREPARE TO WAKE THE SLEEPING GUARDIAN FIENDS.

I WILL SEE WHAT IS BELOW...

YES, MASTER.

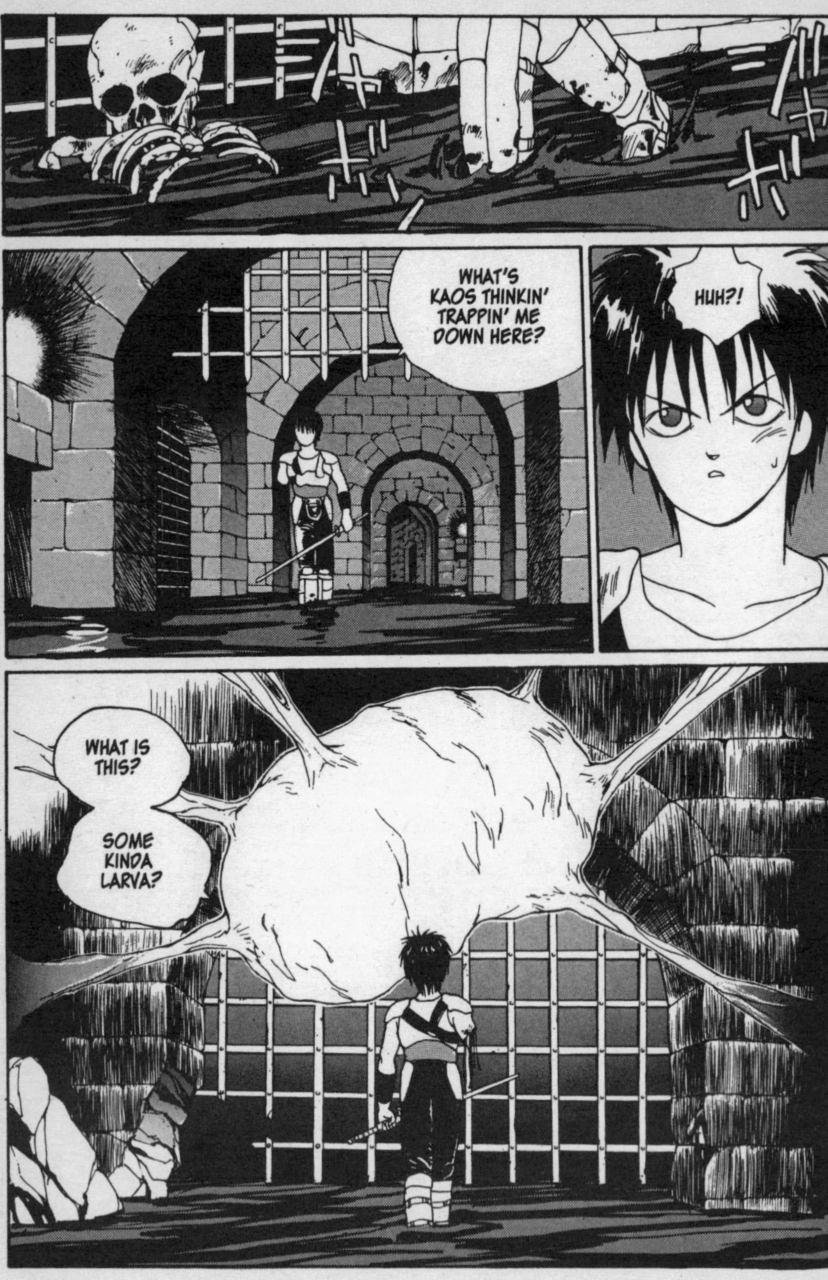
WHAT'S KAOS THINKIN' TRAPPIN' ME DOWN HERE?
HUH?!
WHAT IS THIS?
SOME KINDA LARVA?

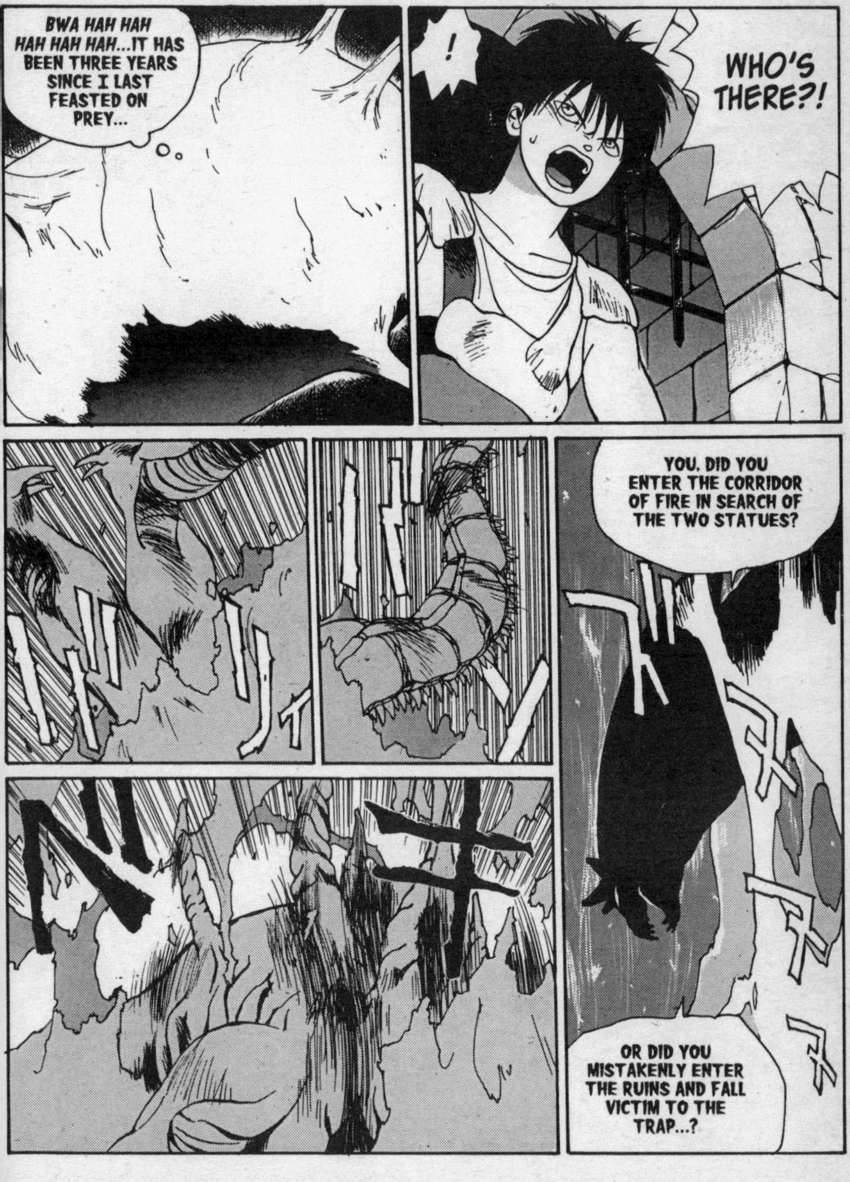
BWA HAH HAH HAH HAH HAH...IT HAS BEEN THREE YEARS SINCE I LAST FEASTED ON PREY...
!
WHO'S THERE?!
YOU, DID YOU ENTER THE CORRIDOR OF FIRE IN SEARCH OF THE TWO STATUES?
OR DID YOU MISTAKENLY ENTER THE RUINS AND FALL VICTIM TO THE TRAP...?

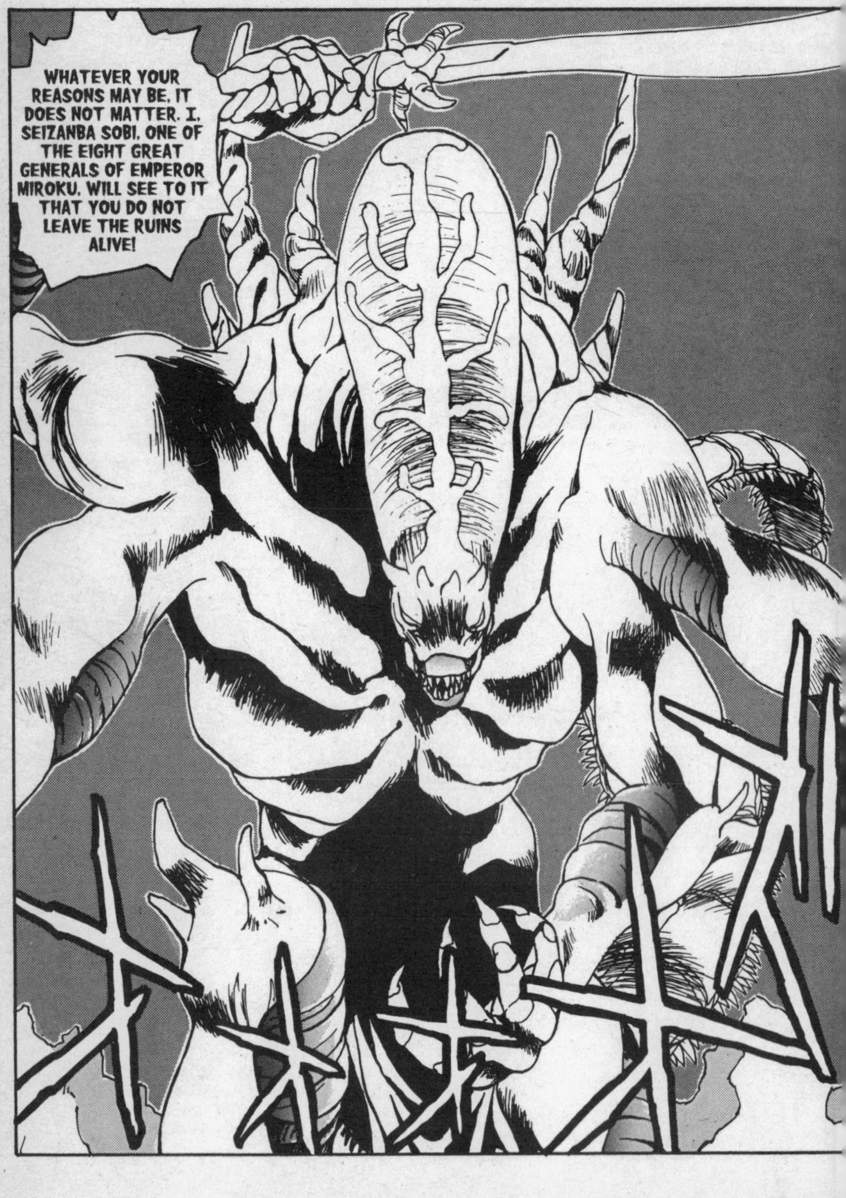
WHATEVER YOUR REASONS MAY BE, IT DOES NOT MATTER. I, SEIZANBA SOBI, ONE OF THE EIGHT GREAT GENERALS OF EMPEROR MIROKU, WILL SEE TO IT THAT YOU DO NOT LEAVE THE RUINS ALIVE!

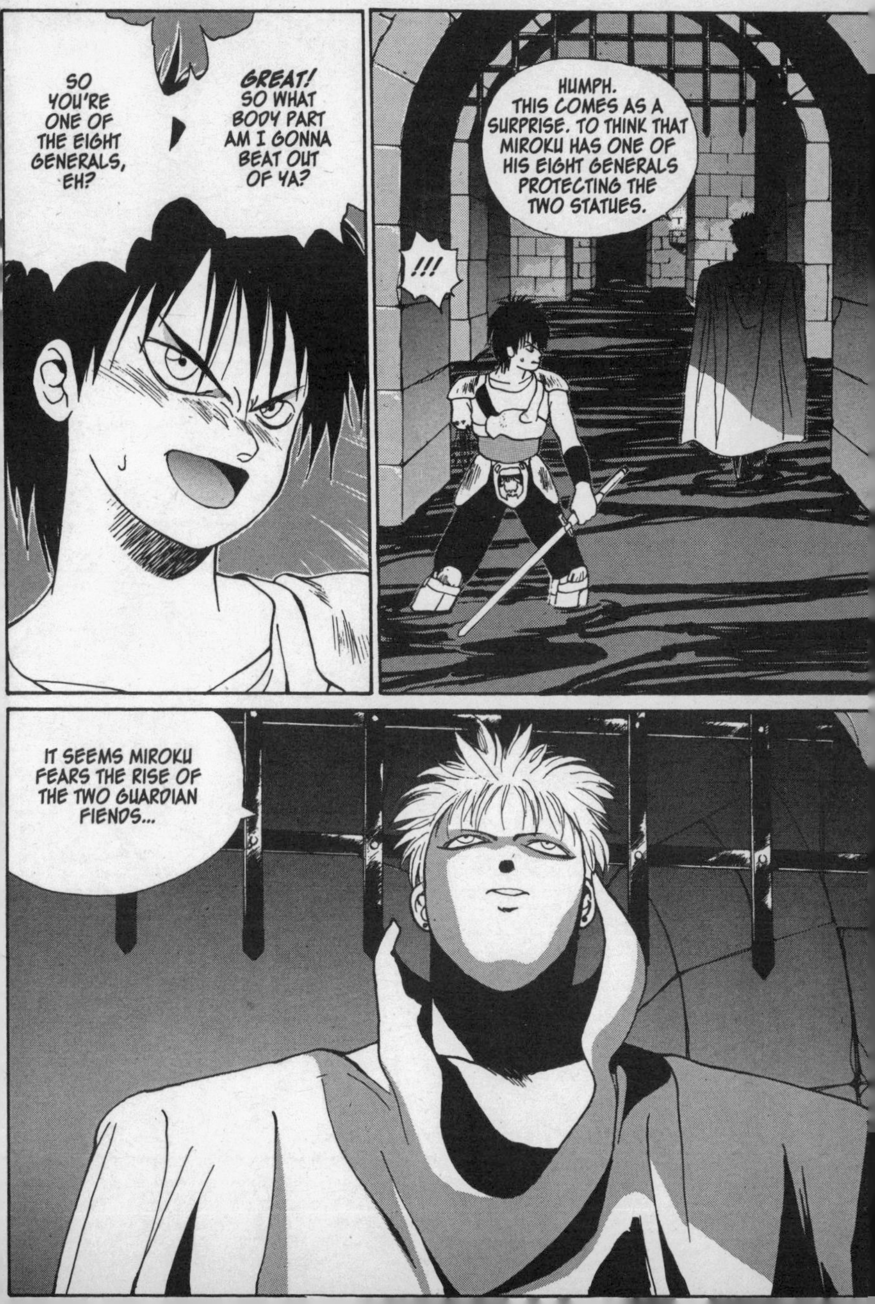
SO YOU'RE ONE OF THE EIGHT GENERALS, EH?
GREAT! SO WHAT BODY PART AM I GONNA BEAT OUT OF YA?
HUMPH. THIS COMES AS A SURPRISE. TO THINK THAT MIROKU HAS ONE OF HIS EIGHT GENERALS PROTECTING THE TWO STATUES.
!!!
IT SEEMS MIROKU FEARS THE RISE OF THE TWO GUARDIAN FIENDS...

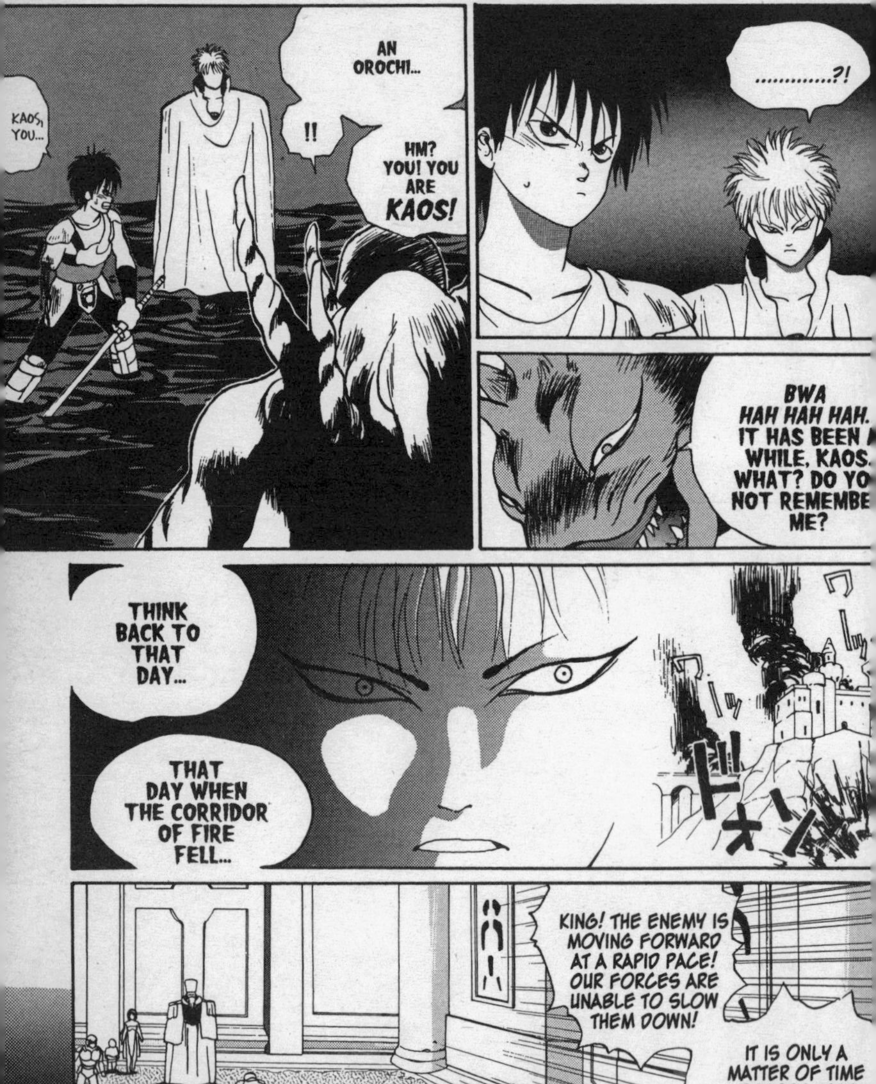
KAOS, YOU...
AN OROCHI...
!!
HM? YOU! YOU ARE KAOS!
..............?!
BWA HAH HAH HAH. IT HAS BEEN A WHILE, KAOS. WHAT? DO YO NOT REMEMBE ME?
THINK BACK TO THAT DAY...
THAT DAY WHEN THE CORRIDOR OF FIRE FELL...
KING! THE ENEMY IS MOVING FORWARD AT A RAPID PACE! OUR FORCES ARE UNABLE TO SLOW THEM DOWN!
IT IS ONLY A MATTER OF TIME BEFORE THEY REACH THE INNER CORRIDOR!

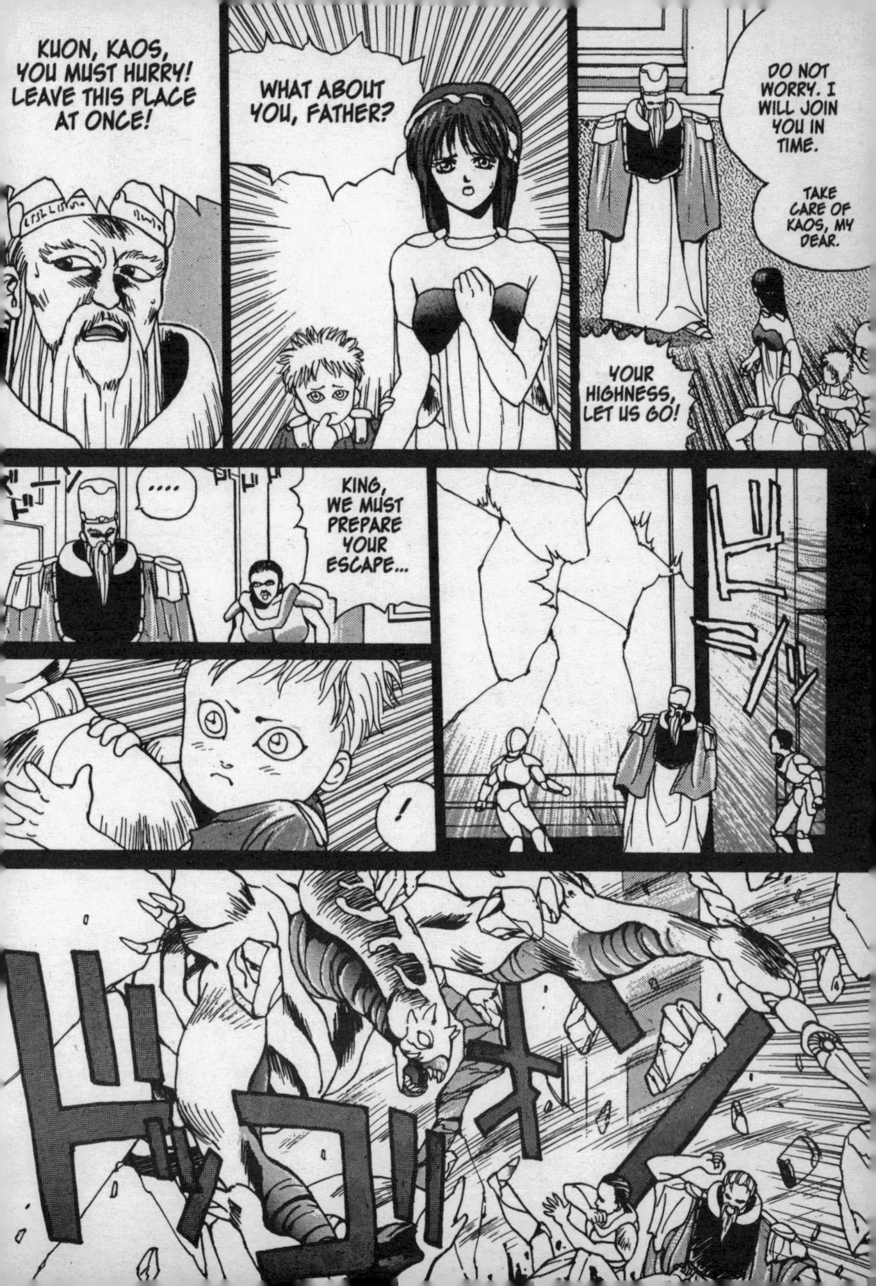
KUON, KAOS, YOU MUST HURRY! LEAVE THIS PLACE AT ONCE!
WHAT ABOUT YOU, FATHER?
DO NOT WORRY. I WILL JOIN YOU IN TIME.
TAKE CARE OF KAOS, MY DEAR.
YOUR HIGHNESS, LET US GO!
....
KING, WE MUST PREPARE YOUR ESCAPE...
!

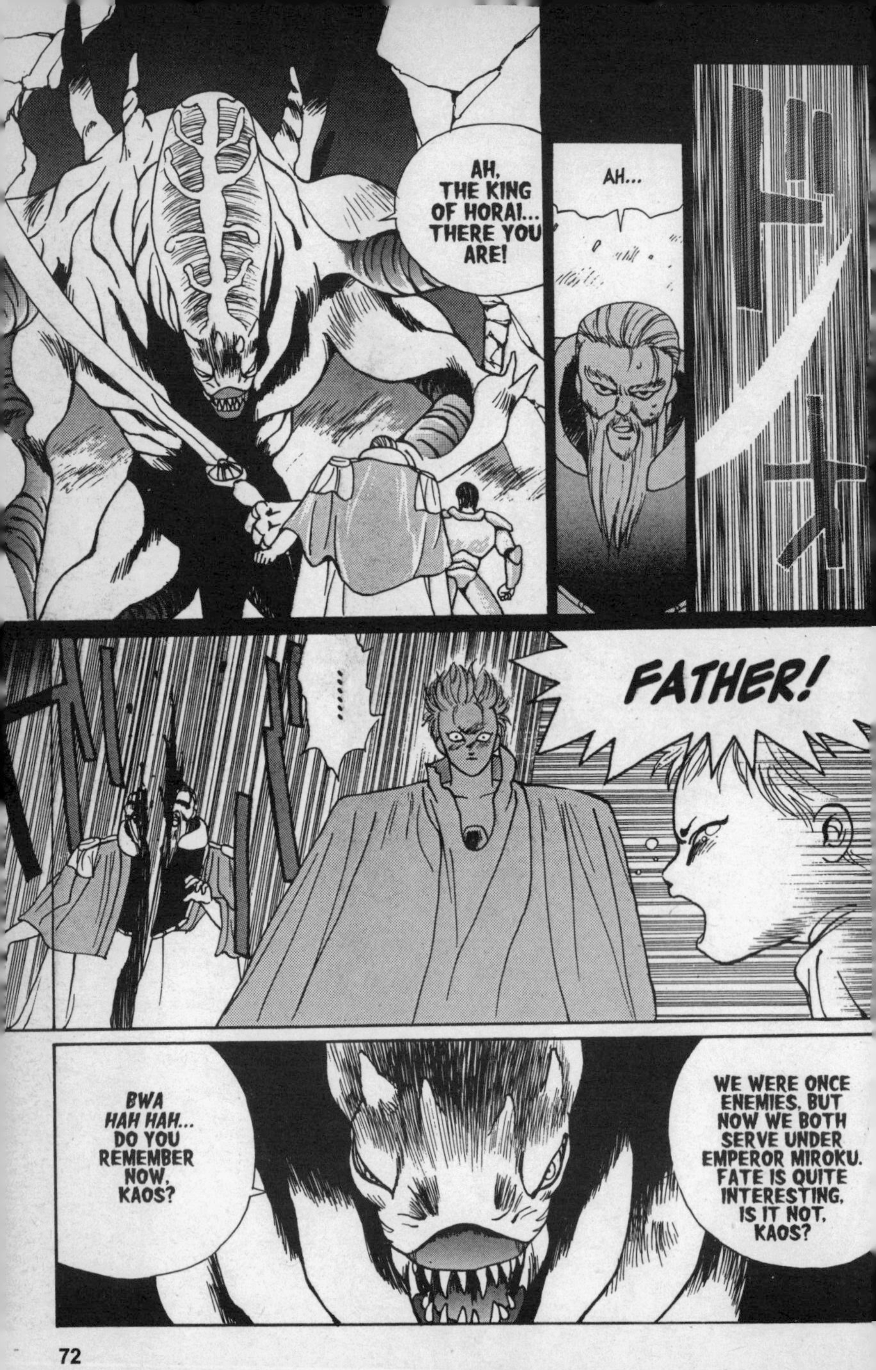
AH, THE KING OF HORAI... THERE YOU ARE!
AH...
......
FATHER!
BWA HAH HAH... DO YOU REMEMBER NOW, KAOS?
WE WERE ONCE ENEMIES, BUT NOW WE BOTH SERVE UNDER EMPEROR MIROKU. FATE IS QUITE INTERESTING, IS IT NOT, KAOS?

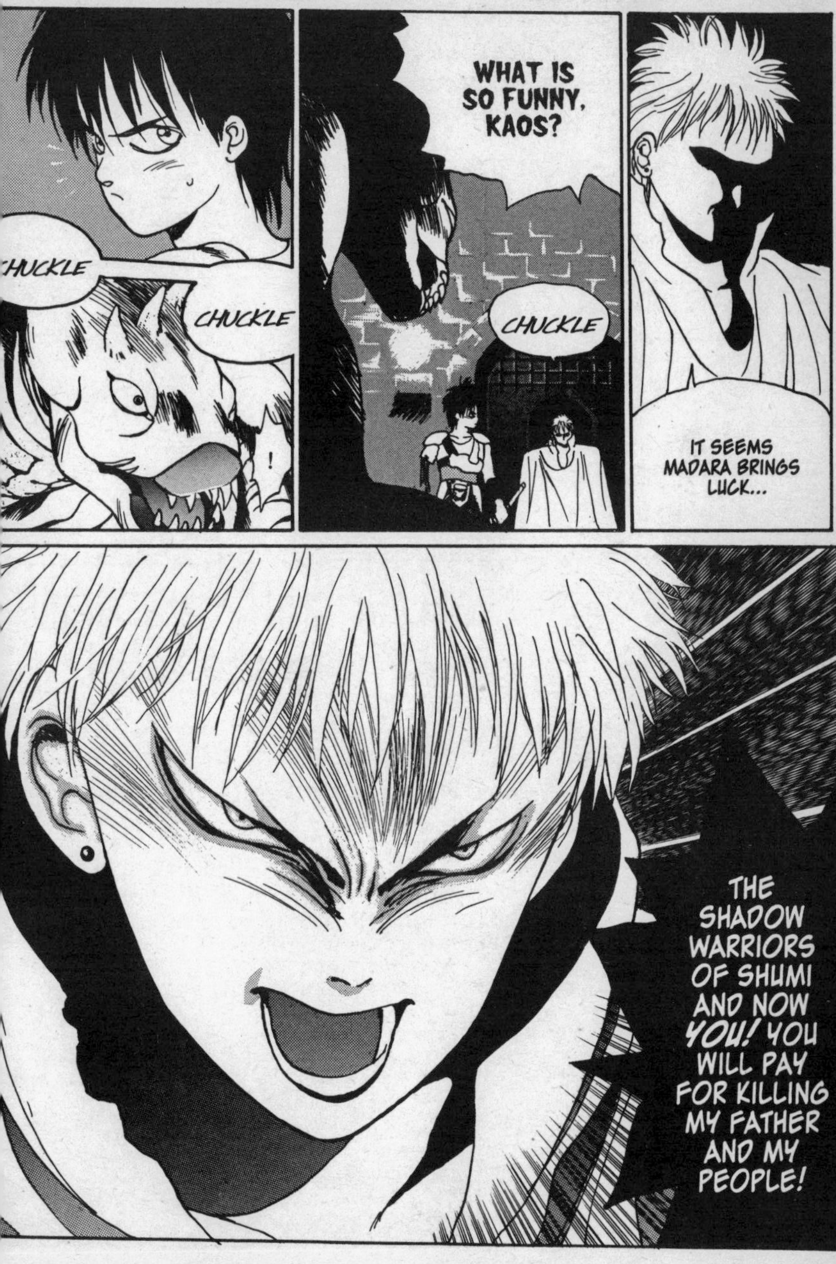
CHUCKLE
CHUCKLE
!
WHAT IS SO FUNNY, KAOS?
CHUCKLE
IT SEEMS MADARA BRINGS LUCK...
THE SHADOW WARRIORS OF SHUMI AND NOW YOU! YOU WILL PAY FOR KILLING MY FATHER AND MY PEOPLE!

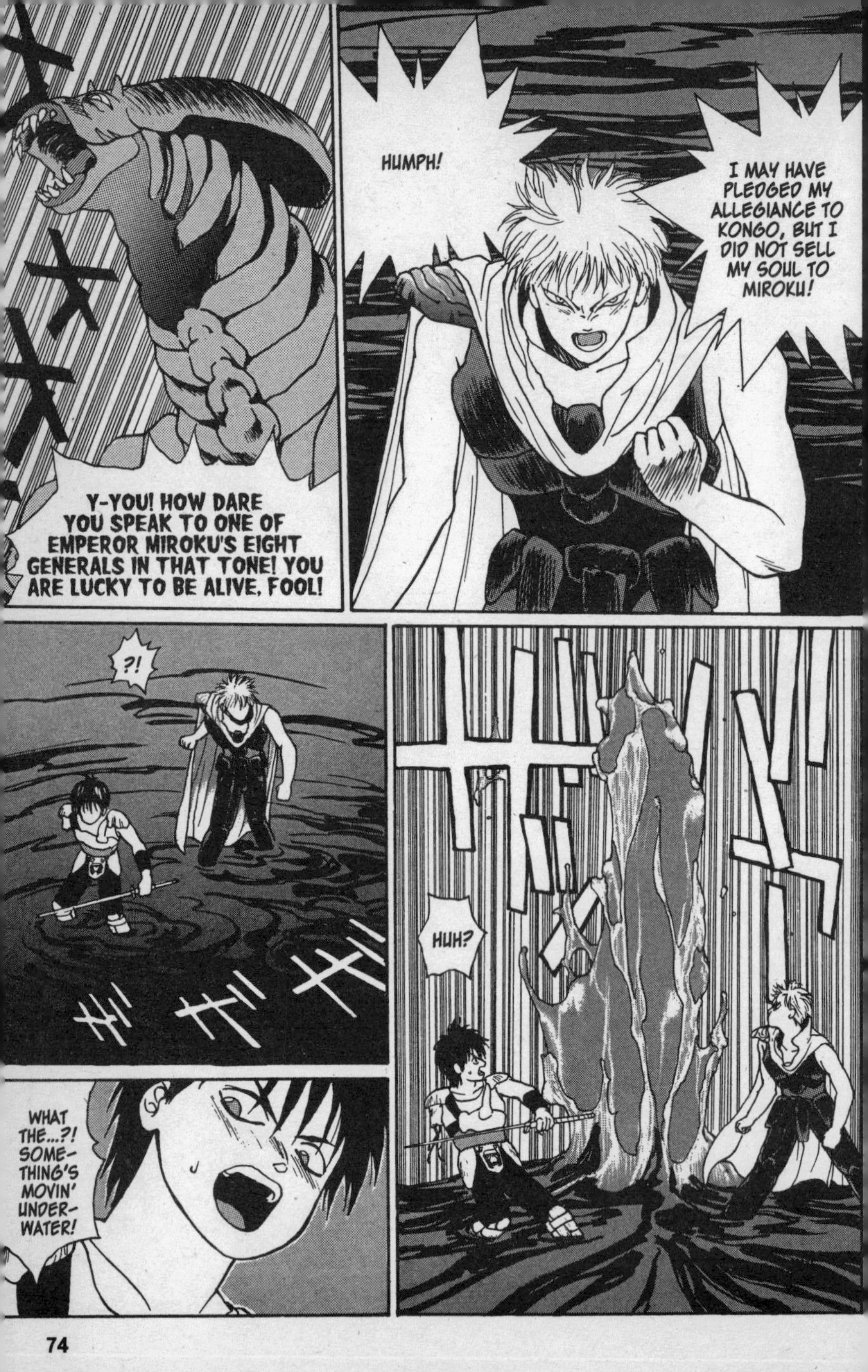
HUMPH!
I MAY HAVE PLEDGED MY ALLEGIANCE TO KONGO, BUT I DID NOT SELL MY SOUL TO MIROKU!
Y-YOU! HOW DARE YOU SPEAK TO ONE OF EMPEROR MIROKU'S EIGHT GENERALS IN THAT TONE! YOU ARE LUCKY TO BE ALIVE, FOOL!
HUH?
?!
WHAT THE...?! SOME-THING'S MOVIN' UNDER-WATER!

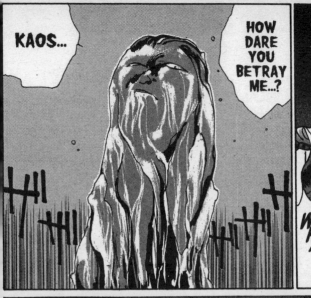

KAOS...

HOW DARE YOU BETRAY ME...?

MIROKU...

WHAT?!

SO THIS IS MIROKU...

I'VE SEEN 'IM IN MY DREAMS BEFORE...

YOU SHALL BE FORGIVEN FOR YOUR KILLING OF THE SHADOW WARRIORS OF SHUMI...

BUT IF YOU INTEND TO WAKE THE TWO GUARDIAN FIENDS AND KILL SEIZANBA SOBI, THEN YOU AND THE OTHER HALF OF YOUR BODY WILL PAY!

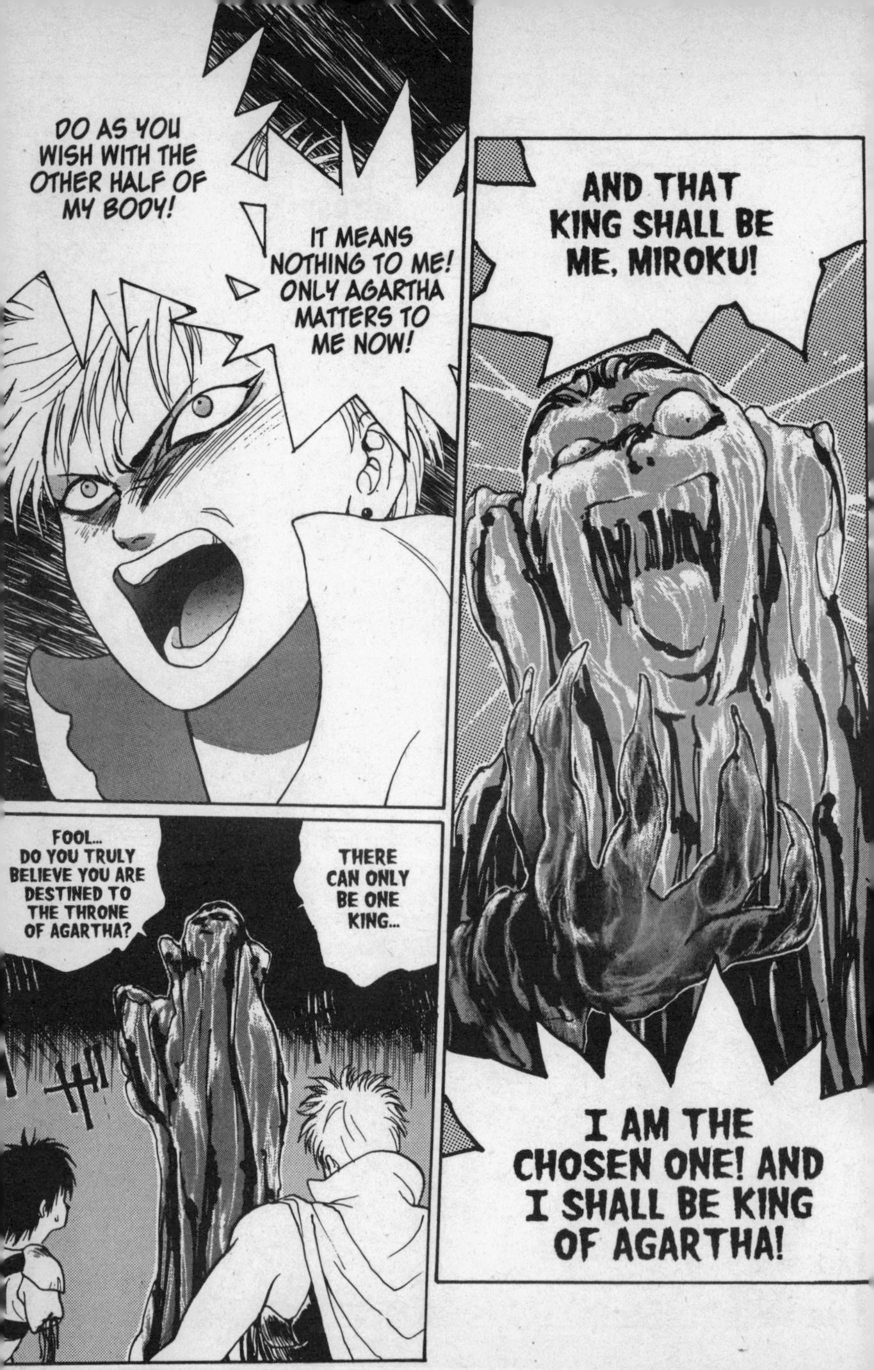
DO AS YOU WISH WITH THE OTHER HALF OF MY BODY!
IT MEANS NOTHING TO ME! ONLY AGARTHA MATTERS TO ME NOW!
FOOL... DO YOU TRULY BELIEVE YOU ARE DESTINED TO THE THRONE OF AGARTHA?
THERE CAN ONLY BE ONE KING...
AND THAT KING SHALL BE ME, MIROKU!
I AM THE CHOSEN ONE! AND I SHALL BE KING OF AGARTHA!

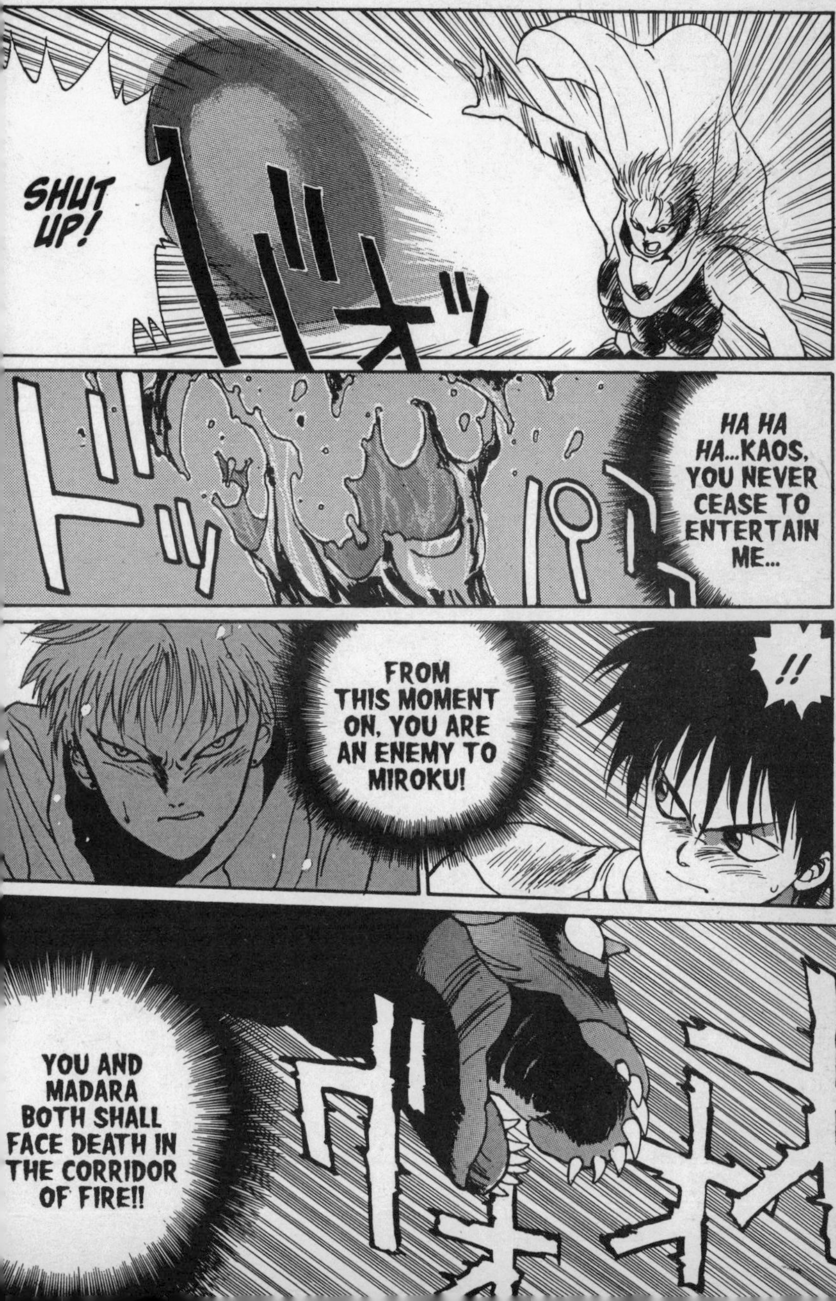
SHUT UP!
HA HA HA...KAOS, YOU NEVER CEASE TO ENTERTAIN ME...
FROM THIS MOMENT ON, YOU ARE AN ENEMY TO MIROKU!
!!
YOU AND MADARA BOTH SHALL FACE DEATH IN THE CORRIDOR OF FIRE!!

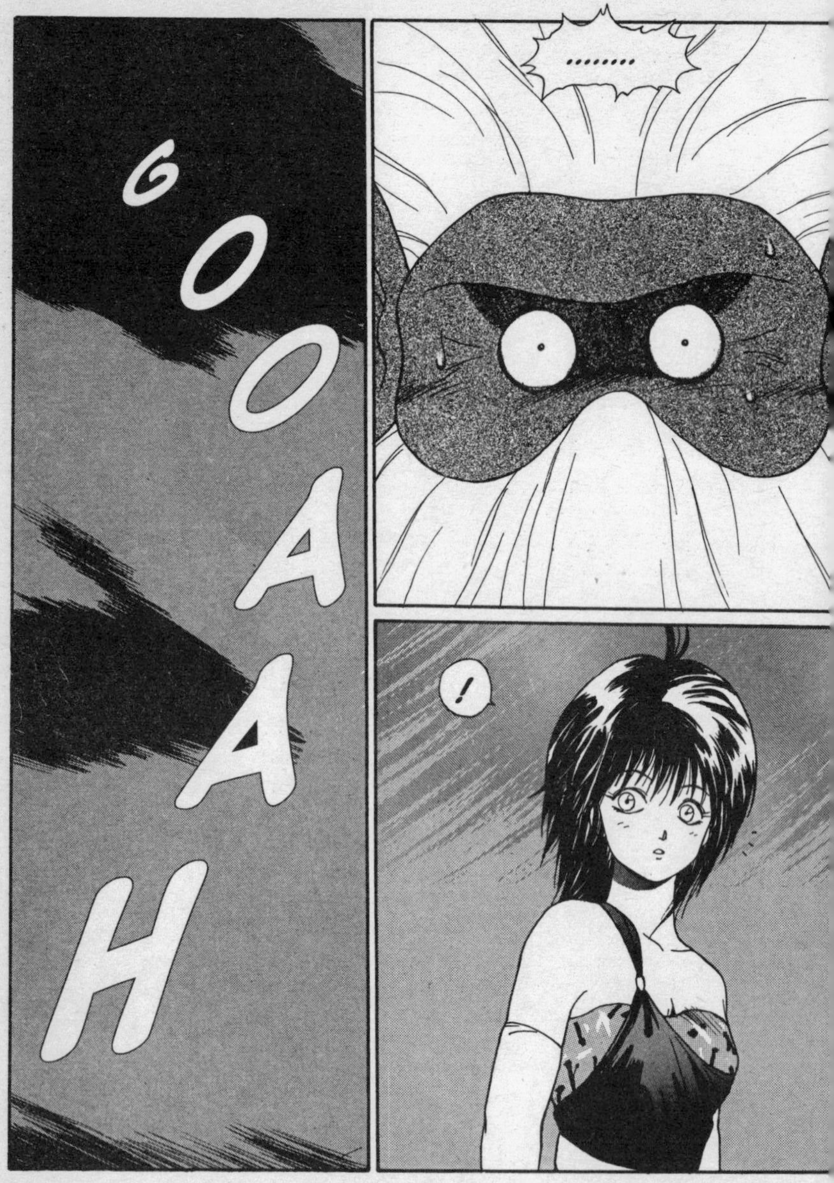
GOOAAH
....
!

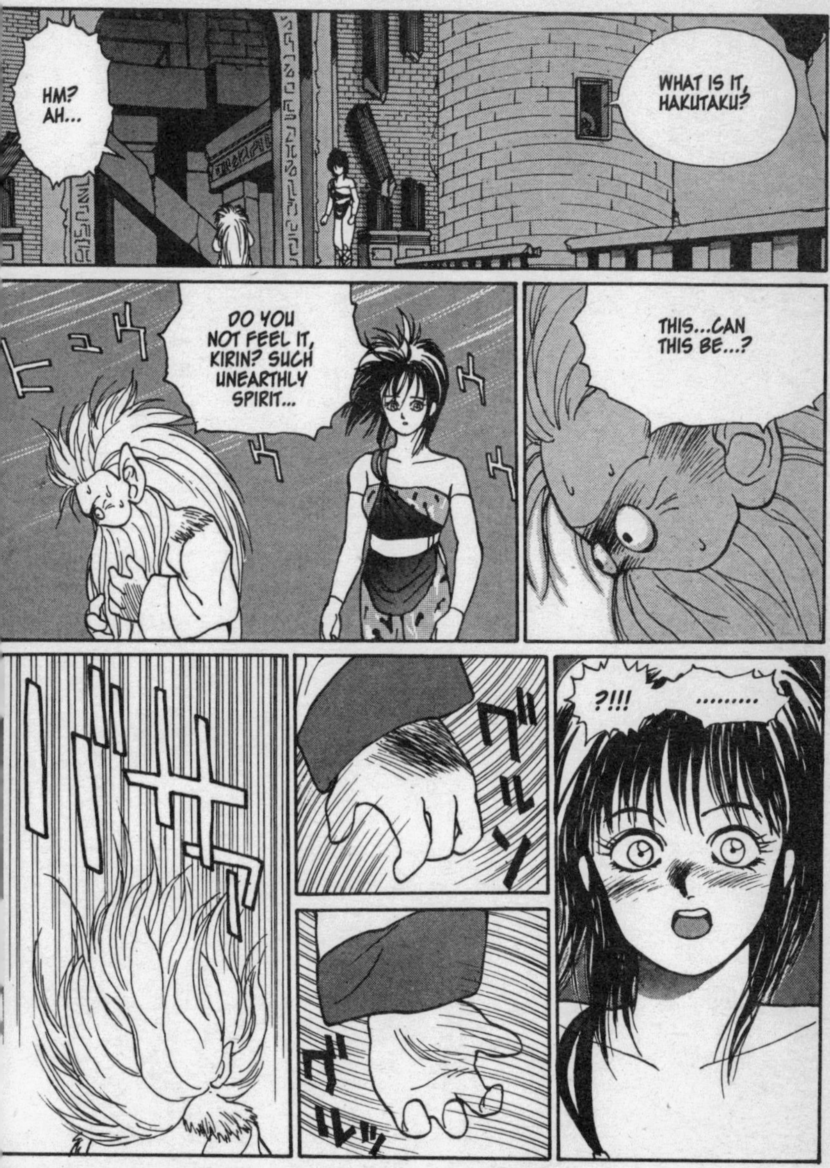
HM? AH...
WHAT IS IT, HAKUTAKU?
DO YOU NOT FEEL IT, KIRIN? SUCH UNEARTHLY SPIRIT...
THIS...CAN THIS BE...?
?!!!
....

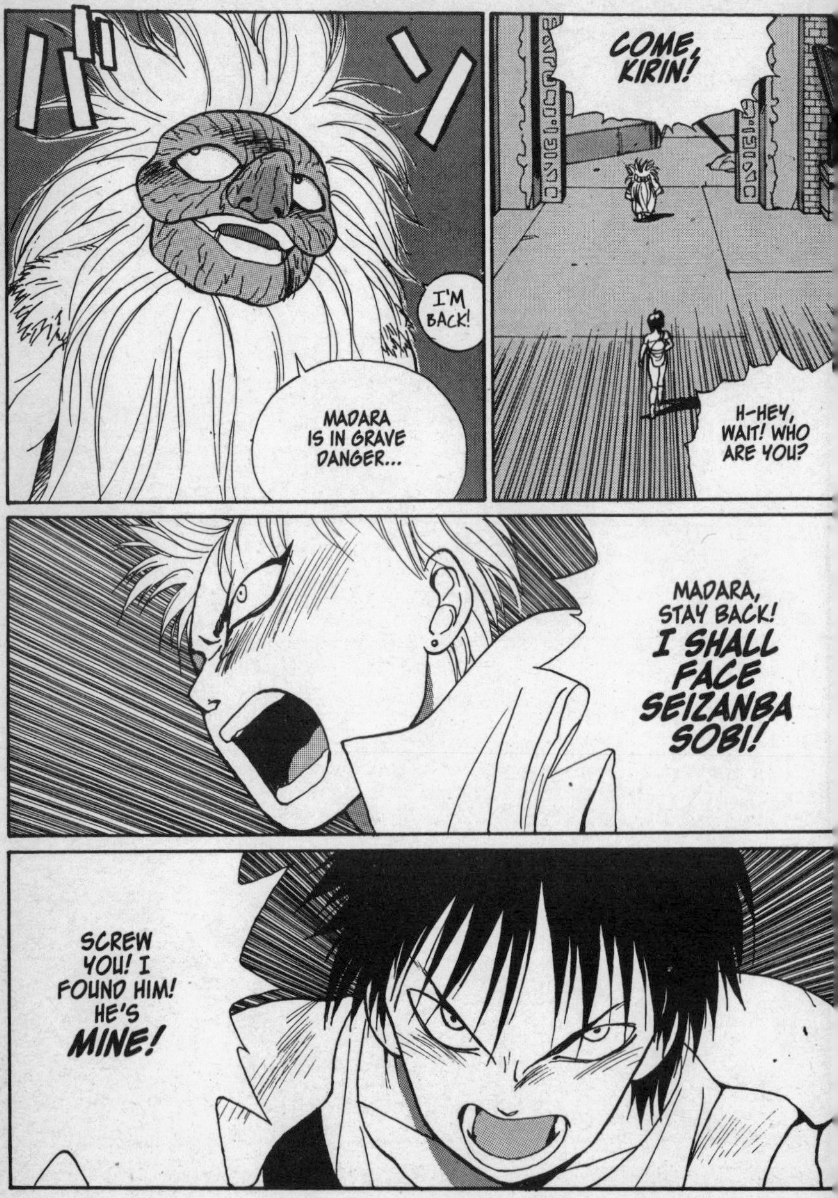
I'M BACK!
MADARA IS IN GRAVE DANGER...
COME, KIRIN!
H-HEY, WAIT! WHO ARE YOU?
MADARA, STAY BACK! I SHALL FACE SEIZANBA SOBI!
SCREW YOU! I FOUND HIM! HE'S MINE!

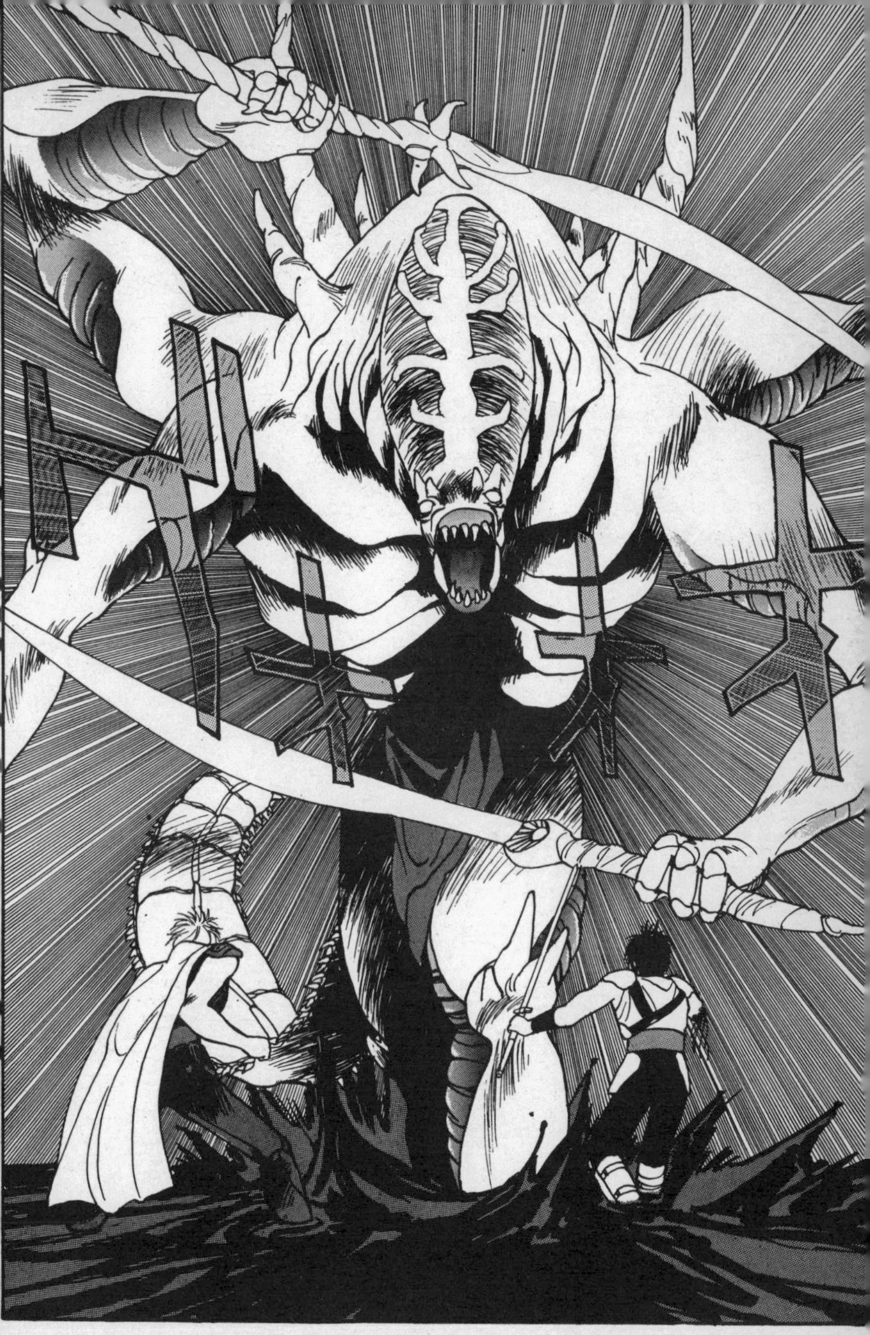

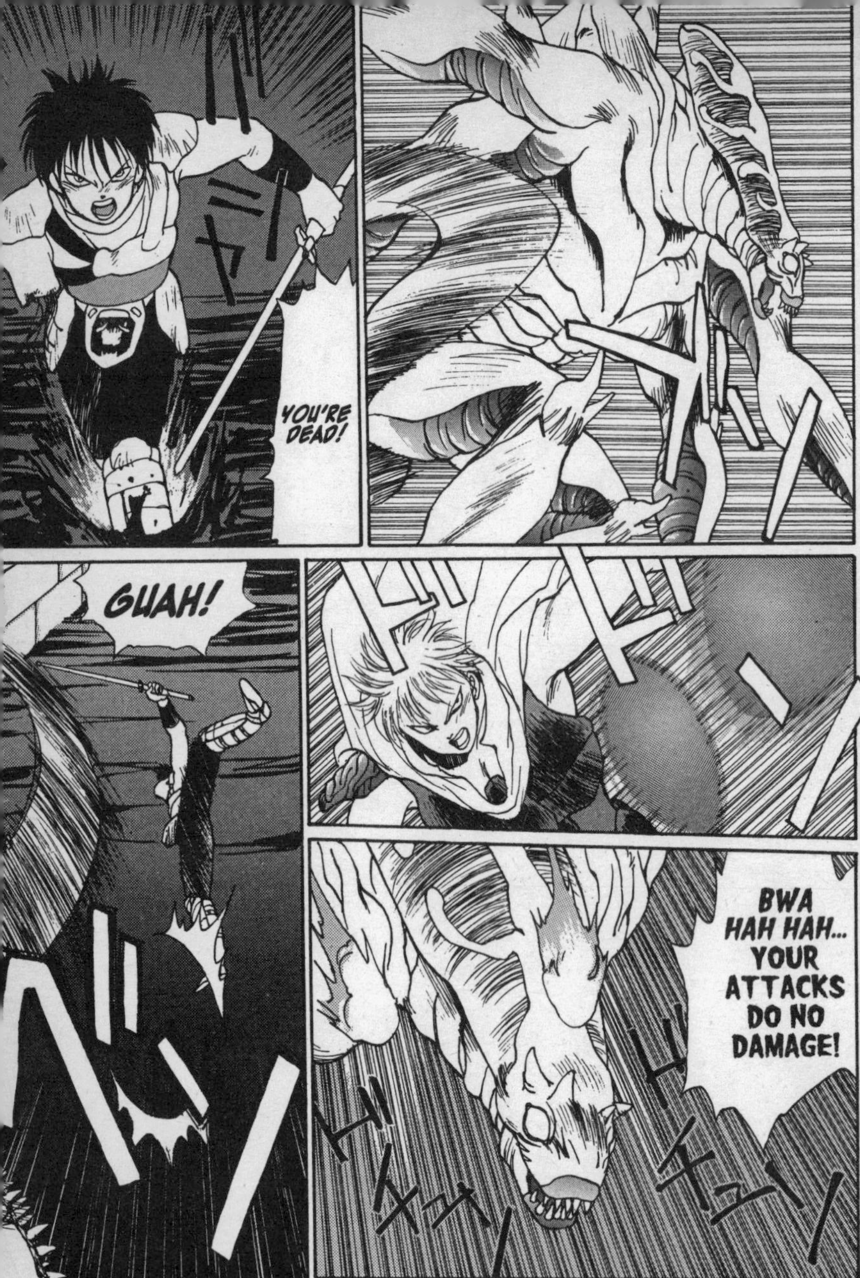
YOU'RE DEAD!
GUAH!
BWA HAH HAH... YOUR ATTACKS DO NO DAMAGE!

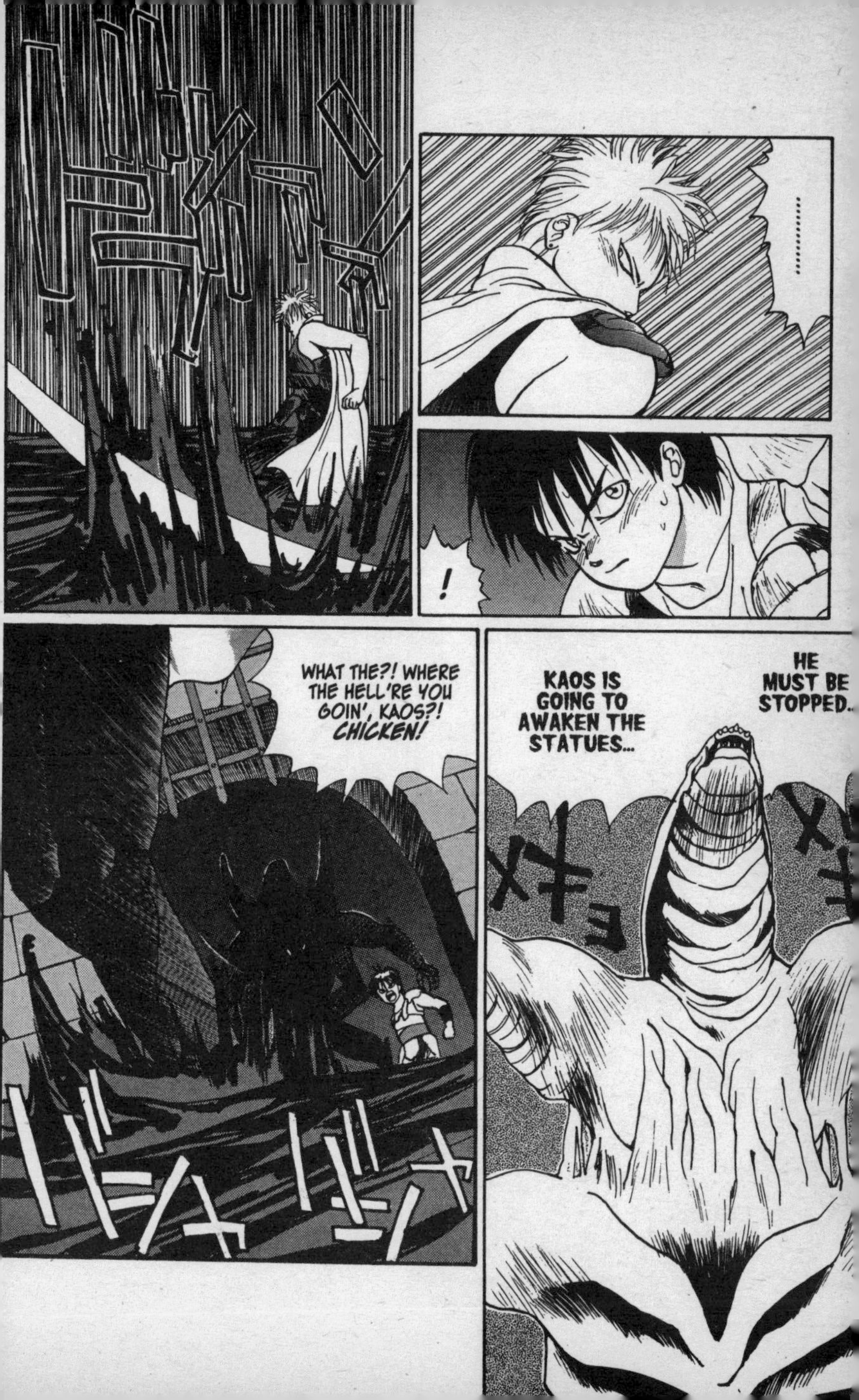
......
!
WHAT THE?! WHERE THE HELL'RE YOU GOIN', KAOS?! CHICKEN!
KAOS IS GOING TO AWAKEN THE STATUES...
HE MUST BE STOPPED...

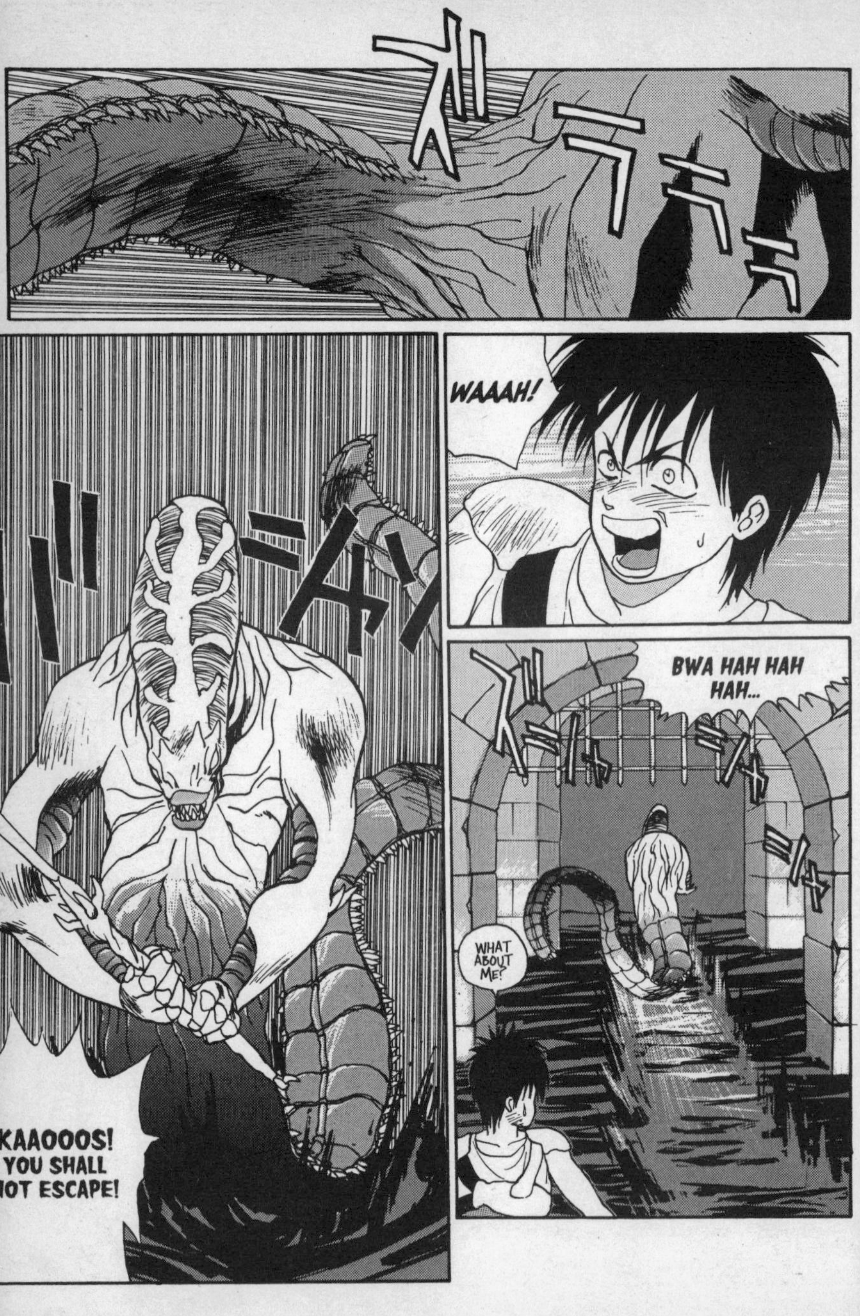
KAAOOOS! YOU SHALL NOT ESCAPE!
WAAAH!
BWA HAH HAH HAH...
WHAT ABOUT ME?

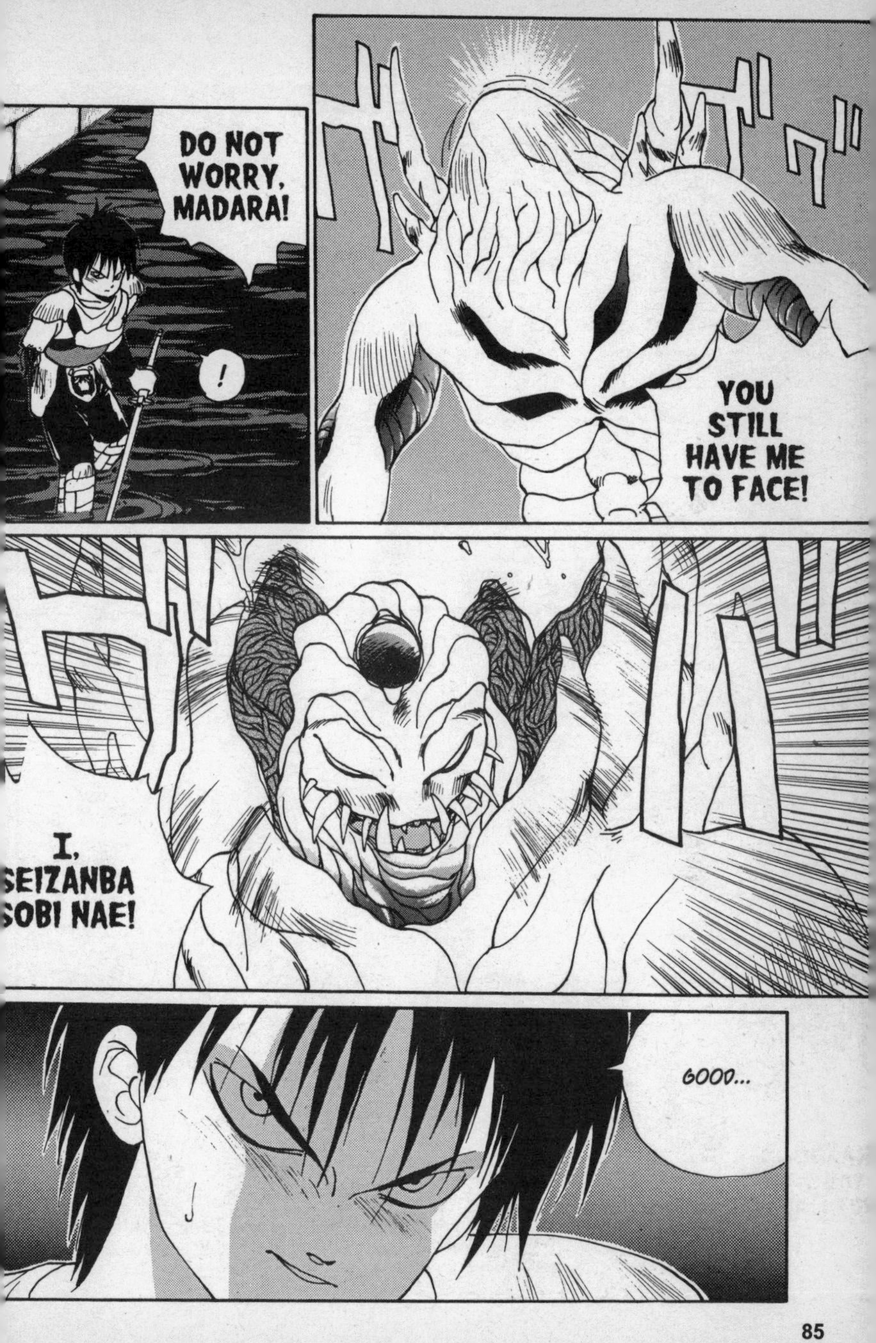
DO NOT WORRY, MADARA!
!
YOU STILL HAVE ME TO FACE!
I, SEIZANBA SOBI NAE!
GOOD...

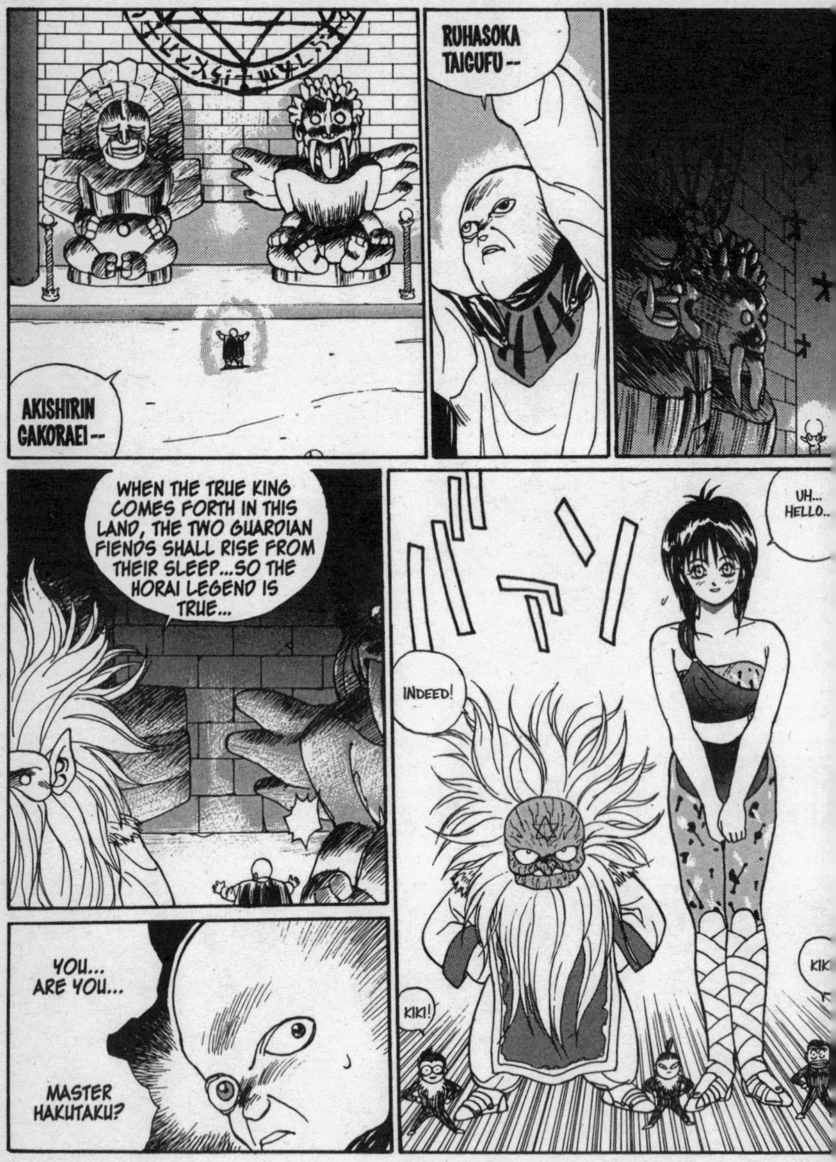

AKISHIRIN GAKORAEI --
RUHASOKA TAIGUFU --
WHEN THE TRUE KING COMES FORTH IN THIS LAND, THE TWO GUARDIAN FIENDS SHALL RISE FROM THEIR SLEEP...SO THE HORAI LEGEND IS TRUE...
YOU... ARE YOU...
MASTER HAKUTAKU?
UH... HELLO..
INDEED!
KIKI!
KIK

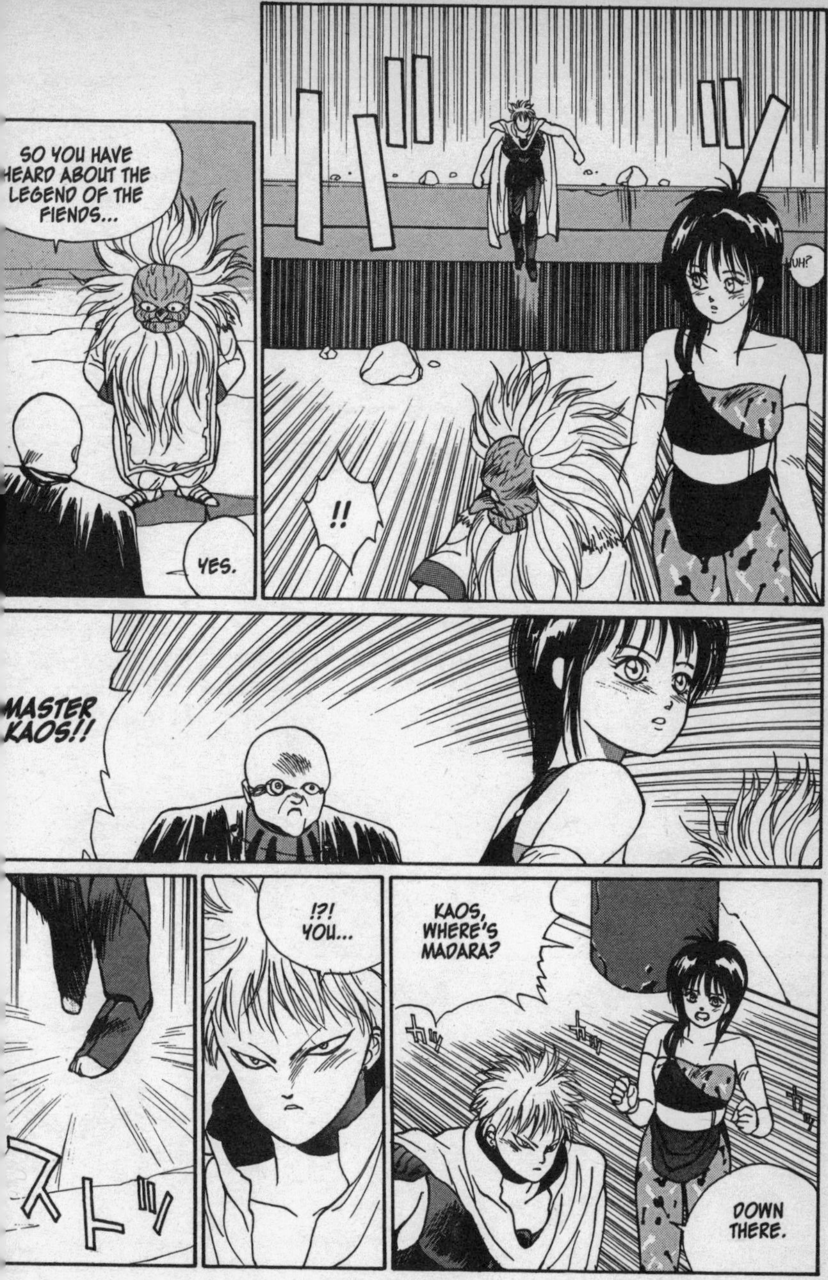
SO YOU HAVE HEARD ABOUT THE LEGEND OF THE FIENDS...
YES.
HUH?
!!
MASTER KAOS!!
ストッ
!?! YOU...
KAOS, WHERE'S MADARA?
カッ
カッ
カッ
DOWN THERE.

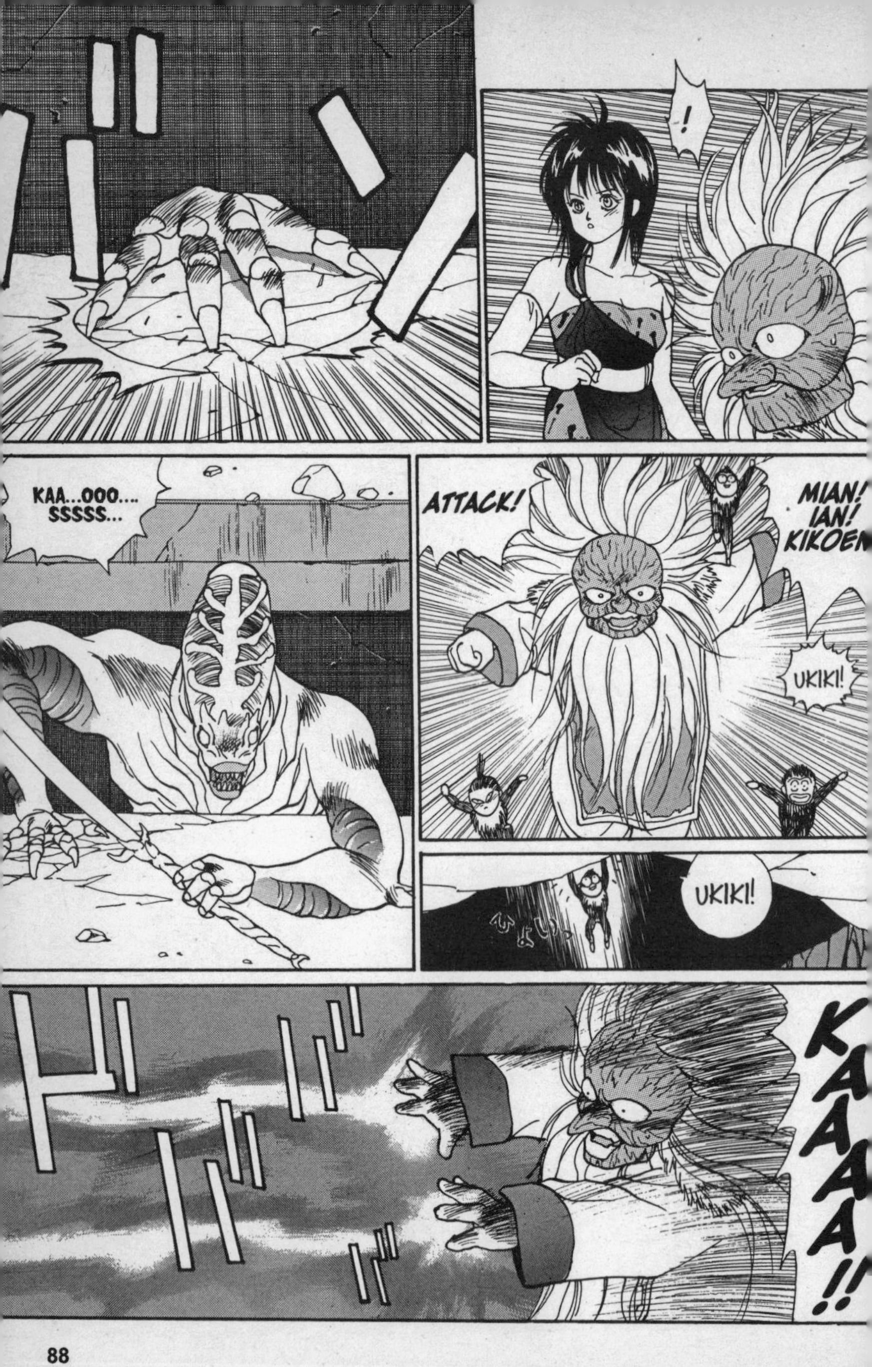
!
KAA...OOO....
SSSSS...
ATTACK!
MIAN!
IAN!
KIKOEN
UKIKI!
UKIKI!
KAAAA!!

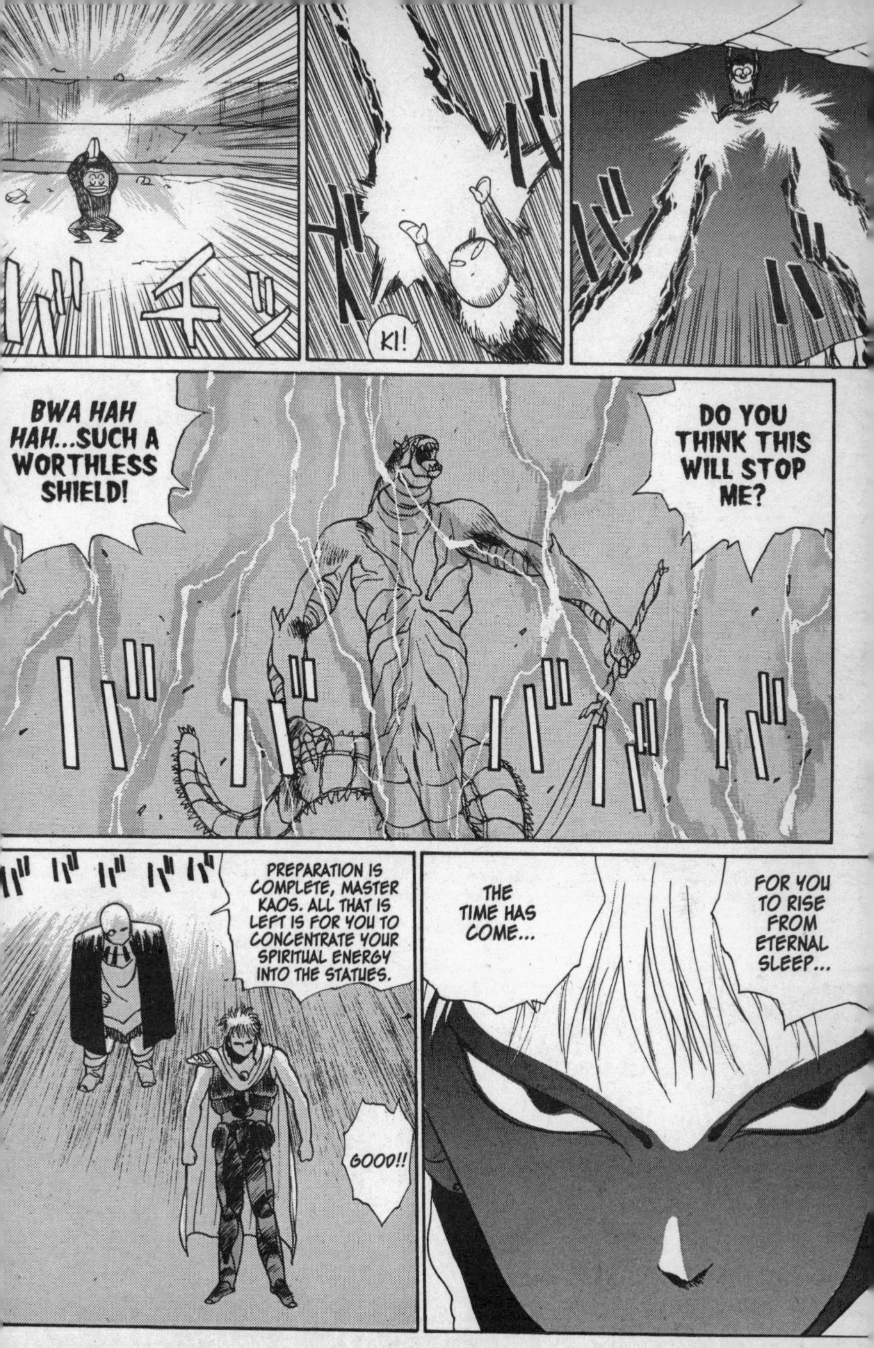
KI!
BWA HAH HAH...SUCH A WORTHLESS SHIELD!
DO YOU THINK THIS WILL STOP ME?
PREPARATION IS COMPLETE, MASTER KAOS. ALL THAT IS LEFT IS FOR YOU TO CONCENTRATE YOUR SPIRITUAL ENERGY INTO THE STATUES.
GOOD!!
THE TIME HAS COME...
FOR YOU TO RISE FROM ETERNAL SLEEP...

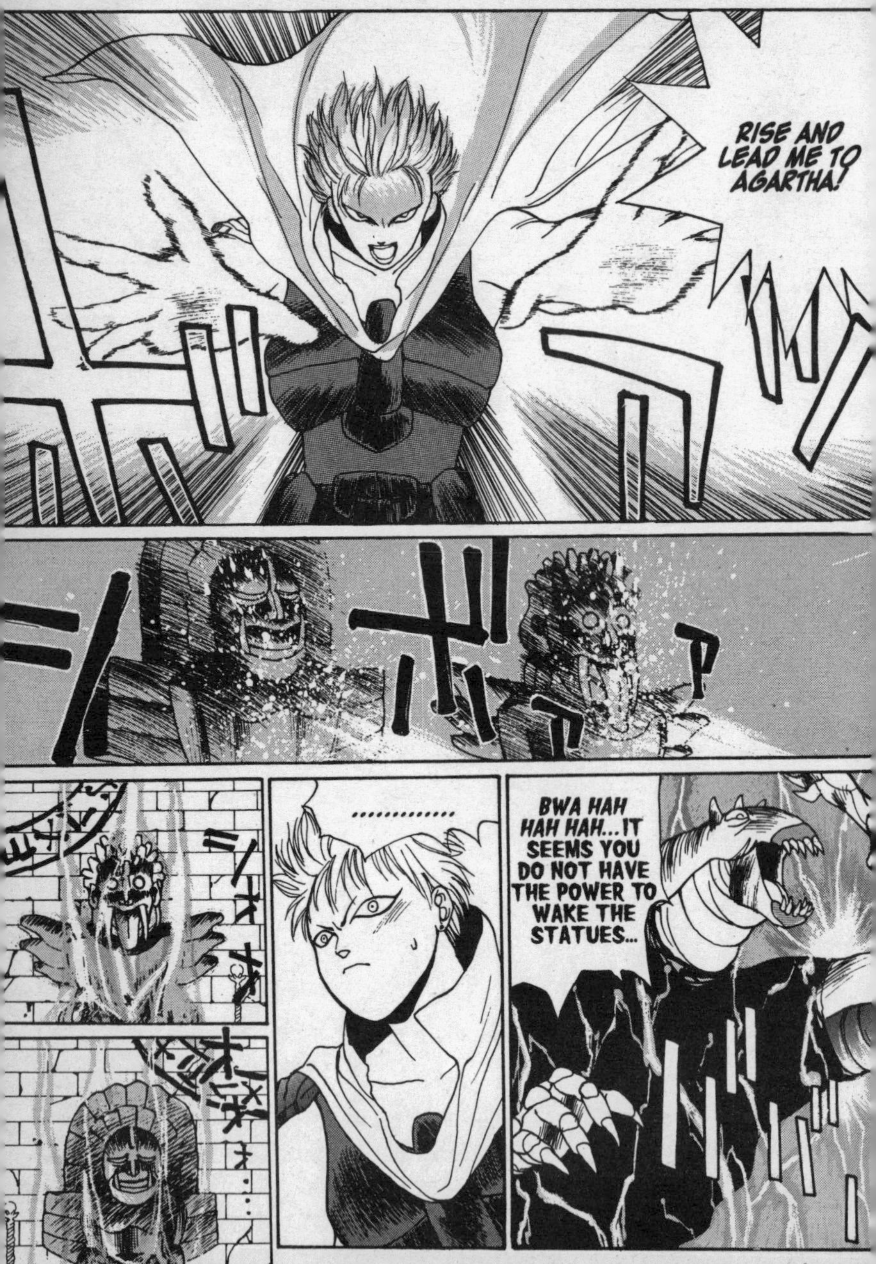
RISE AND LEAD ME TO AGARTHA!
....
BWA HAH HAH HAH...IT SEEMS YOU DO NOT HAVE THE POWER TO WAKE THE STATUES...

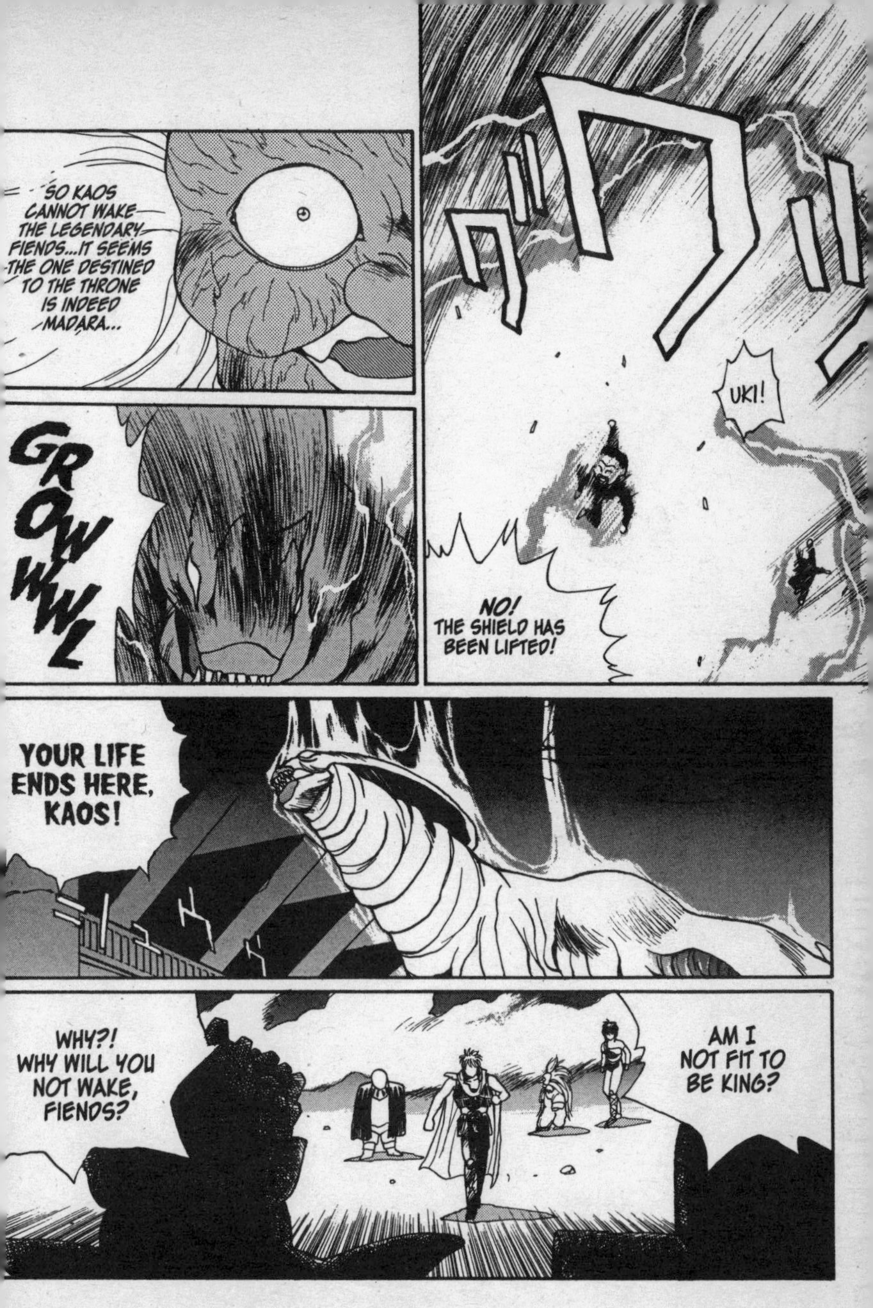
SO KAOS CANNOT WAKE THE LEGENDARY FIENDS...IT SEEMS THE ONE DESTINED TO THE THRONE IS INDEED MADARA...
GROWWWL
UKI!
NO! THE SHIELD HAS BEEN LIFTED!
YOUR LIFE ENDS HERE, KAOS!
WHY?! WHY WILL YOU NOT WAKE, FIENDS?
AM I NOT FIT TO BE KING?

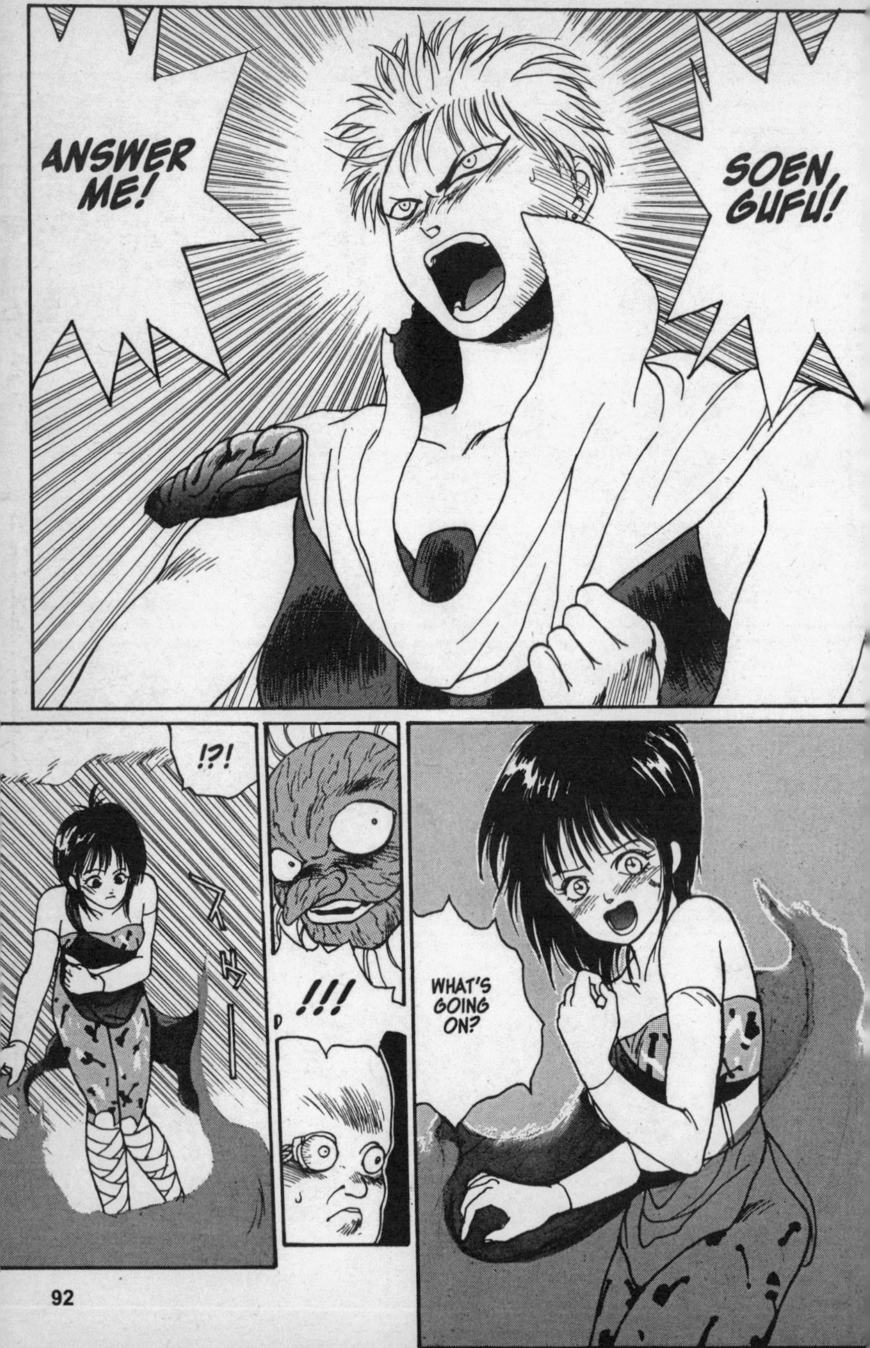
ANSWER ME!
SOEN GUFU!
!?!
!!!
WHAT'S GOING ON?

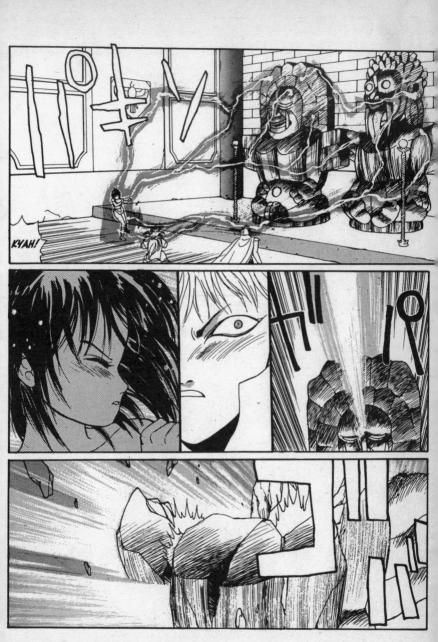

KYAH!

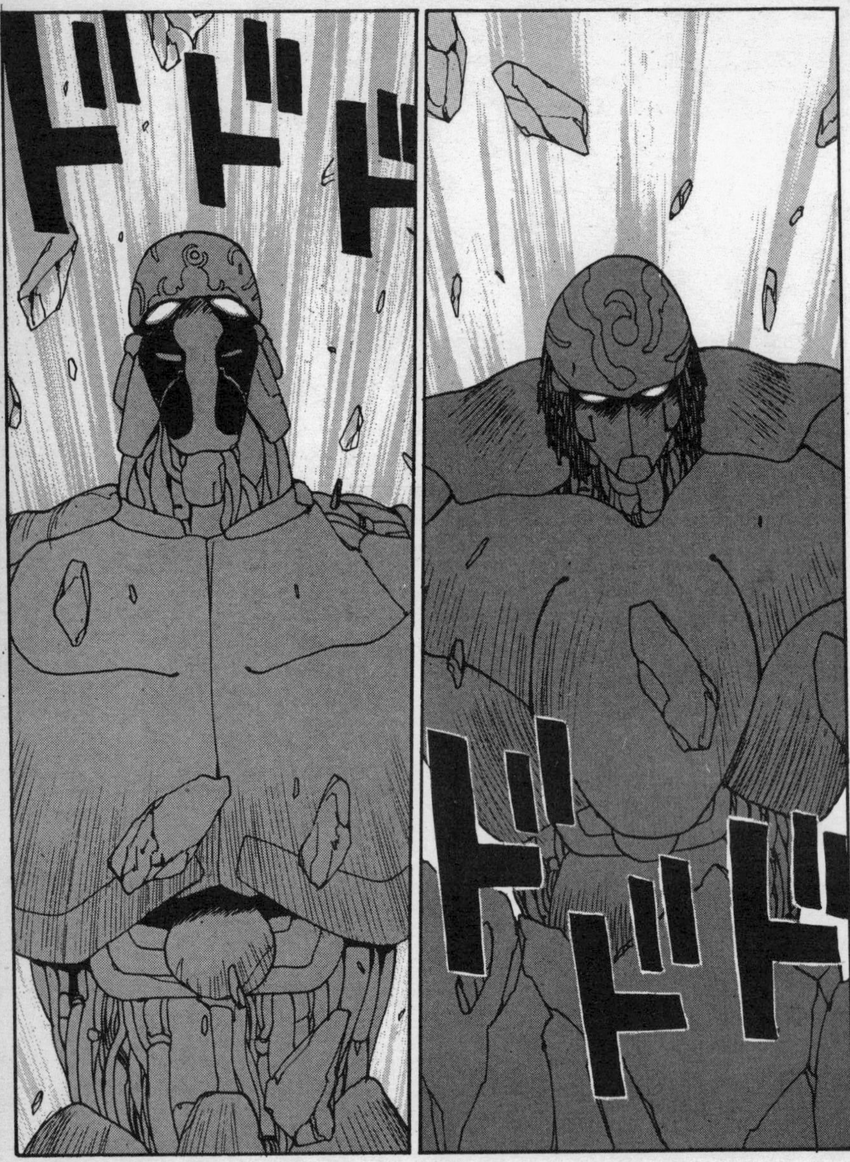
ドドド
ドドド

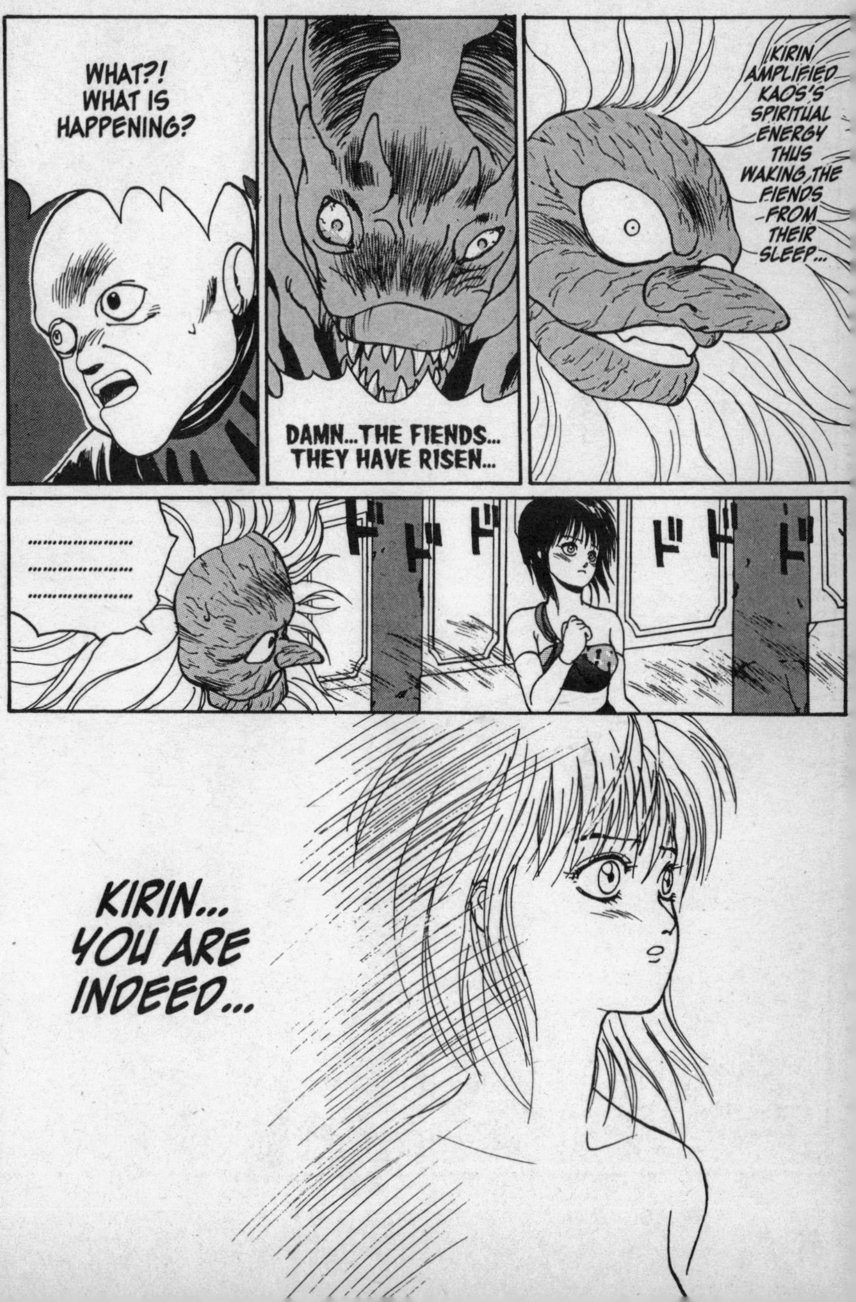
WHAT?! WHAT IS HAPPENING?
DAMN... THE FIENDS... THEY HAVE RISEN...
KIRIN AMPLIFIED KAOS'S SPIRITUAL ENERGY THUS WAKING THE FIENDS FROM THEIR SLEEP...
....
KIRIN... YOU ARE INDEED...

THE ENEMY IS ONE OF THE EIGHT GENERALS OF THE KINGDOM OF KONGO...

BATTLE WEAPONS CARRIED BY THE INISHE FROM AGARTHA...

SOEN AND GUFU...THE TIME HAS COME FOR YOU TO *RISE!!*

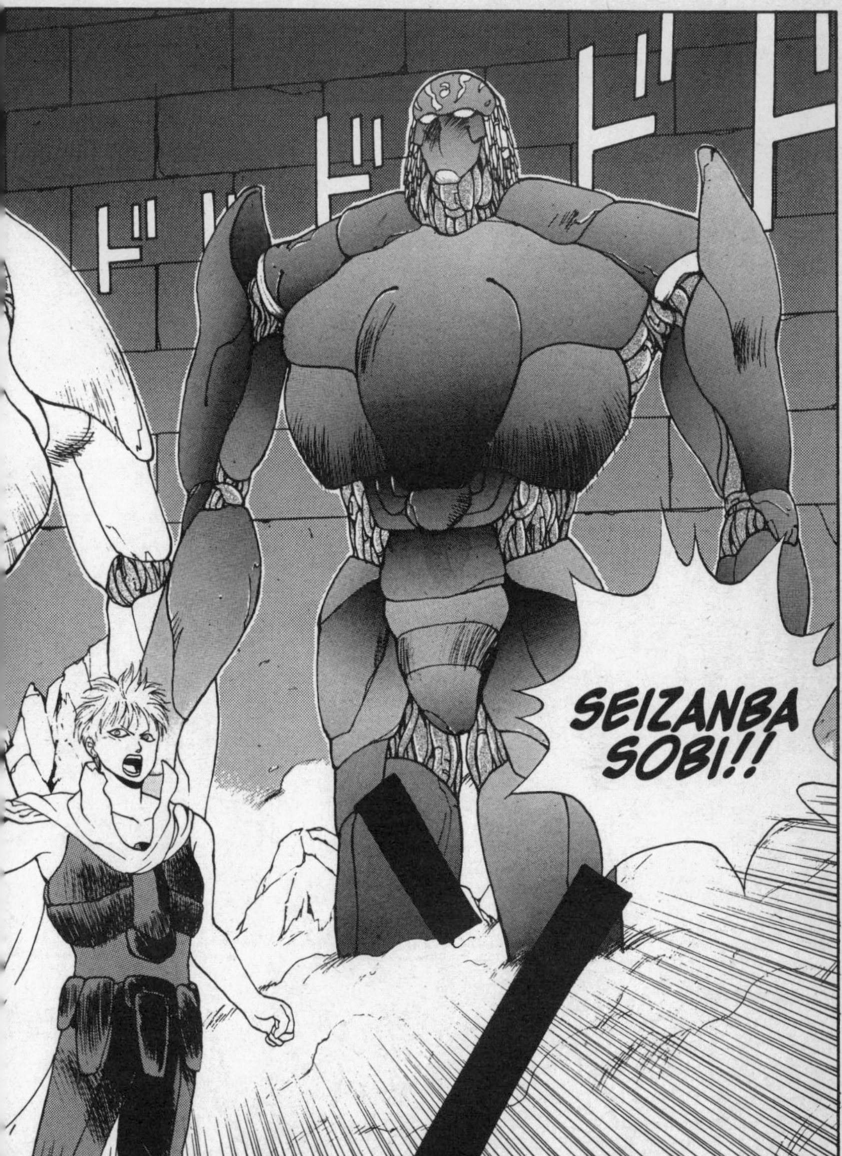
ドドドド
SEIZANBA SOBI!!

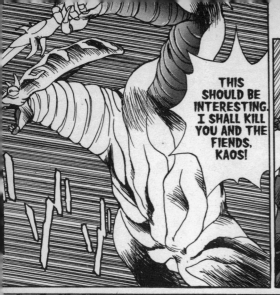

THIS SHOULD BE INTERESTING. I SHALL KILL YOU AND THE FIENDS, KAOS!

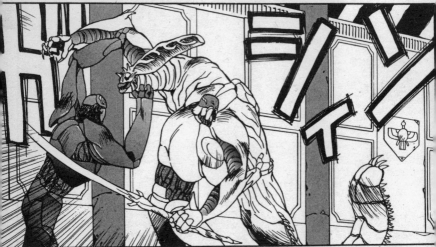

UARRRRGH!

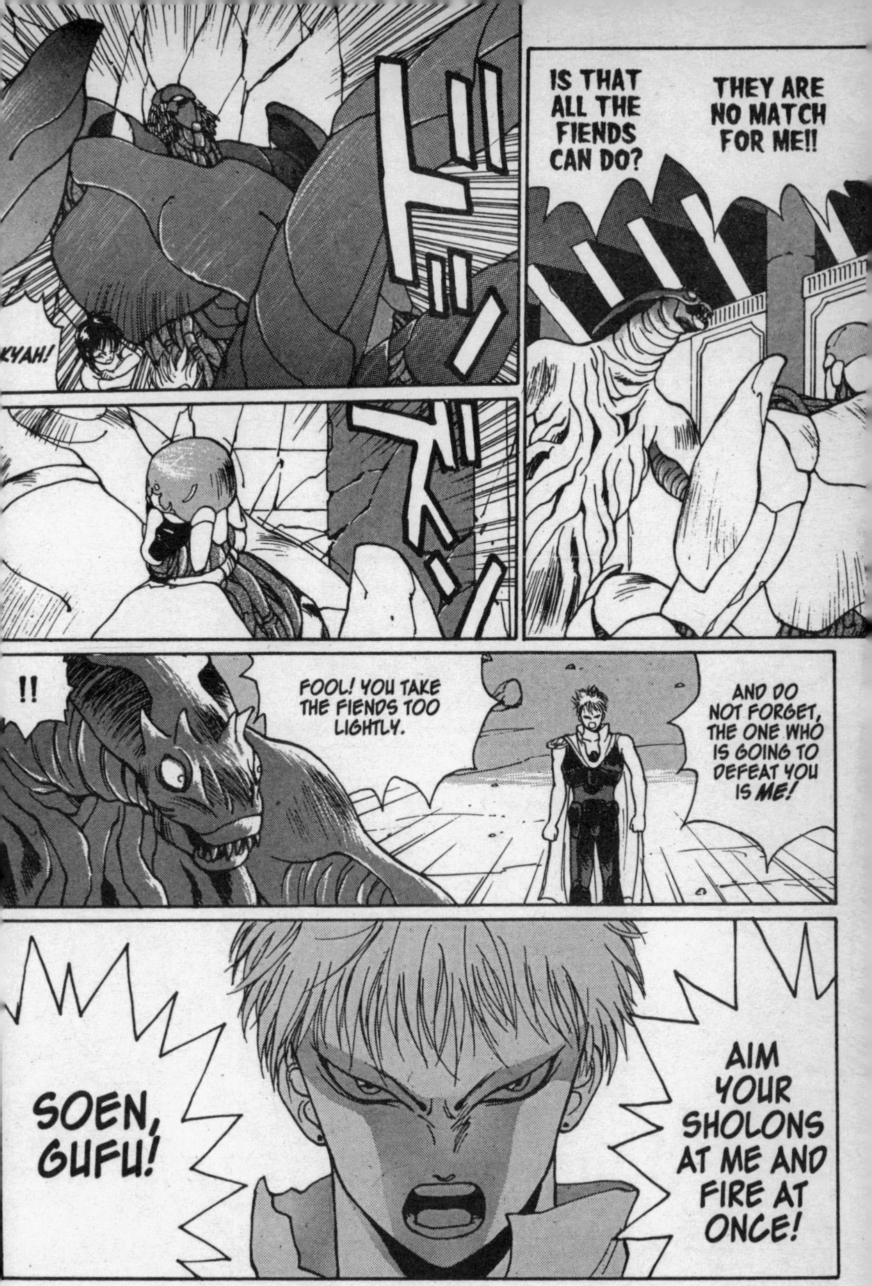
KYAH!
IS THAT ALL THE FIENDS CAN DO?
THEY ARE NO MATCH FOR ME!!
!!
FOOL! YOU TAKE THE FIENDS TOO LIGHTLY.
AND DO NOT FORGET, THE ONE WHO IS GOING TO DEFEAT YOU IS ME!
SOEN, GUFU!
AIM YOUR SHOLONS AT ME AND FIRE AT ONCE!

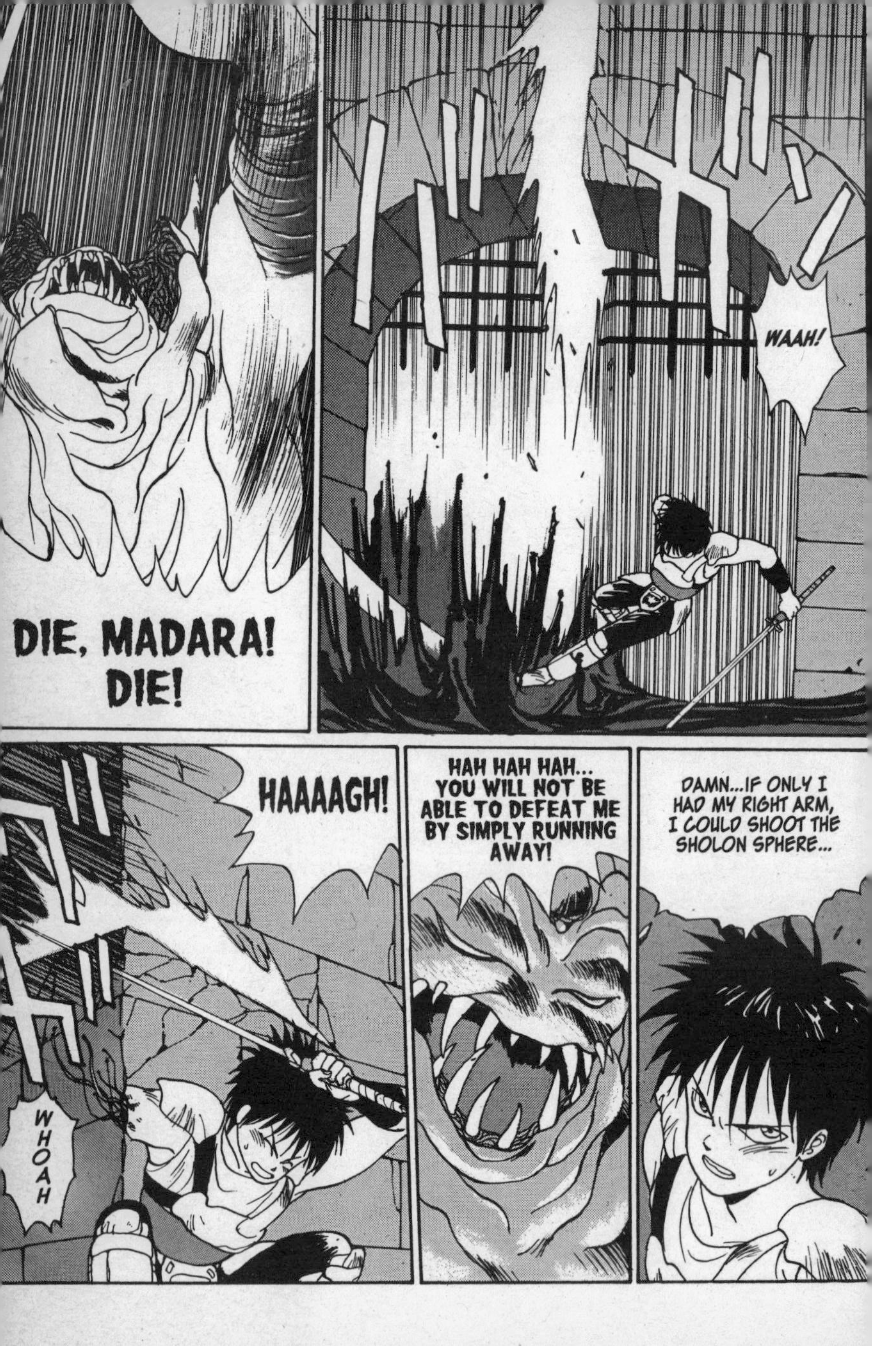

DIE, MADARA! DIE!
WAAH!
HAAAAGH!
WHOAH
HAH HAH HAH... YOU WILL NOT BE ABLE TO DEFEAT ME BY SIMPLY RUNNING AWAY!
DAMN...IF ONLY I HAD MY RIGHT ARM, I COULD SHOOT THE SHOLON SPHERE...

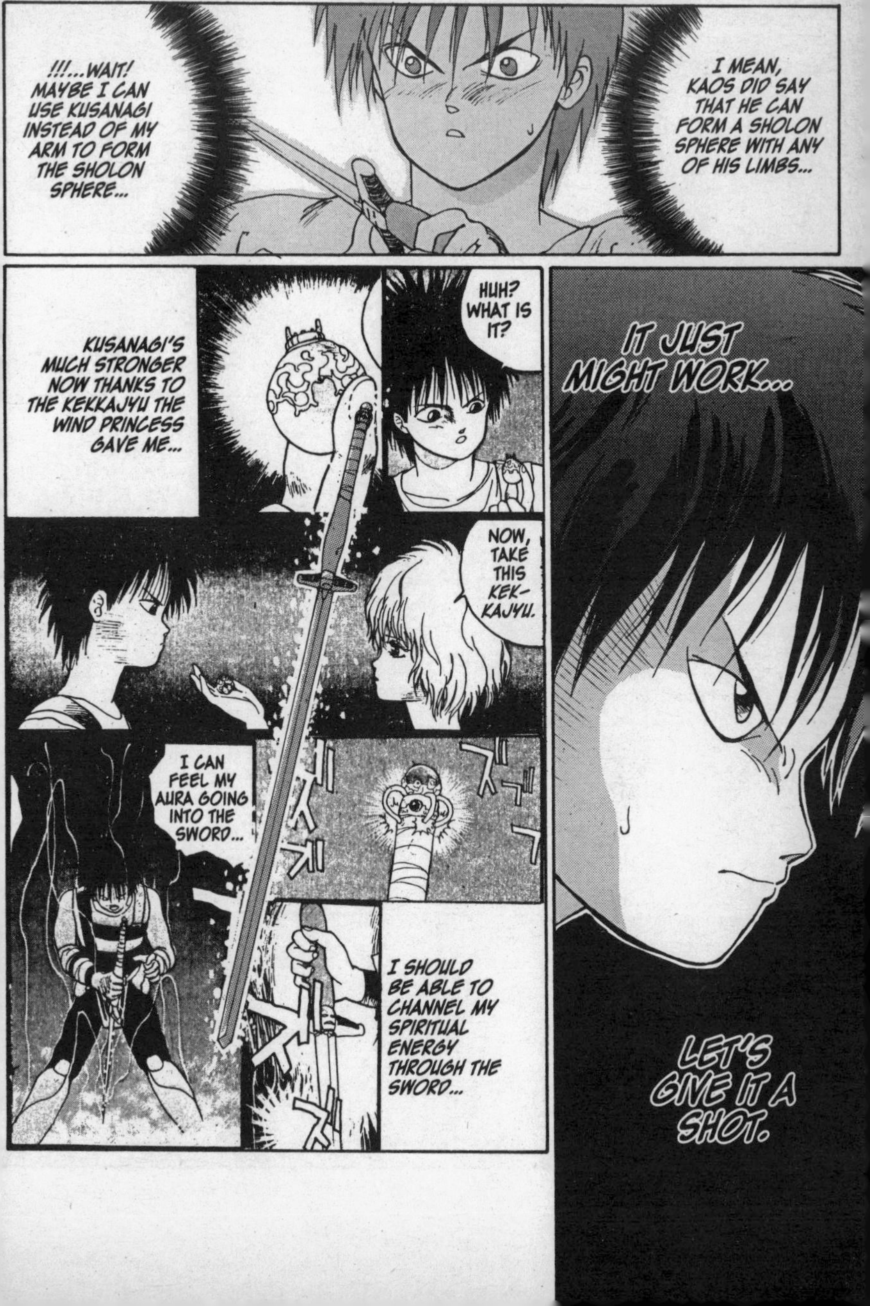
!!!...WAIT! MAYBE I CAN USE KUSANAGI INSTEAD OF MY ARM TO FORM THE SHOLON SPHERE...
I MEAN, KAOS DID SAY THAT HE CAN FORM A SHOLON SPHERE WITH ANY OF HIS LIMBS...
KUSANAGI'S MUCH STRONGER NOW THANKS TO THE KEKKAJYU THE WIND PRINCESS GAVE ME...
HUH? WHAT IS IT?
NOW, TAKE THIS KEK-KAJYU.
I CAN FEEL MY AURA GOING INTO THE SWORD...
I SHOULD BE ABLE TO CHANNEL MY SPIRITUAL ENERGY THROUGH THE SWORD...
IT JUST MIGHT WORK...
LET'S GIVE IT A SHOT.

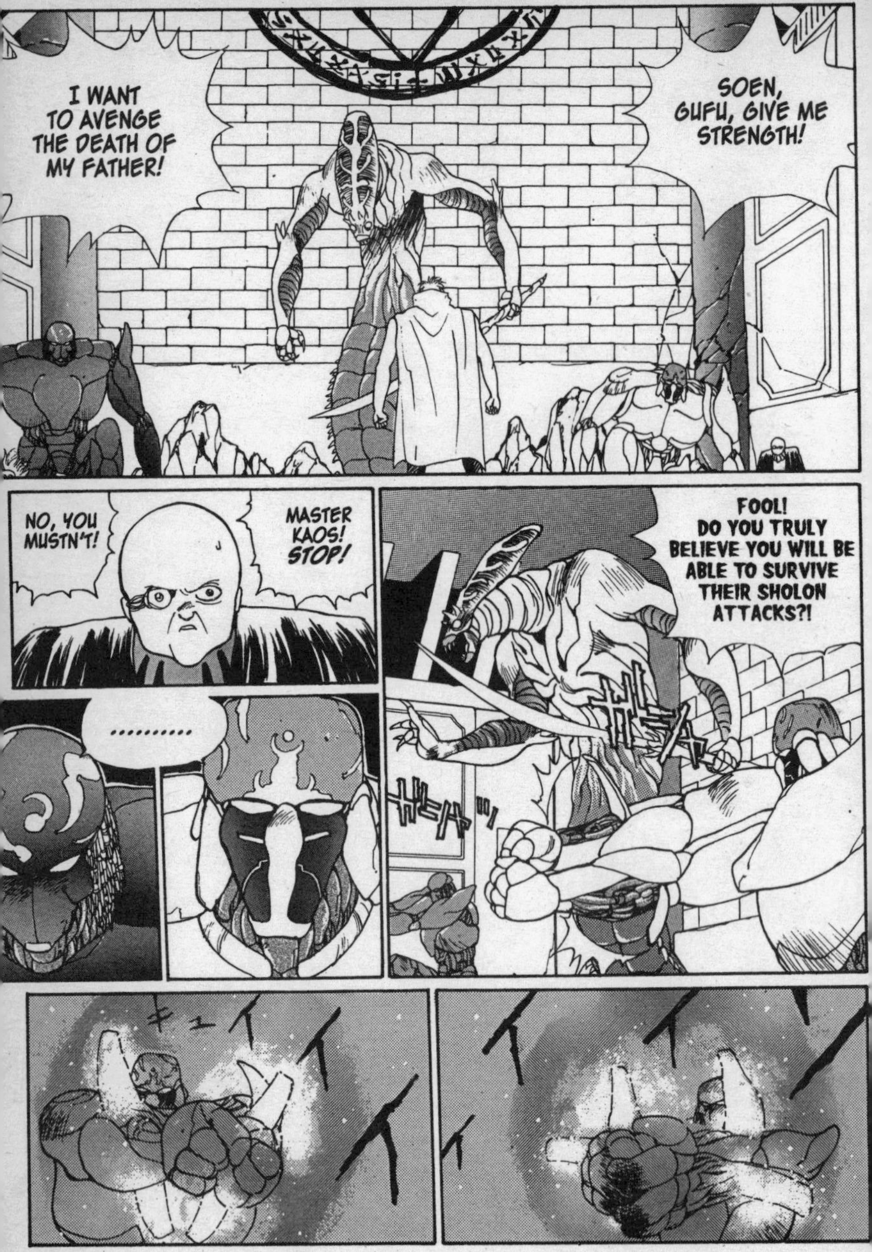

I WANT TO AVENGE THE DEATH OF MY FATHER!
SOEN, GUFU, GIVE ME STRENGTH!
NO, YOU MUSTN'T!
MASTER KAOS! STOP!
....
FOOL! DO YOU TRULY BELIEVE YOU WILL BE ABLE TO SURVIVE THEIR SHOLON ATTACKS?!

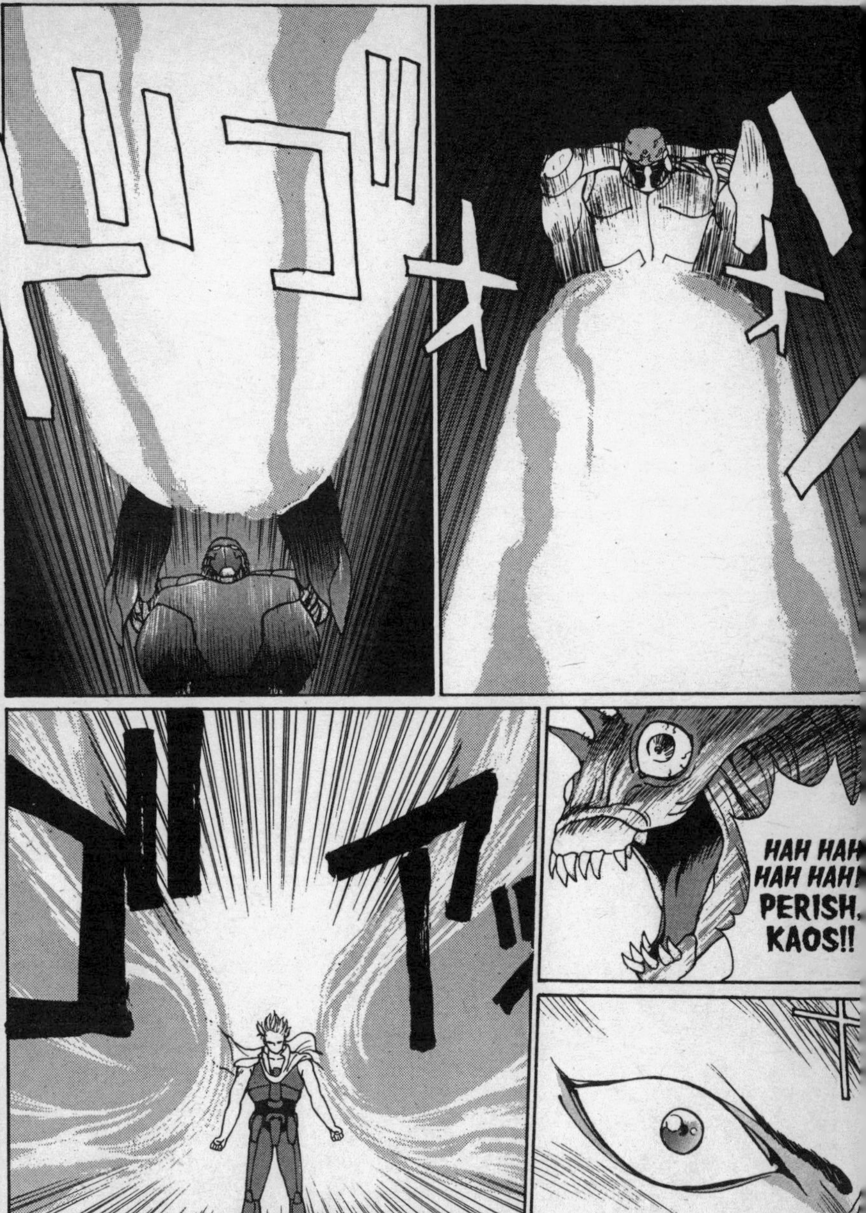
HAH HAH HAH HAH! PERISH, KAOS!!

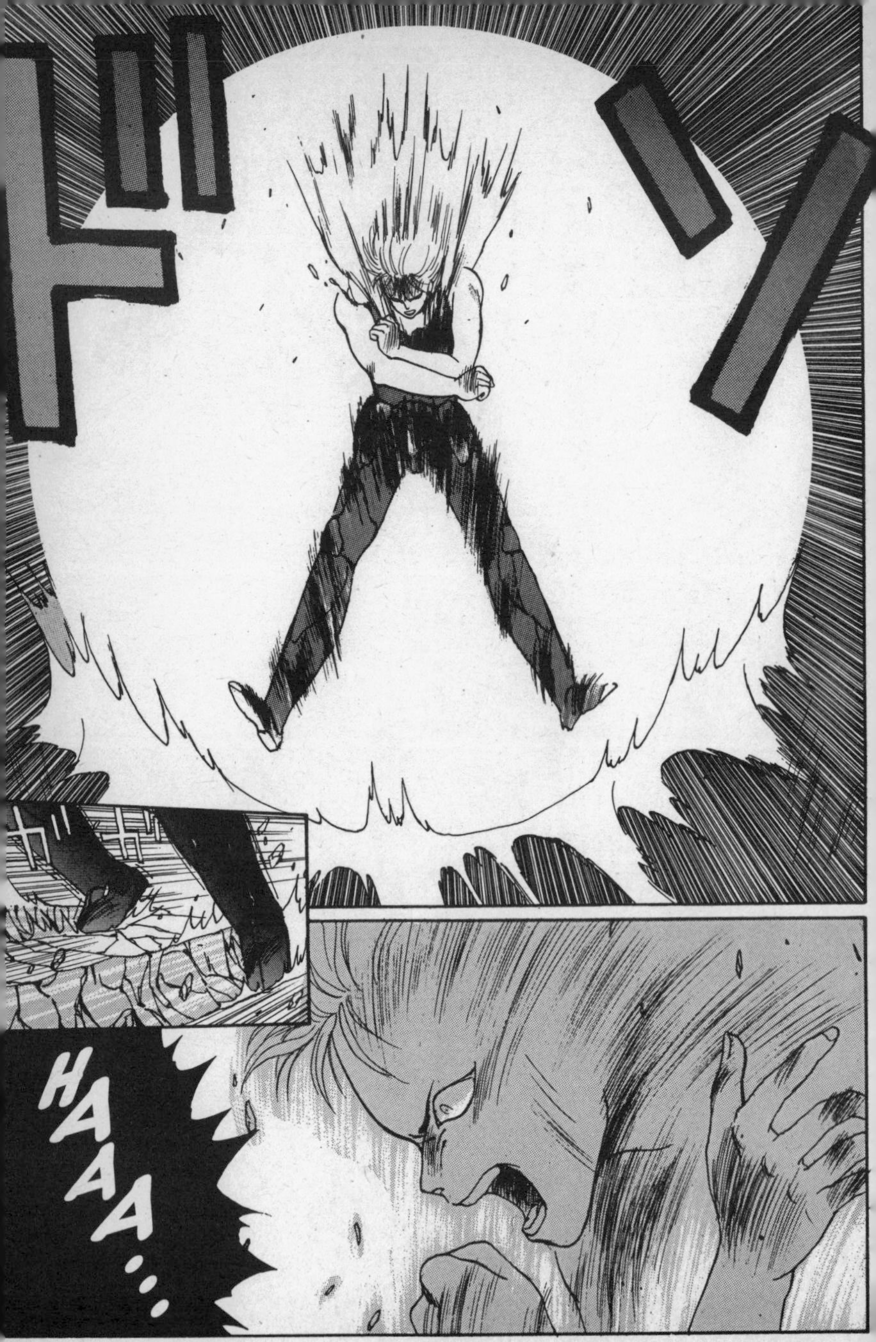
ドン
HAAA...

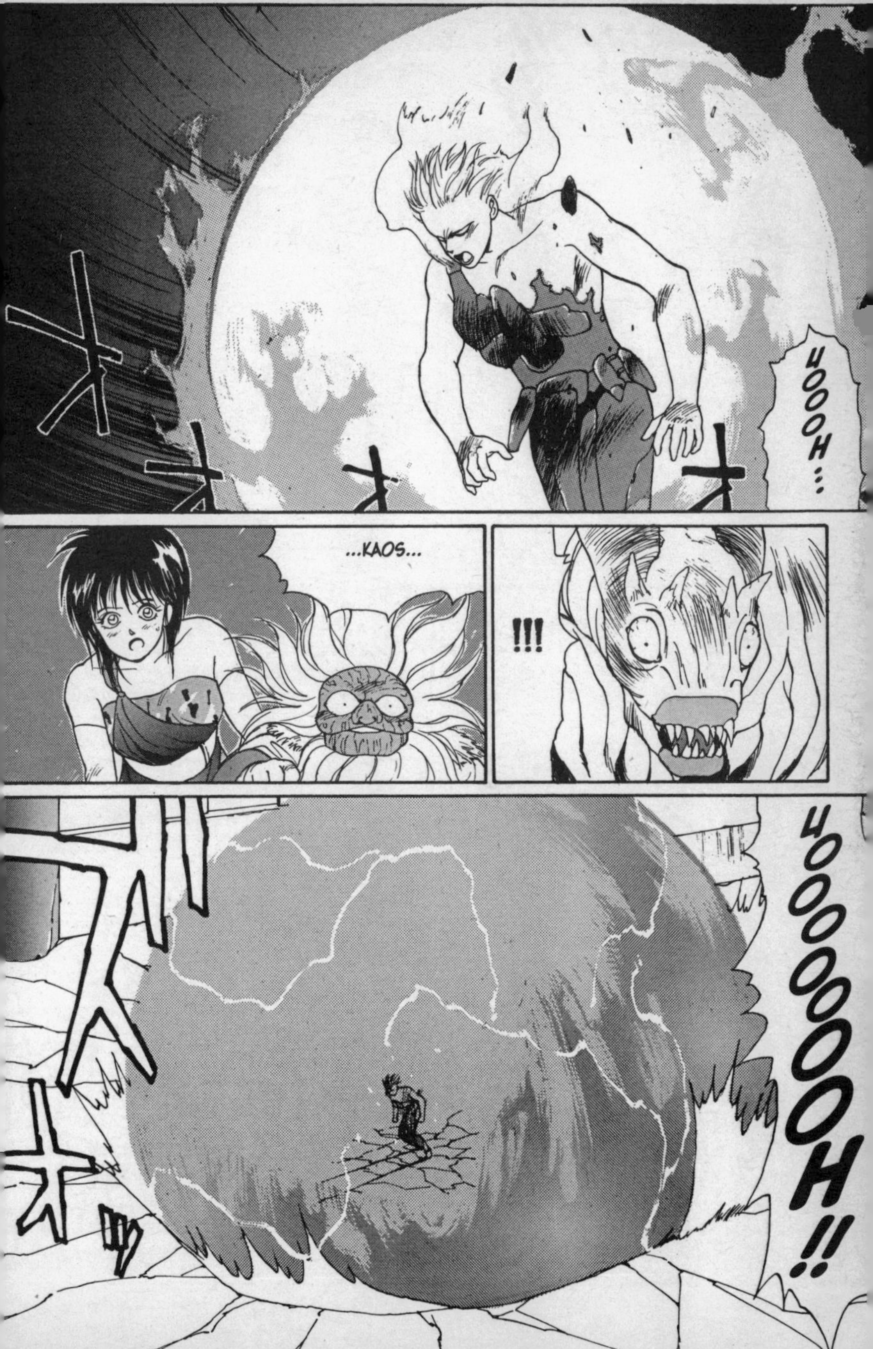
UOOOH...
...KAOS...
!!!
UOOOOOOOOOOH!!

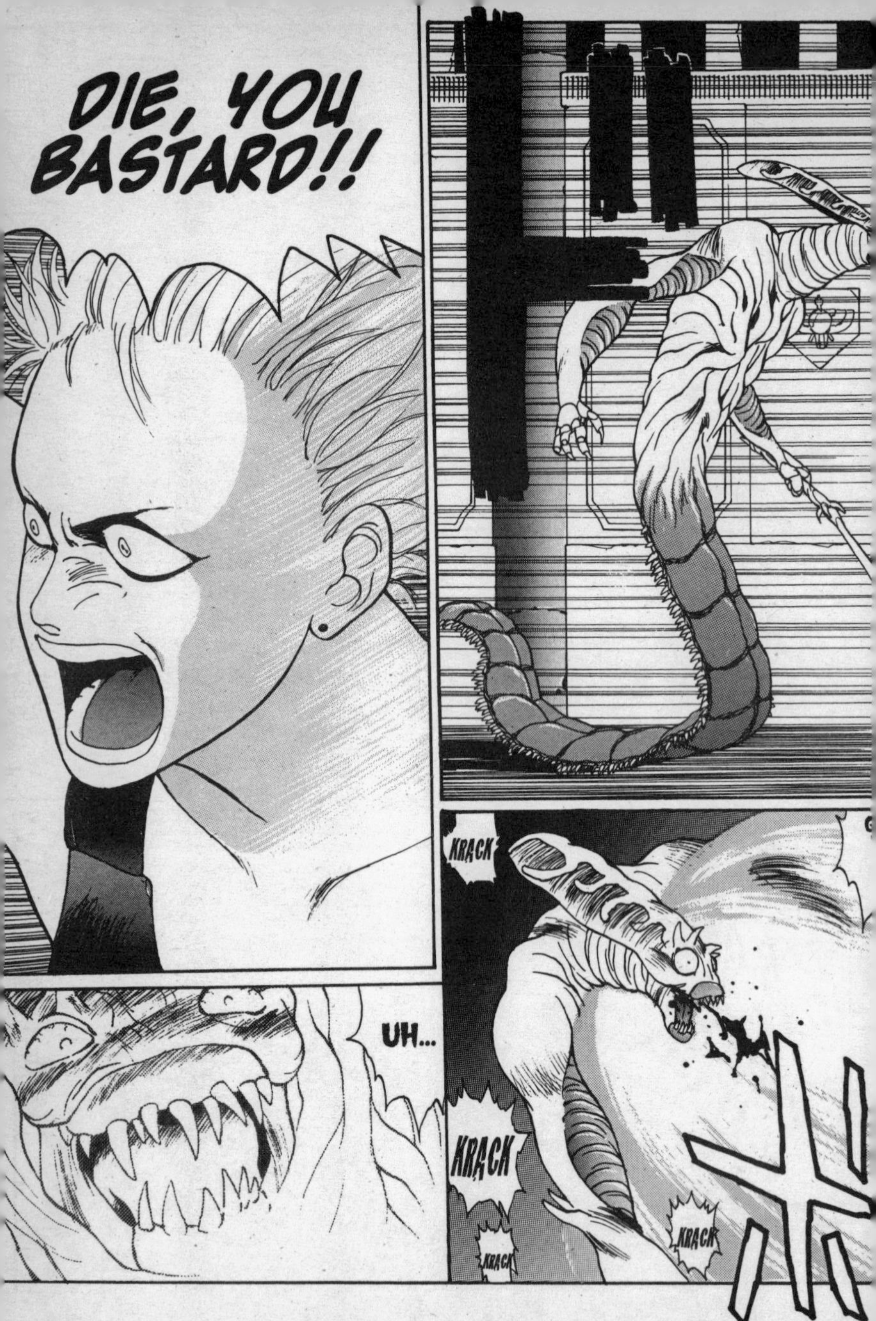
DIE, YOU BASTARD!!
KRACK
KRACK
KRACK
KRACK
UH...

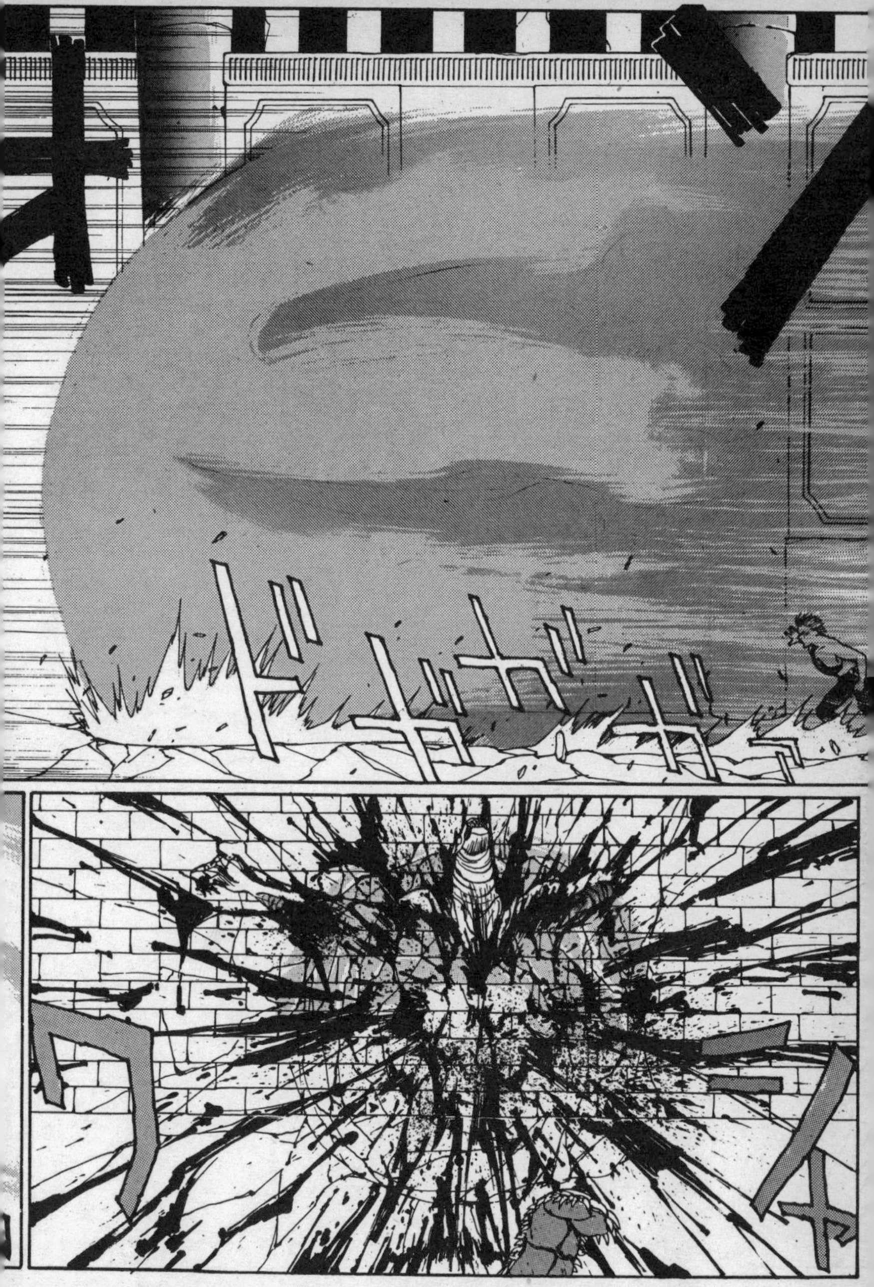
ドガガガァ

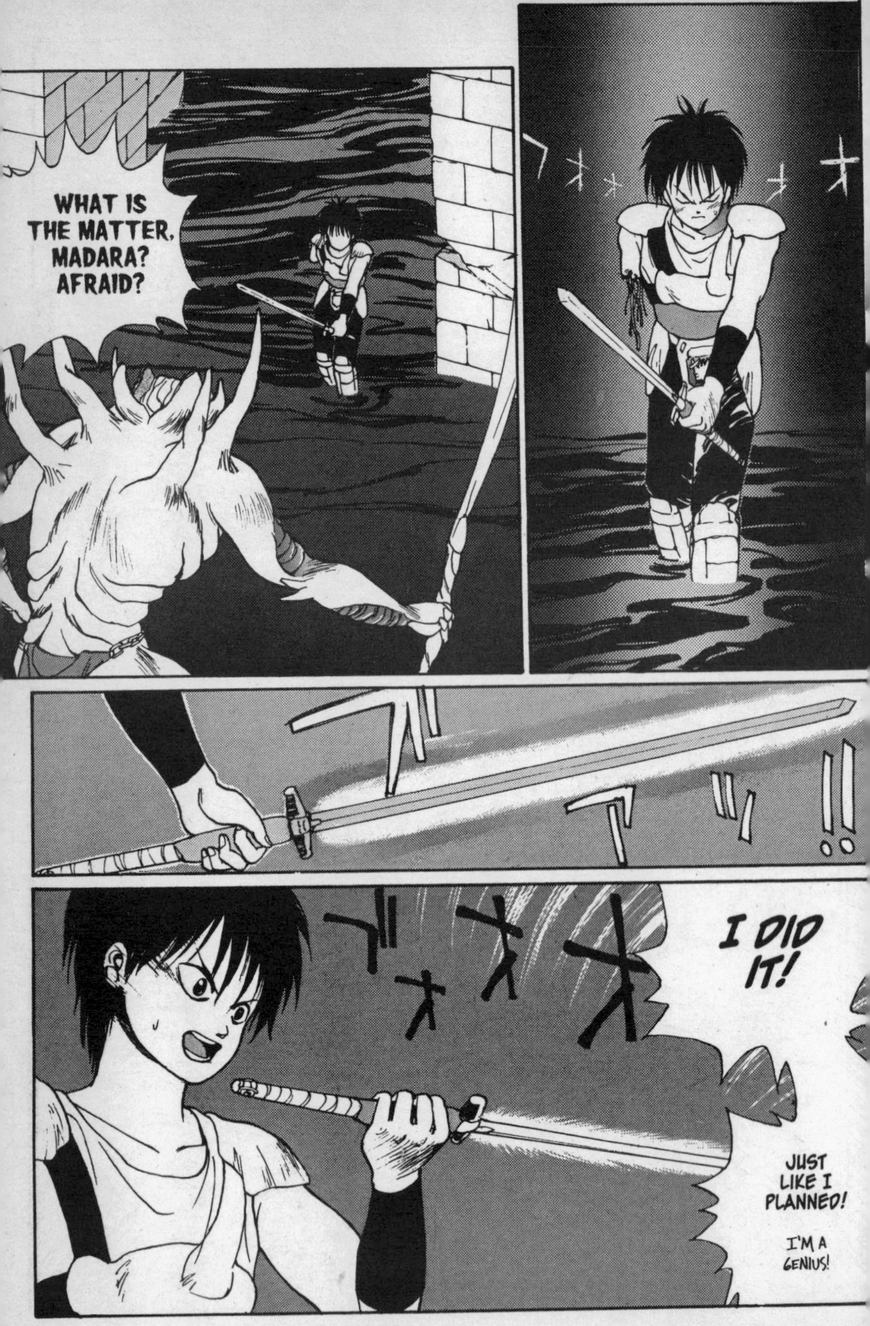
WHAT IS THE MATTER, MADARA? AFRAID?
I DID IT!
JUST LIKE I PLANNED!
I'M A GENIUS!

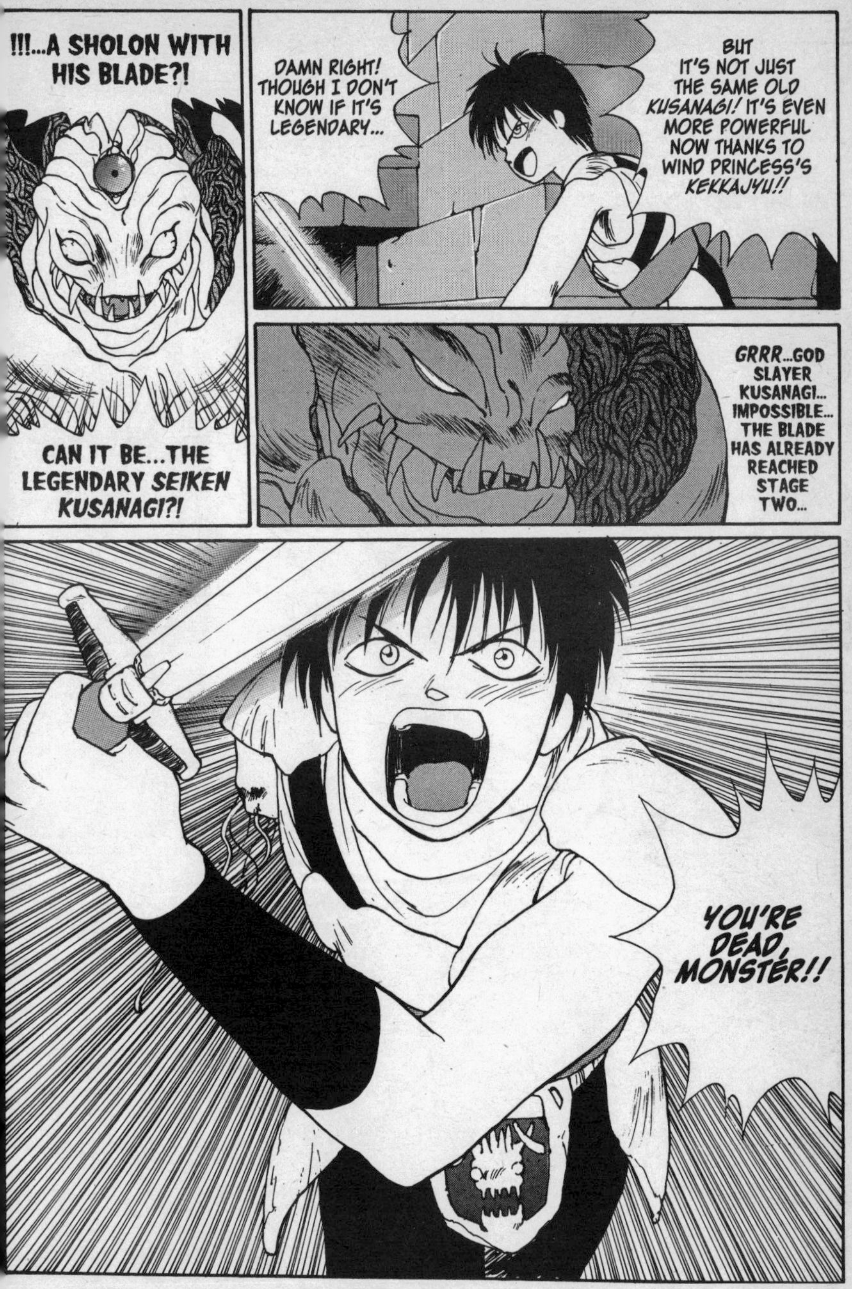
!!!...A SHOLON WITH HIS BLADE?!
CAN IT BE...THE LEGENDARY *SEIKEN KUSANAGI*?!
DAMN RIGHT! THOUGH I DON'T KNOW IF IT'S LEGENDARY...
BUT IT'S NOT JUST THE SAME OLD *KUSANAGI!* IT'S EVEN MORE POWERFUL NOW THANKS TO WIND PRINCESS'S *KEKKAJYU!!*
GRRR...GOD SLAYER KUSANAGI... IMPOSSIBLE... THE BLADE HAS ALREADY REACHED STAGE TWO...
YOU'RE DEAD, MONSTER!!

第四章 業報譚

Chapter 4: **The Tale of Fate**

"The true king shall be engulfed by
a sphere of light and sleep one thousand
days and one thousand nights. Following
his slumber, the king shall descend upon
the world once more and begin his
quest for unification."

– From text written on the stone tablet found on the
Island of the Prophets

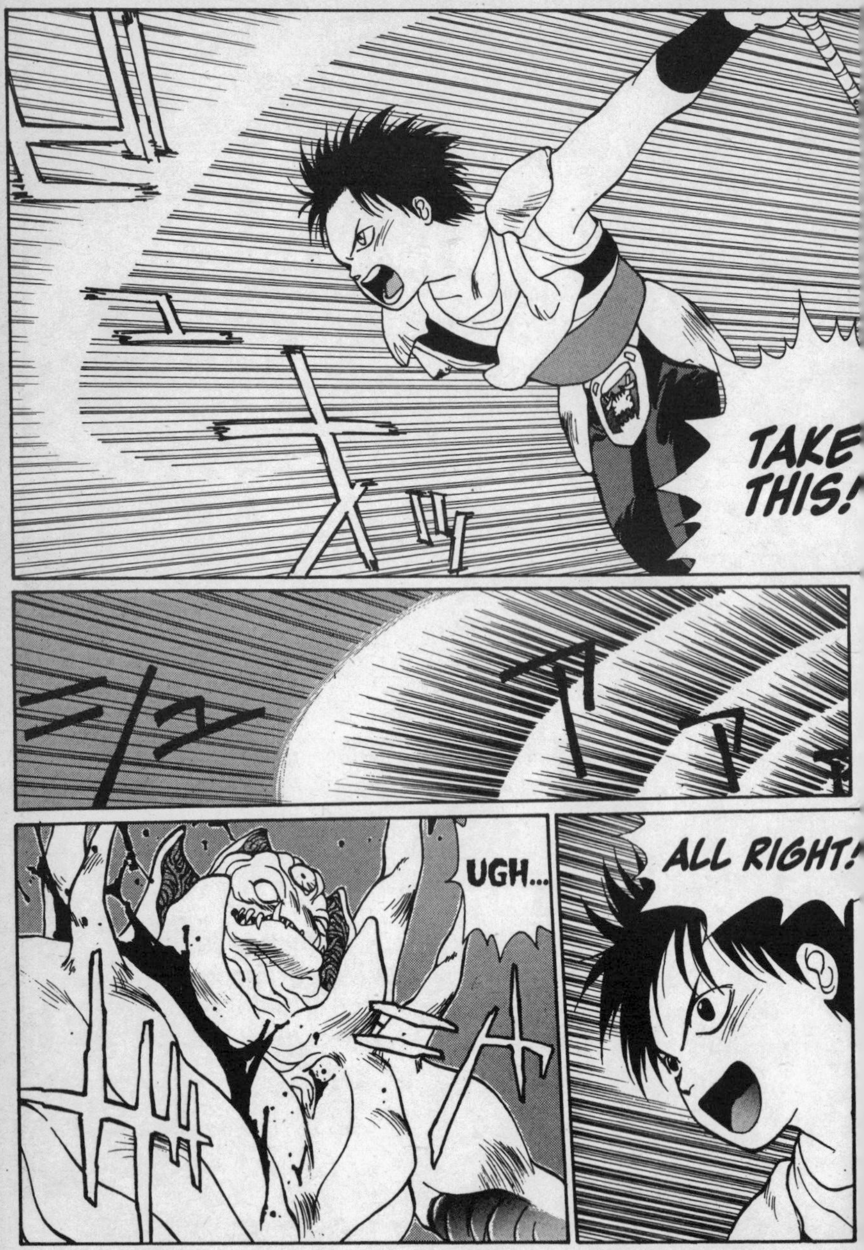
TAKE THIS!
UGH...
ALL RIGHT!

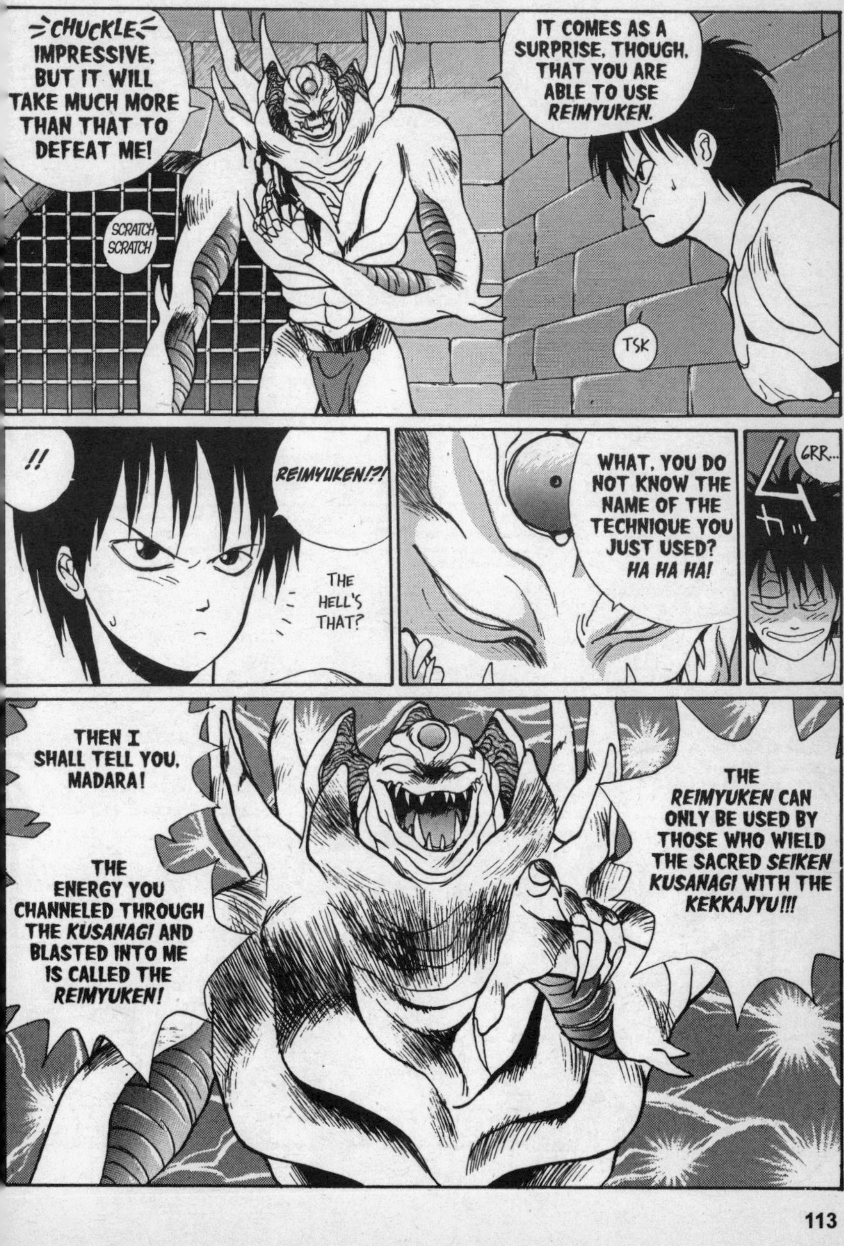

CHUCKLE
IMPRESSIVE, BUT IT WILL TAKE MUCH MORE THAN THAT TO DEFEAT ME!
SCRATCH SCRATCH
IT COMES AS A SURPRISE, THOUGH, THAT YOU ARE ABLE TO USE *REIMYUKEN.*
TSK
!!
REIMYUKEN!?!
THE HELL'S THAT?
WHAT, YOU DO NOT KNOW THE NAME OF THE TECHNIQUE YOU JUST USED? *HA HA HA!*
GRR...
THEN I SHALL TELL YOU, MADARA!
THE ENERGY YOU CHANNELED THROUGH THE *KUSANAGI* AND BLASTED INTO ME IS CALLED THE *REIMYUKEN!*
THE *REIMYUKEN* CAN ONLY BE USED BY THOSE WHO WIELD THE SACRED *SEIKEN KUSANAGI* WITH THE *KEKKAJYU!!!*

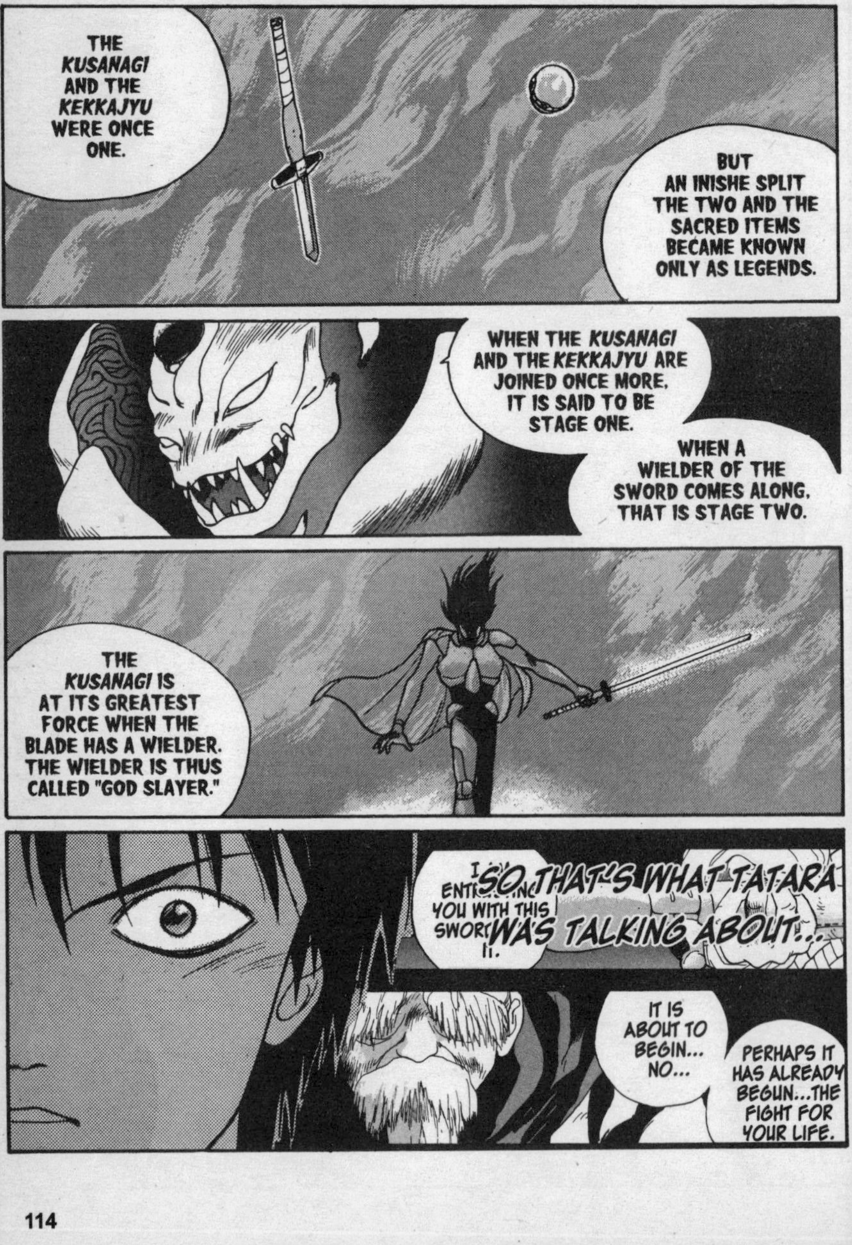
THE *KUSANAGI* AND THE *KEKKAJYU* WERE ONCE ONE.
BUT AN INISHE SPLIT THE TWO AND THE SACRED ITEMS BECAME KNOWN ONLY AS LEGENDS.
WHEN THE *KUSANAGI* AND THE *KEKKAJYU* ARE JOINED ONCE MORE, IT IS SAID TO BE STAGE ONE.
WHEN A WIELDER OF THE SWORD COMES ALONG, THAT IS STAGE TWO.
THE *KUSANAGI* IS AT ITS GREATEST FORCE WHEN THE BLADE HAS A WIELDER. THE WIELDER IS THUS CALLED "GOD SLAYER."
YOU WITH THIS
SO THAT'S WHAT TATARA WAS TALKING ABOUT...
IT IS ABOUT TO BEGIN... NO...
PERHAPS IT HAS ALREADY BEGUN...THE FIGHT FOR YOUR LIFE.

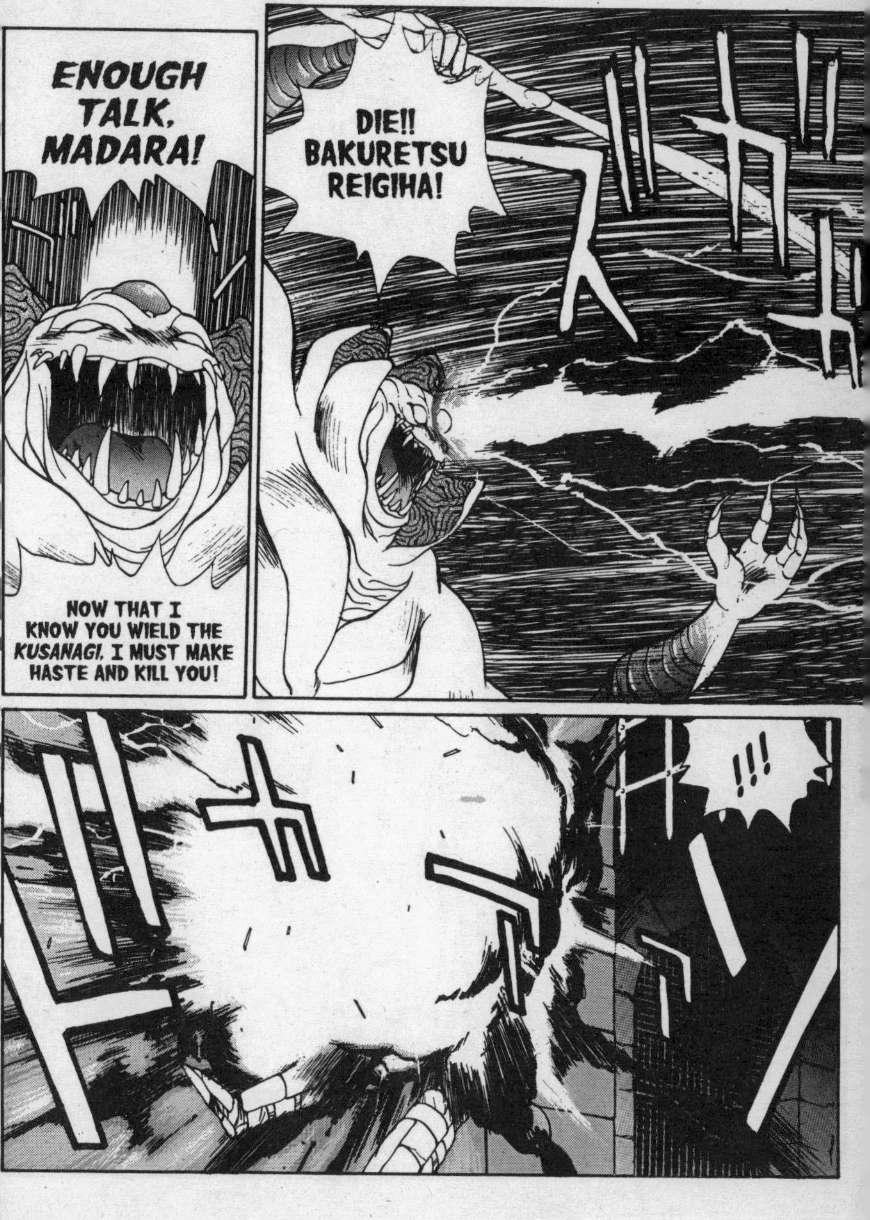

ENOUGH TALK, MADARA!
NOW THAT I KNOW YOU WIELD THE *KUSANAGI*, I MUST MAKE HASTE AND KILL YOU!
DIE!! BAKURETSU REIGIHA!
!!!

A...R...G...H...

UGH...

K-KAOSSS...

HUMPH.
STILL
ALIVE, EH?

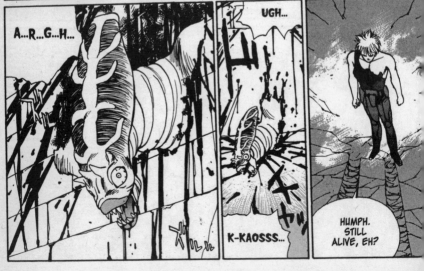

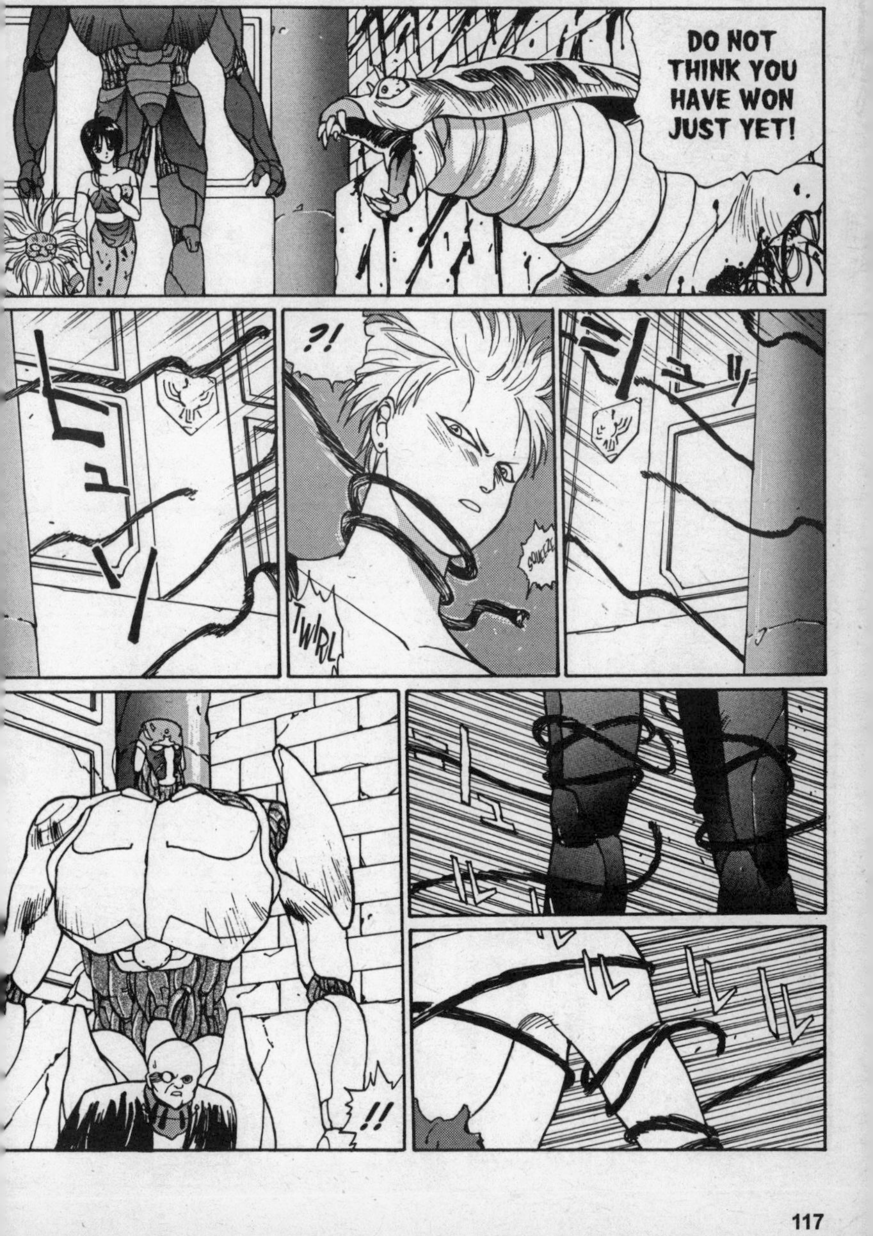

DO NOT THINK YOU HAVE WON JUST YET!
?!
SQUEEZE
TWIRL
!!

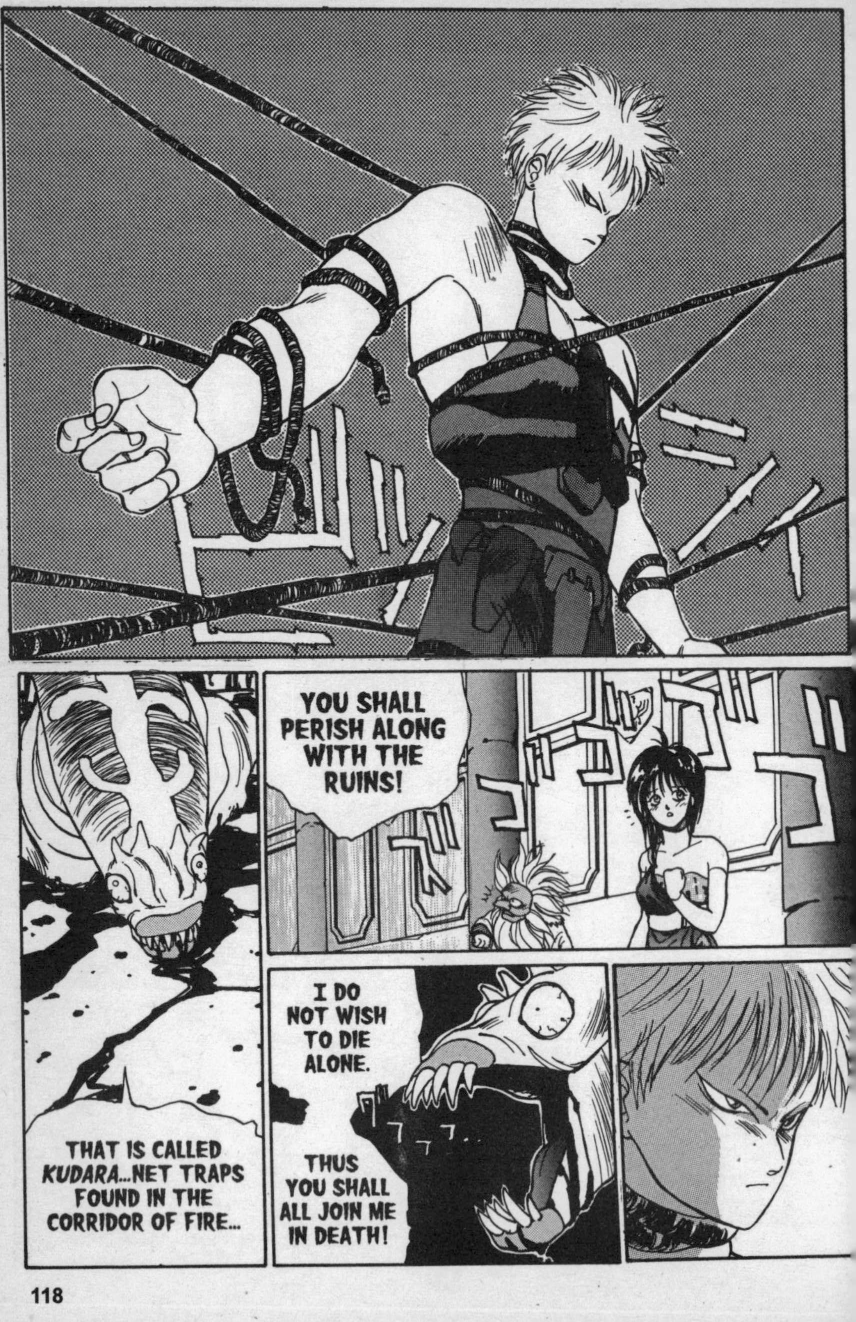

YOU SHALL PERISH ALONG WITH THE RUINS!
THAT IS CALLED KUDARA...NET TRAPS FOUND IN THE CORRIDOR OF FIRE...
I DO NOT WISH TO DIE ALONE.
THUS YOU SHALL ALL JOIN ME IN DEATH!

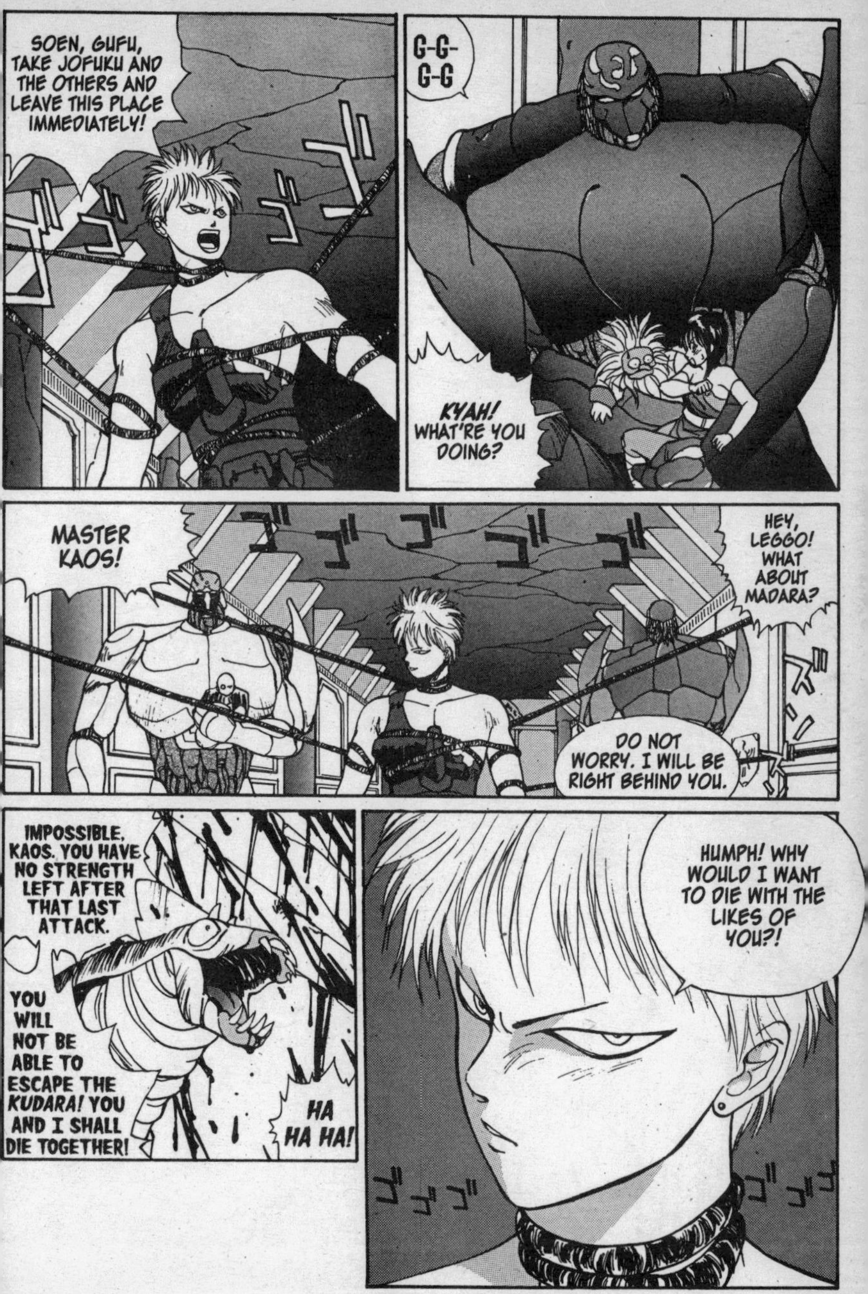
SOEN, GUFU, TAKE JOFUKU AND THE OTHERS AND LEAVE THIS PLACE IMMEDIATELY!
G-G-G-G
KYAH! WHAT'RE YOU DOING?
MASTER KAOS!
HEY, LEGGO! WHAT ABOUT MADARA?
DO NOT WORRY. I WILL BE RIGHT BEHIND YOU.
IMPOSSIBLE, KAOS. YOU HAVE NO STRENGTH LEFT AFTER THAT LAST ATTACK.
YOU WILL NOT BE ABLE TO ESCAPE THE KUDARA! YOU AND I SHALL DIE TOGETHER!
HA HA HA!
HUMPH! WHY WOULD I WANT TO DIE WITH THE LIKES OF YOU?!

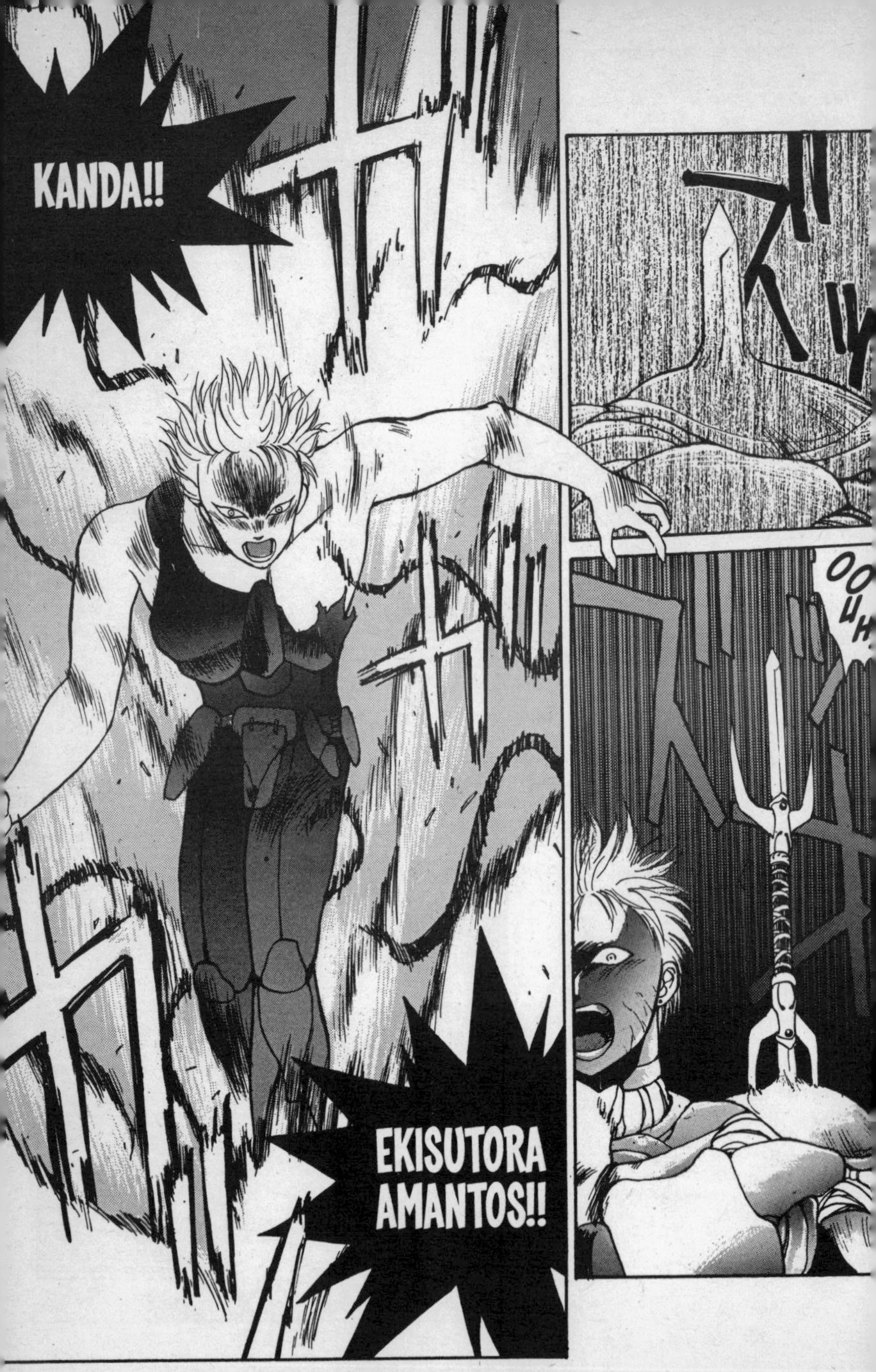
KANDA!!
EKISUTORA AMANTOS!!
OOUH

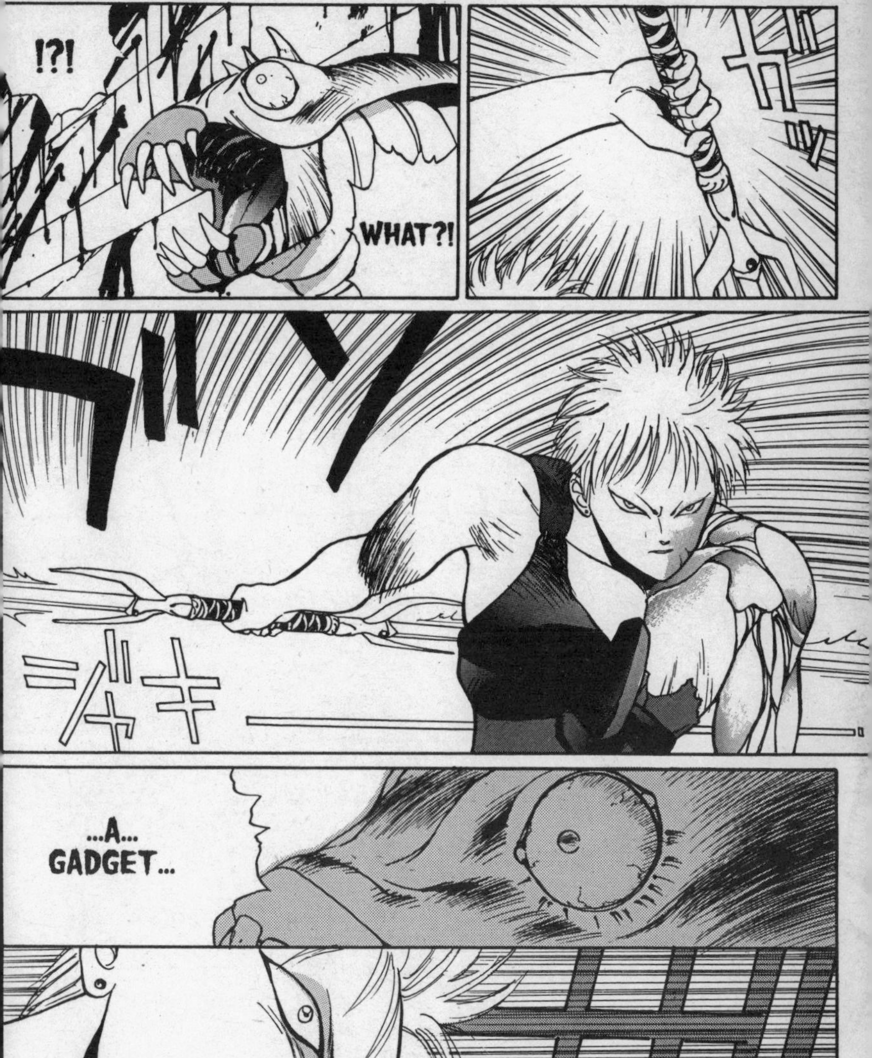
!?!
WHAT?!
...A...
GADGET...

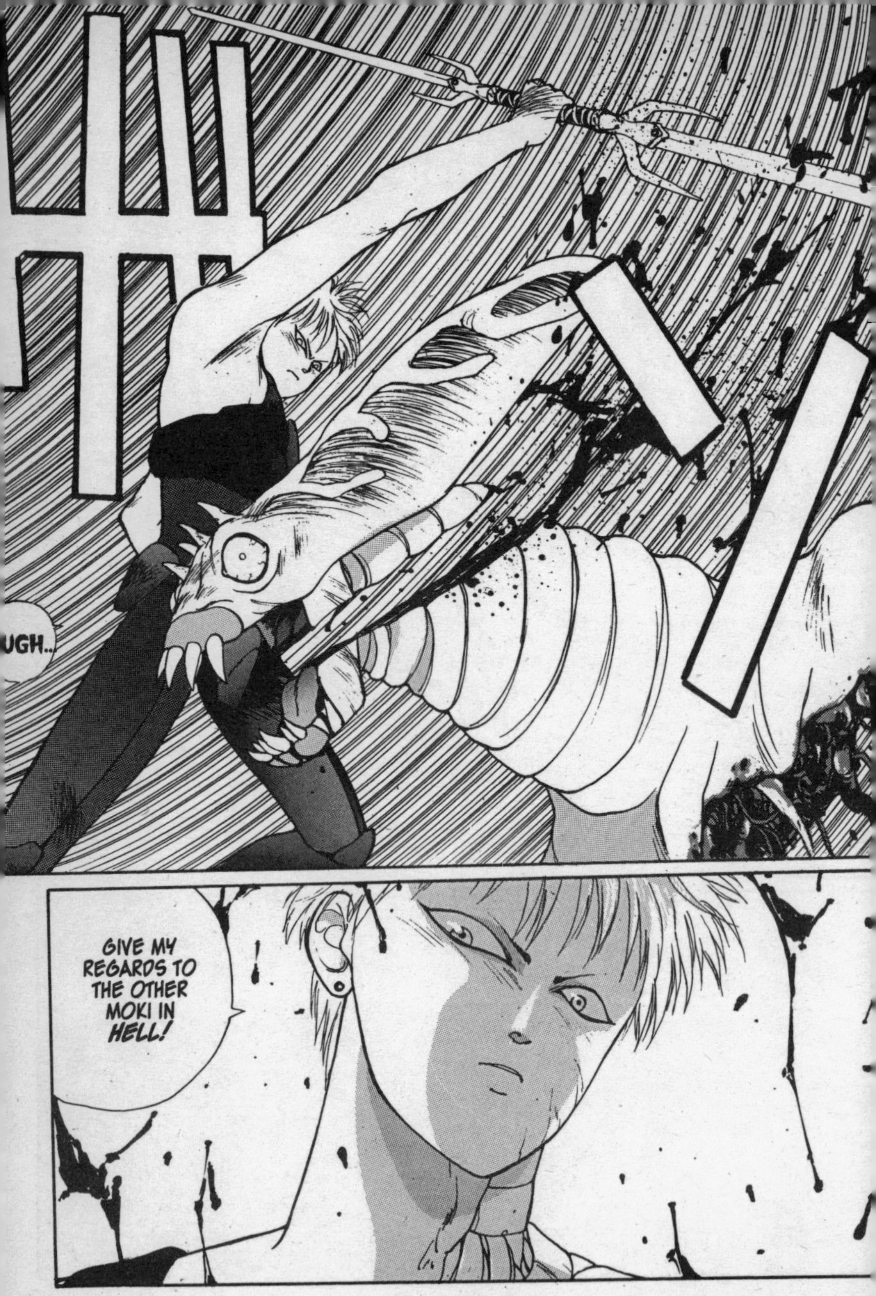
UGH...
GIVE MY REGARDS TO THE OTHER MOKI IN HELL!

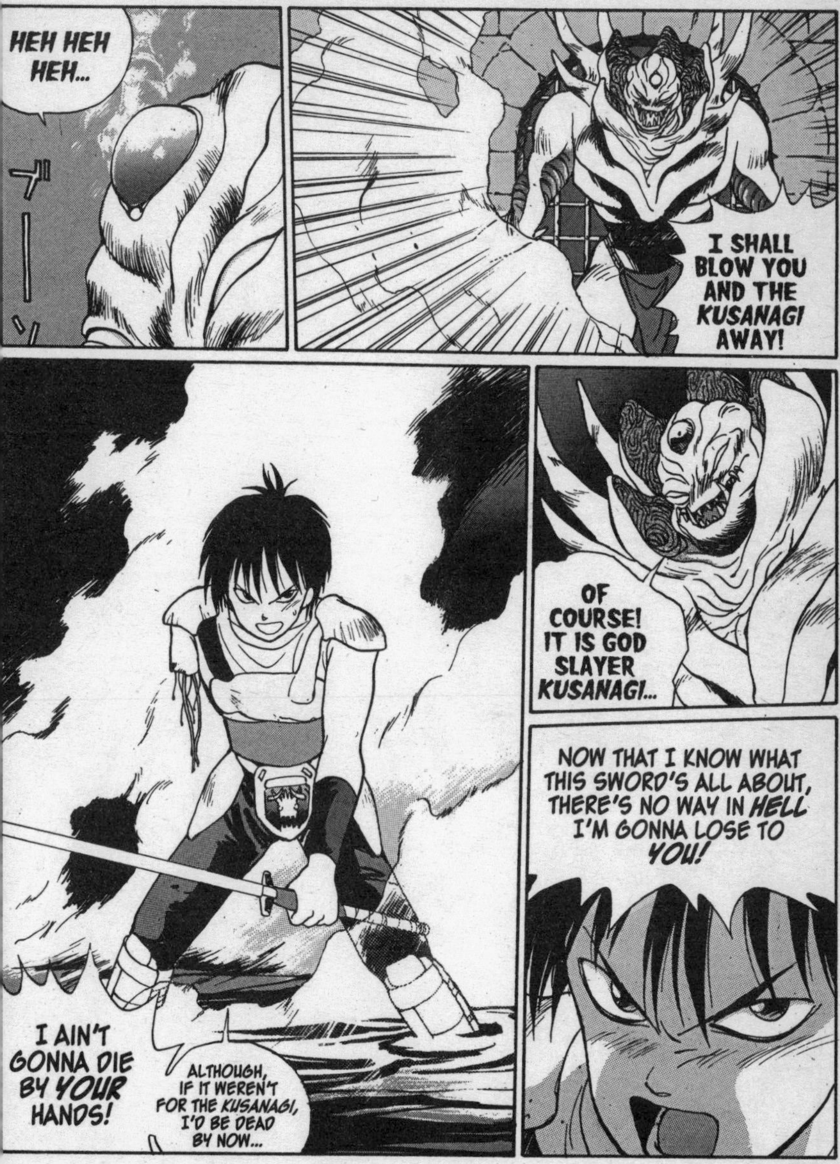
HEH HEH HEH...
I SHALL BLOW YOU AND THE *KUSANAGI* AWAY!
I AIN'T GONNA DIE BY *YOUR* HANDS!
ALTHOUGH, IF IT WEREN'T FOR THE *KUSANAGI*, I'D BE DEAD BY NOW...
OF COURSE! IT IS GOD SLAYER *KUSANAGI*...
NOW THAT I KNOW WHAT THIS SWORD'S ALL ABOUT, THERE'S NO WAY IN *HELL* I'M GONNA LOSE TO *YOU!*

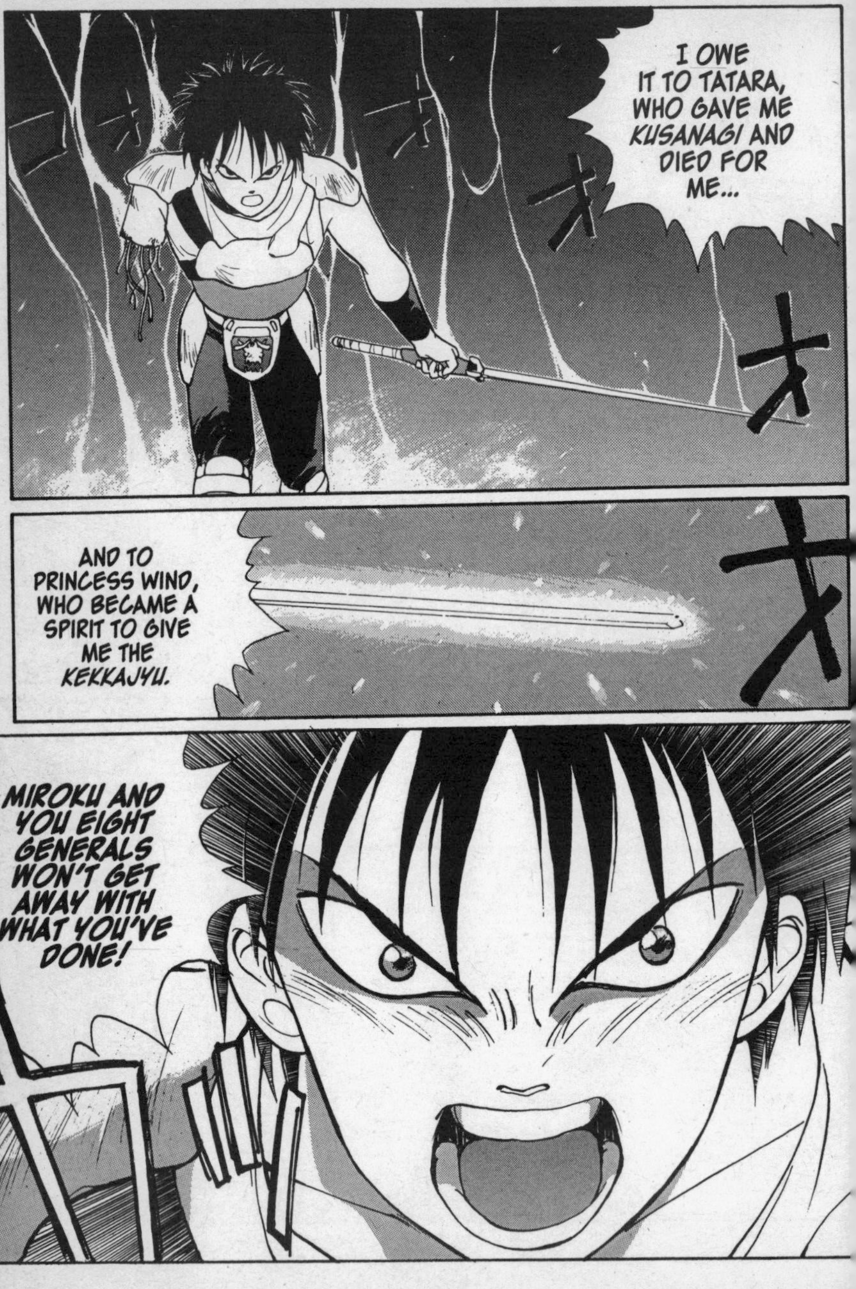
I OWE IT TO TATARA, WHO GAVE ME KUSANAGI AND DIED FOR ME...
AND TO PRINCESS WIND, WHO BECAME A SPIRIT TO GIVE ME THE KEKKAJYU.
MIROKU AND YOU EIGHT GENERALS WON'T GET AWAY WITH WHAT YOU'VE DONE!

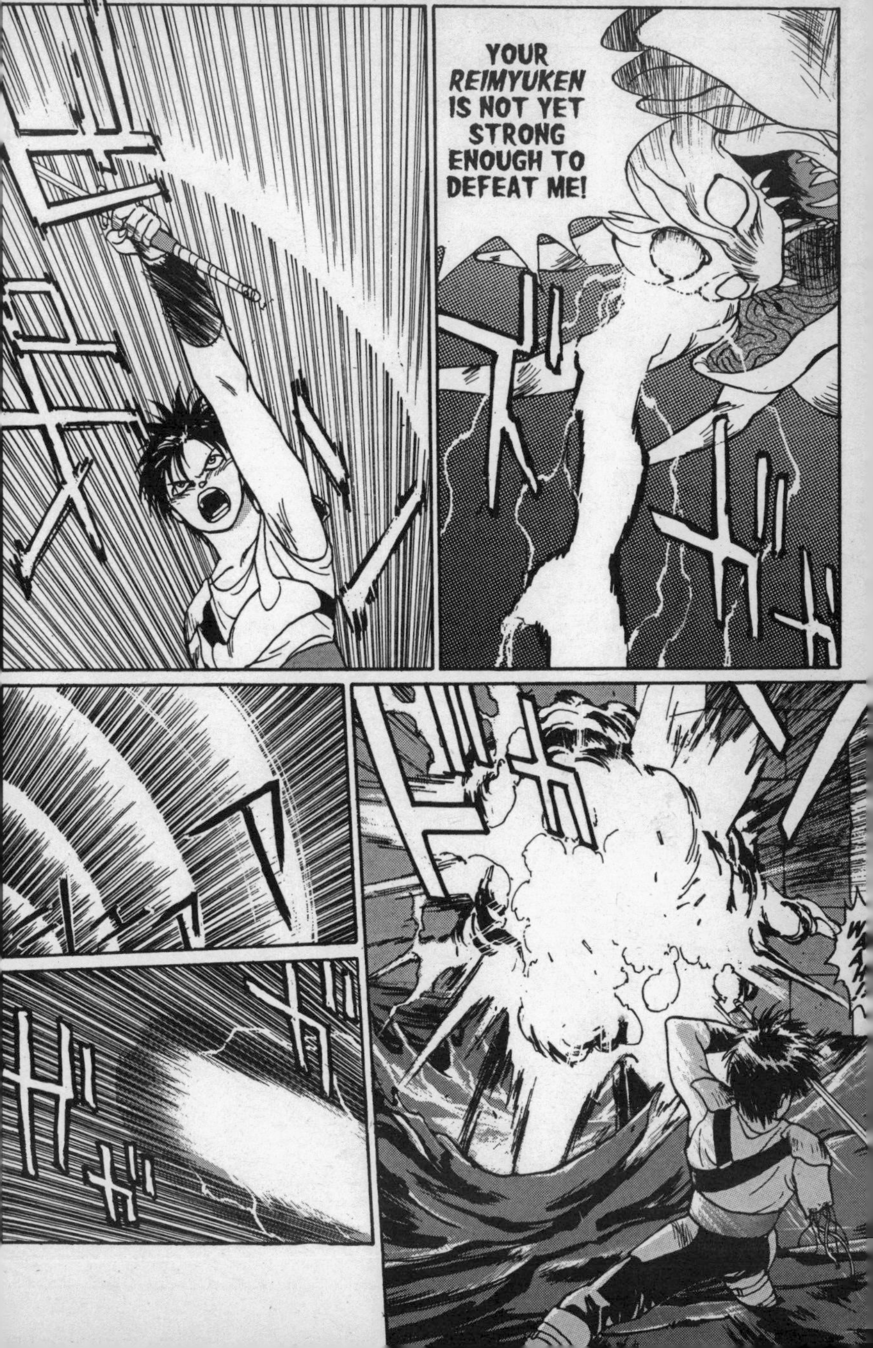
YOUR REIMYUKEN IS NOT YET STRONG ENOUGH TO DEFEAT ME!
WAAH!!

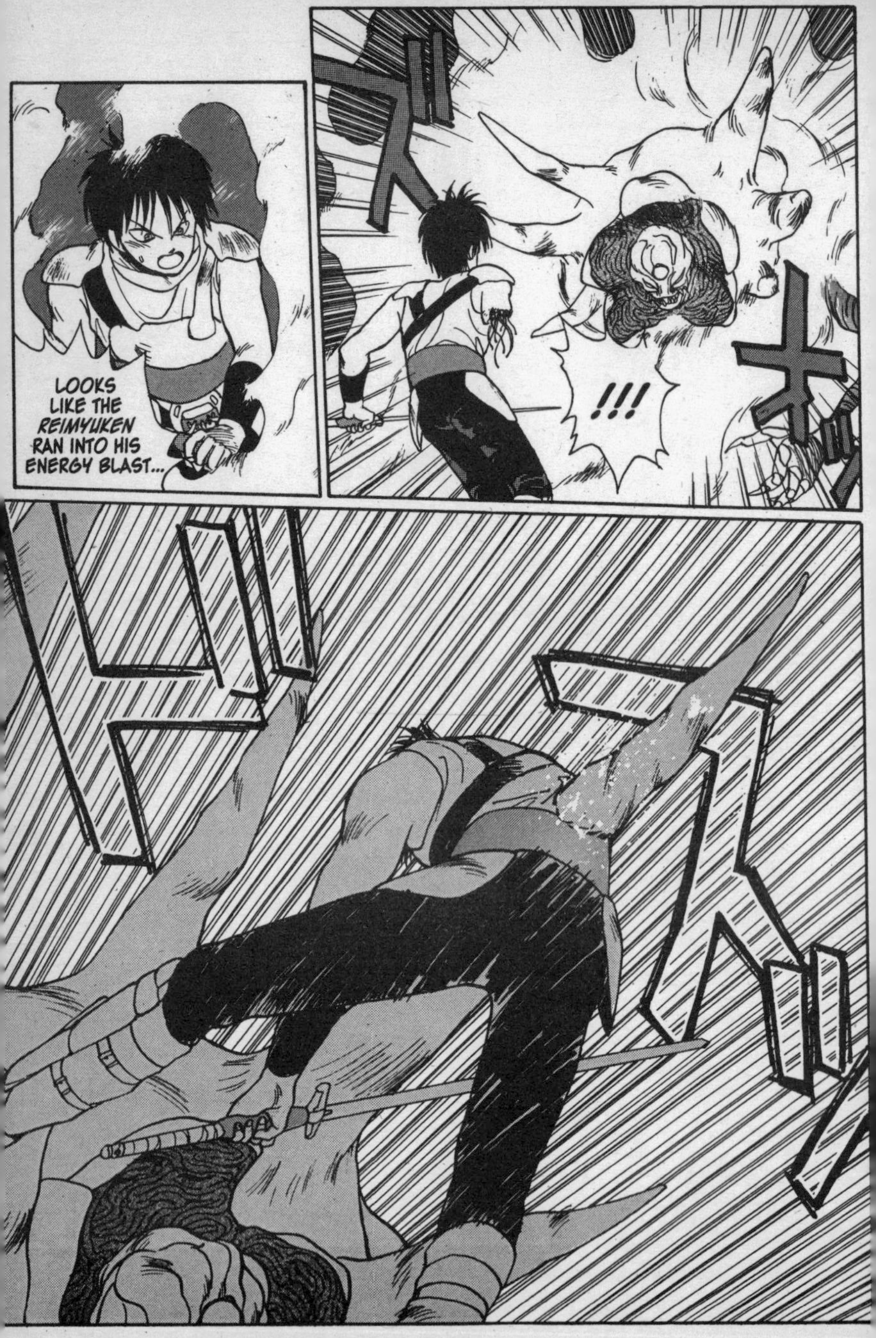
LOOKS LIKE THE REIMYUKEN RAN INTO HIS ENERGY BLAST...
!!!

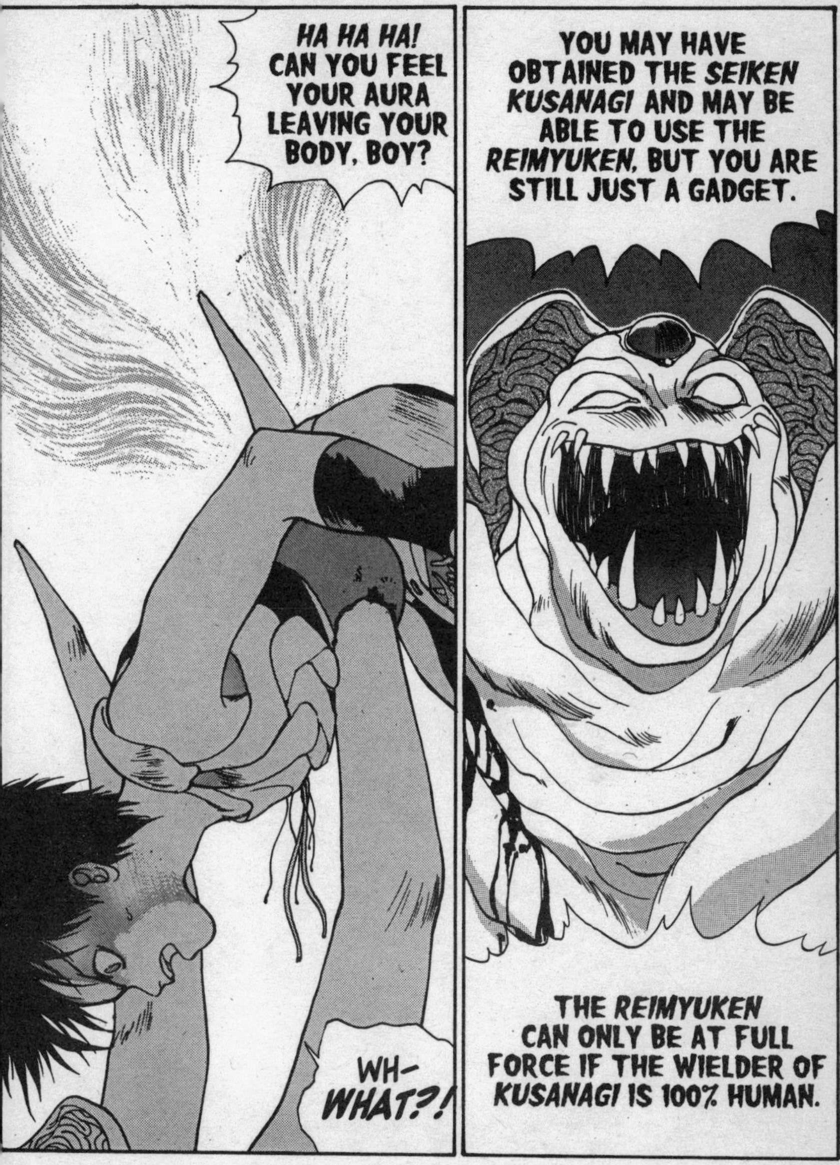
HA HA HA! CAN YOU FEEL YOUR AURA LEAVING YOUR BODY, BOY?
WH- WHAT?!
YOU MAY HAVE OBTAINED THE SEIKEN KUSANAGI AND MAY BE ABLE TO USE THE REIMYUKEN, BUT YOU ARE STILL JUST A GADGET.
THE REIMYUKEN CAN ONLY BE AT FULL FORCE IF THE WIELDER OF KUSANAGI IS 100% HUMAN.

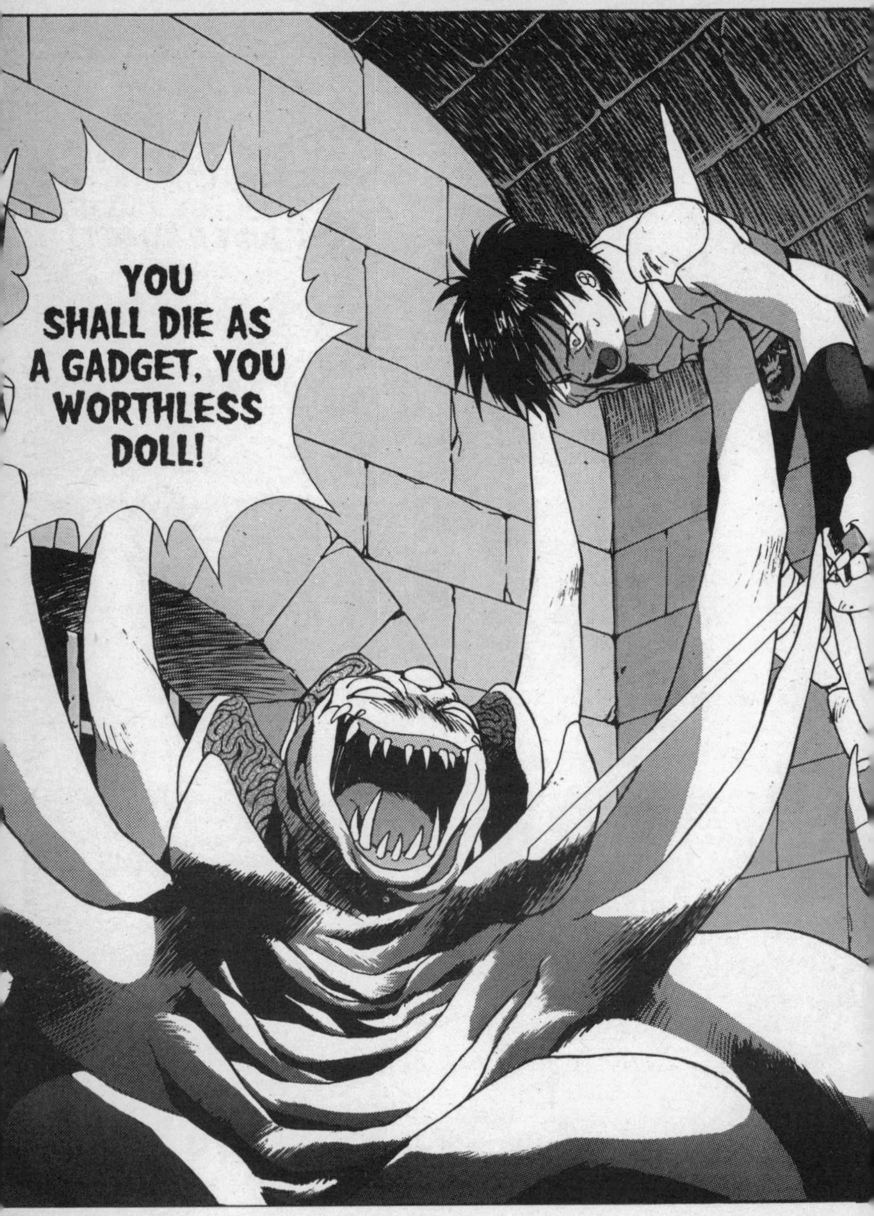
YOU SHALL DIE AS A GADGET, YOU WORTHLESS DOLL!

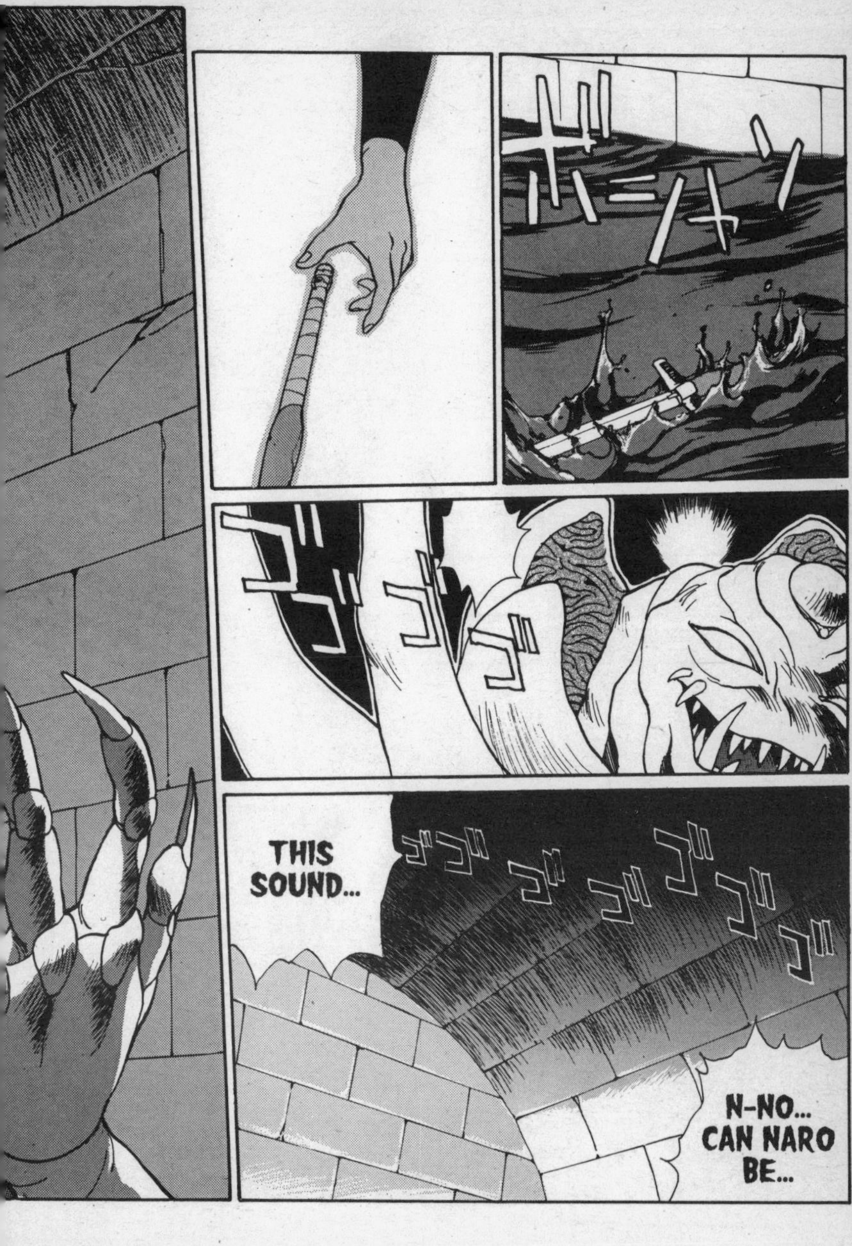
THIS SOUND...
N-NO... CAN NARO BE...

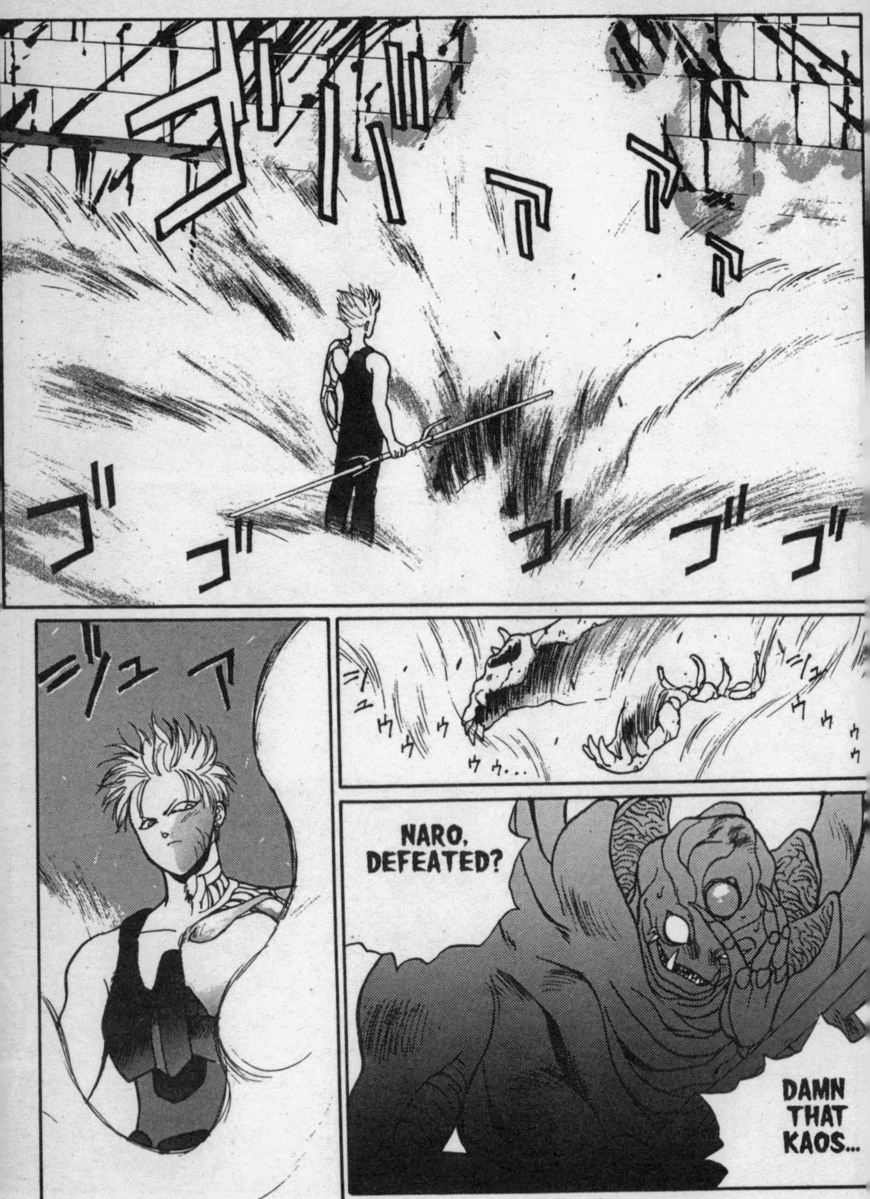
ゴゴゴゴゴ
ジュア
NARO, DEFEATED?
DAMN THAT KAOS...

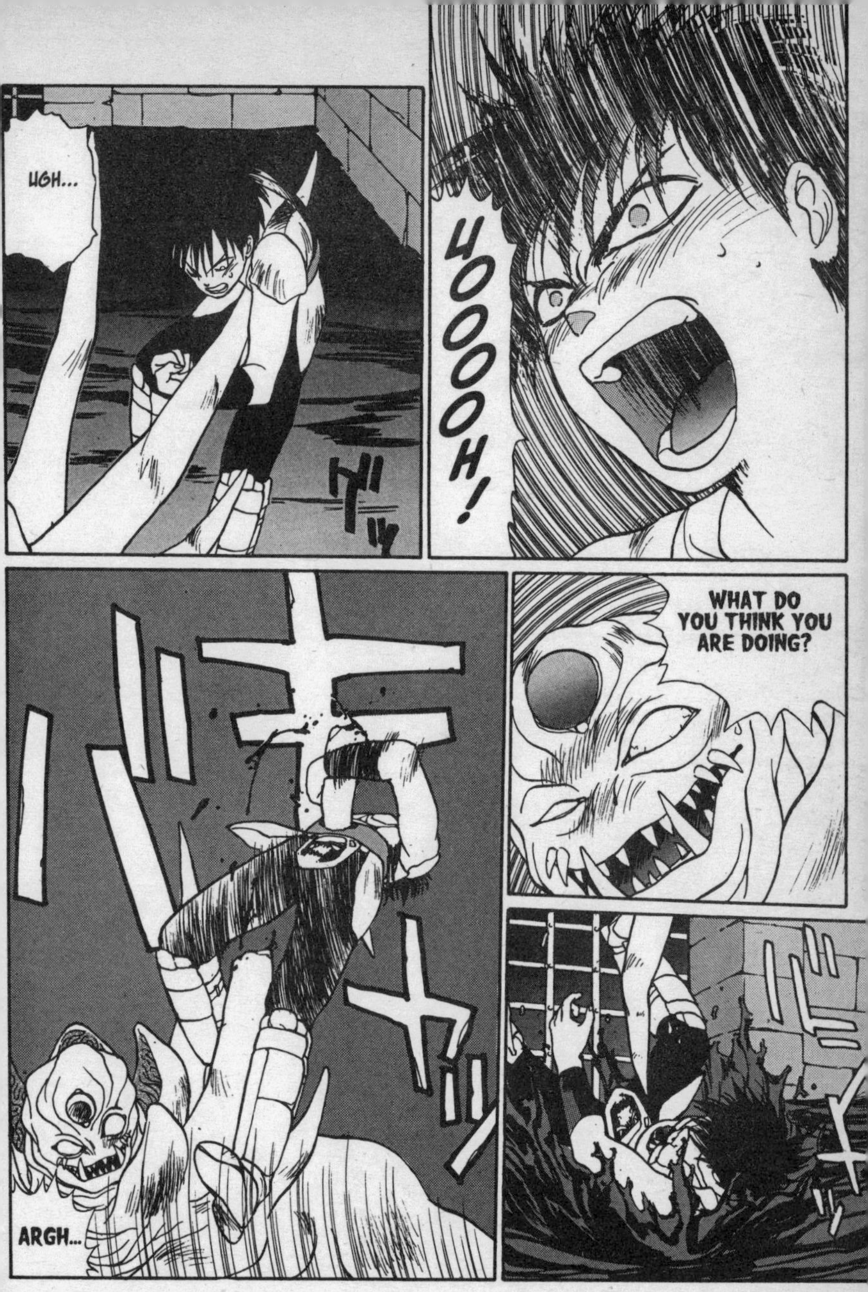
UGH...
UOOOOOH!
ARGH...
WHAT DO YOU THINK YOU ARE DOING?

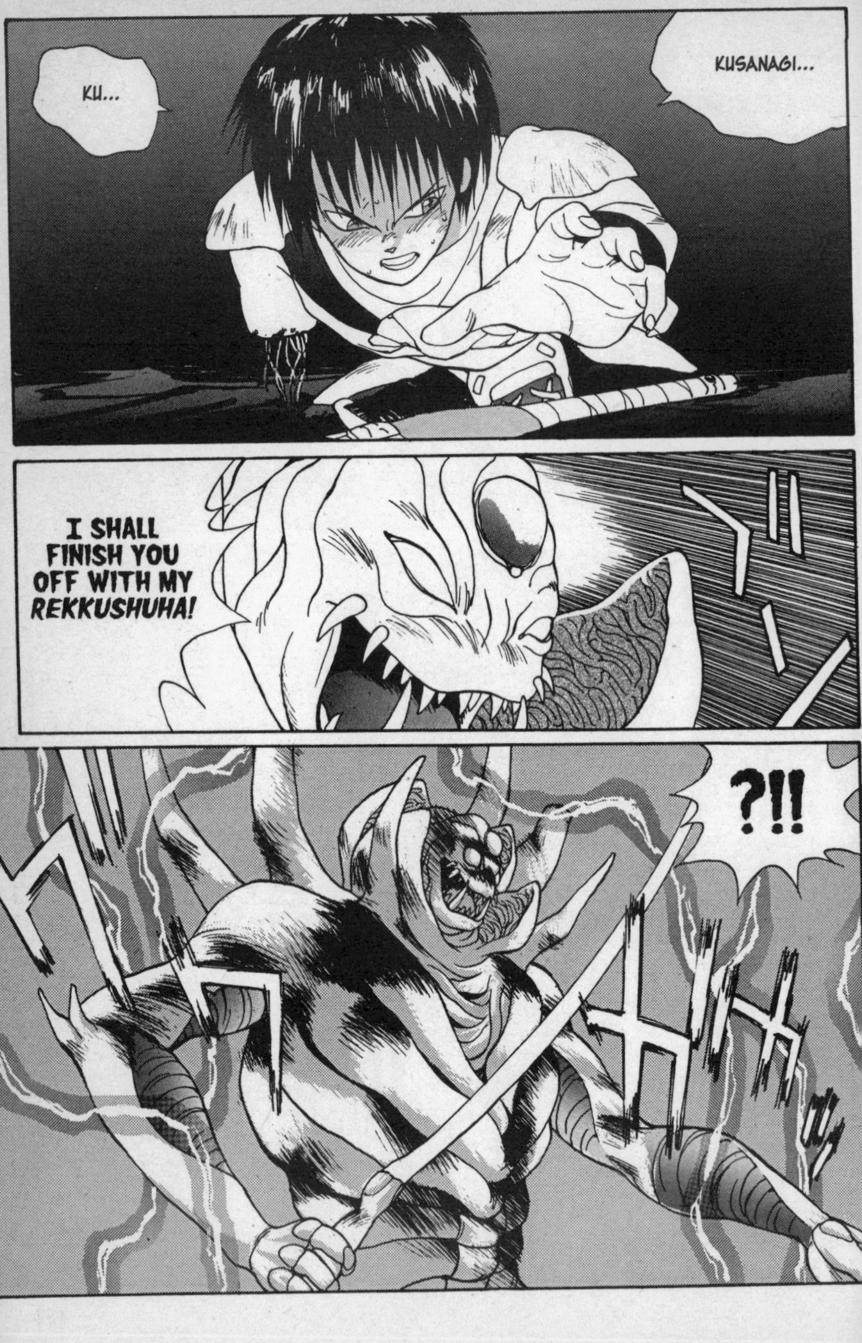
KU...
KUSANAGI...
I SHALL FINISH YOU OFF WITH MY *REKKUSHUHA!*
?!!

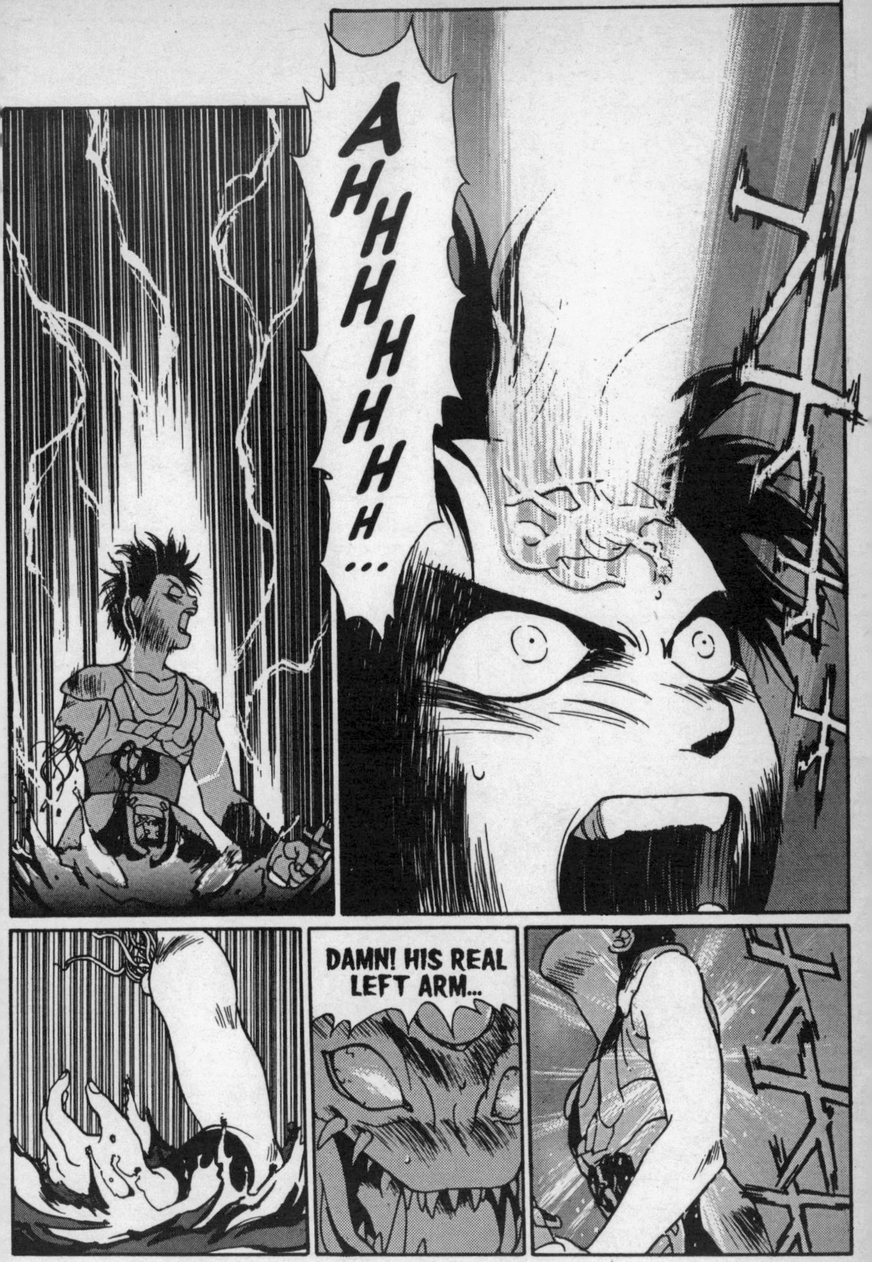
AHHHHHHH...
DAMN! HIS REAL LEFT ARM...

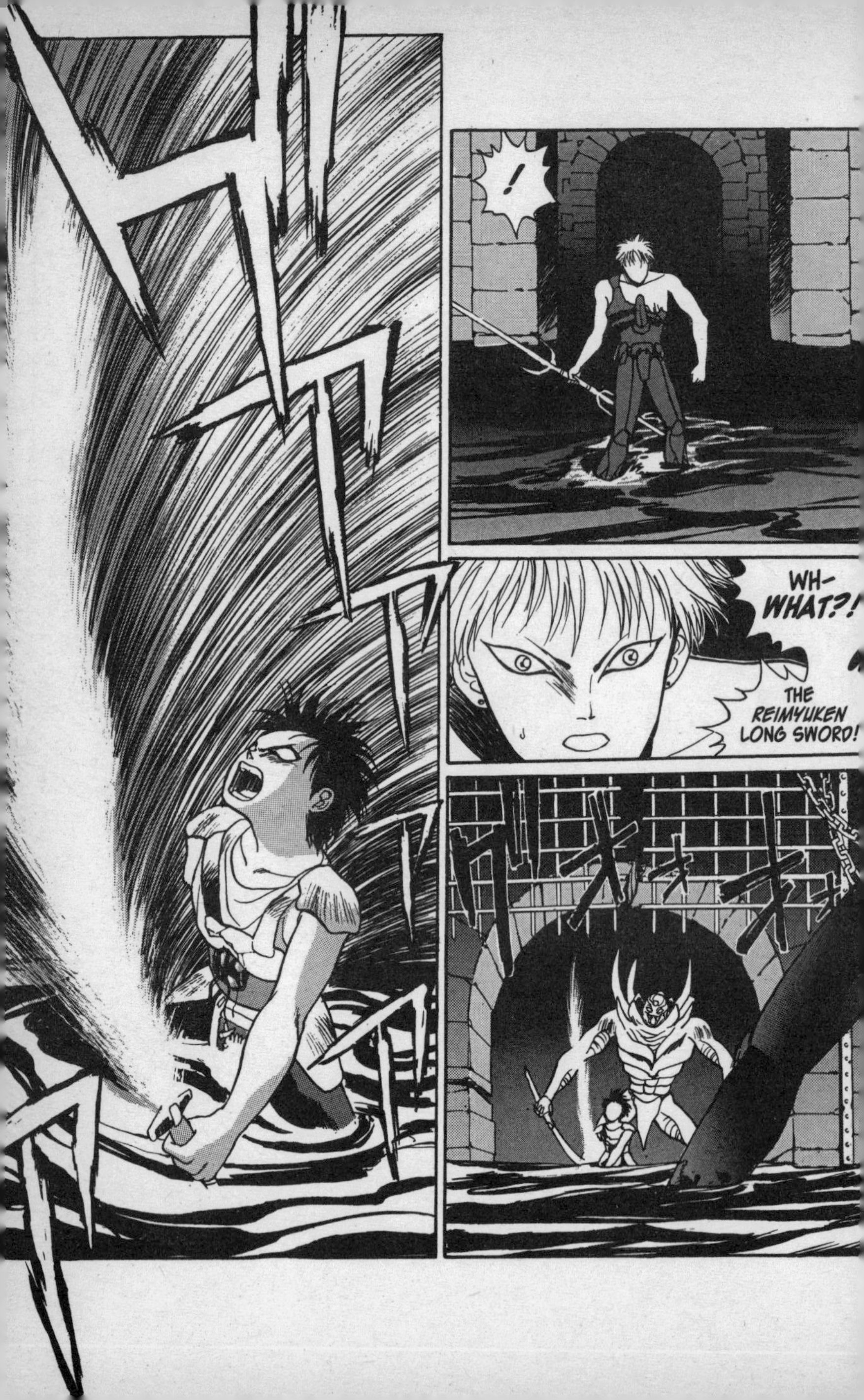
!
WH-
WHAT?!
THE
REIMYUKEN
LONG SWORD!

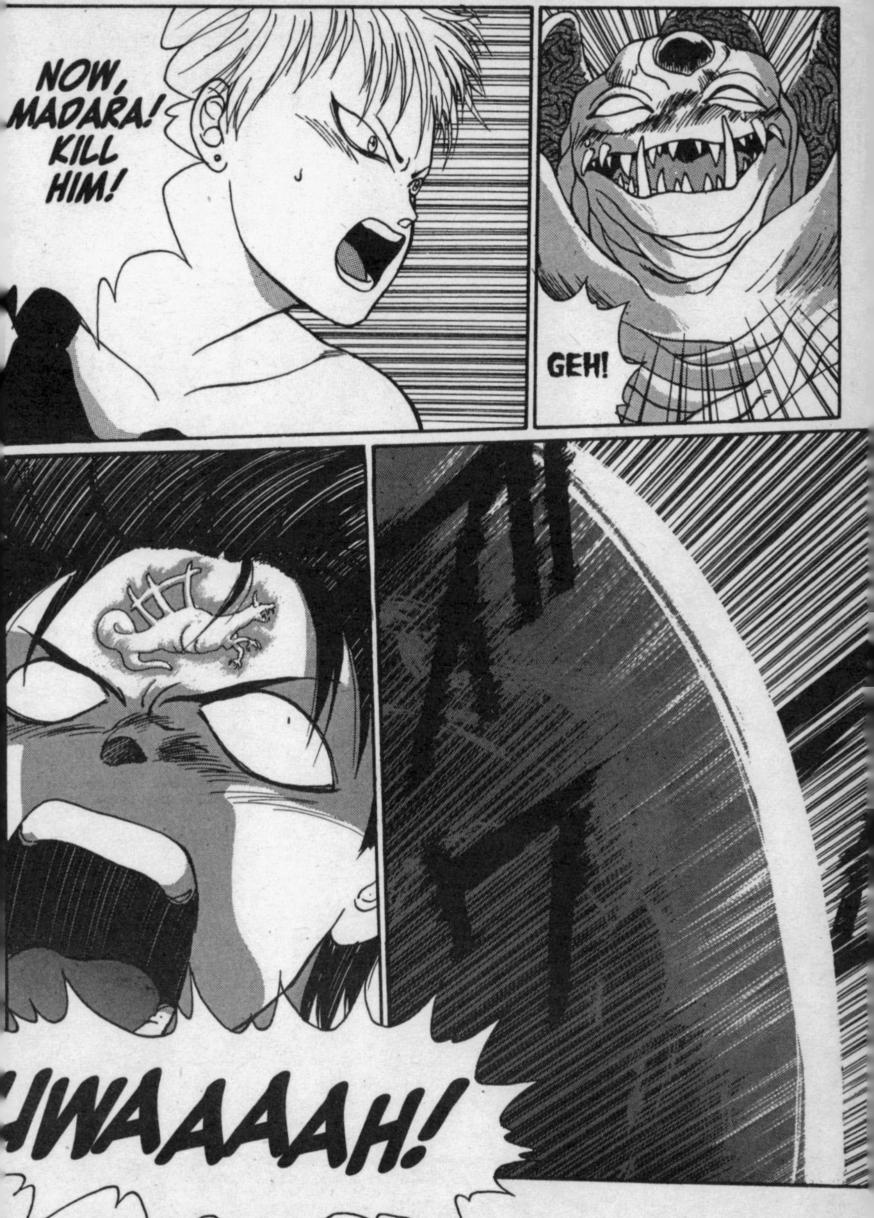
NOW, MADARA! KILL HIM!
GEH!
WAAAAAH!

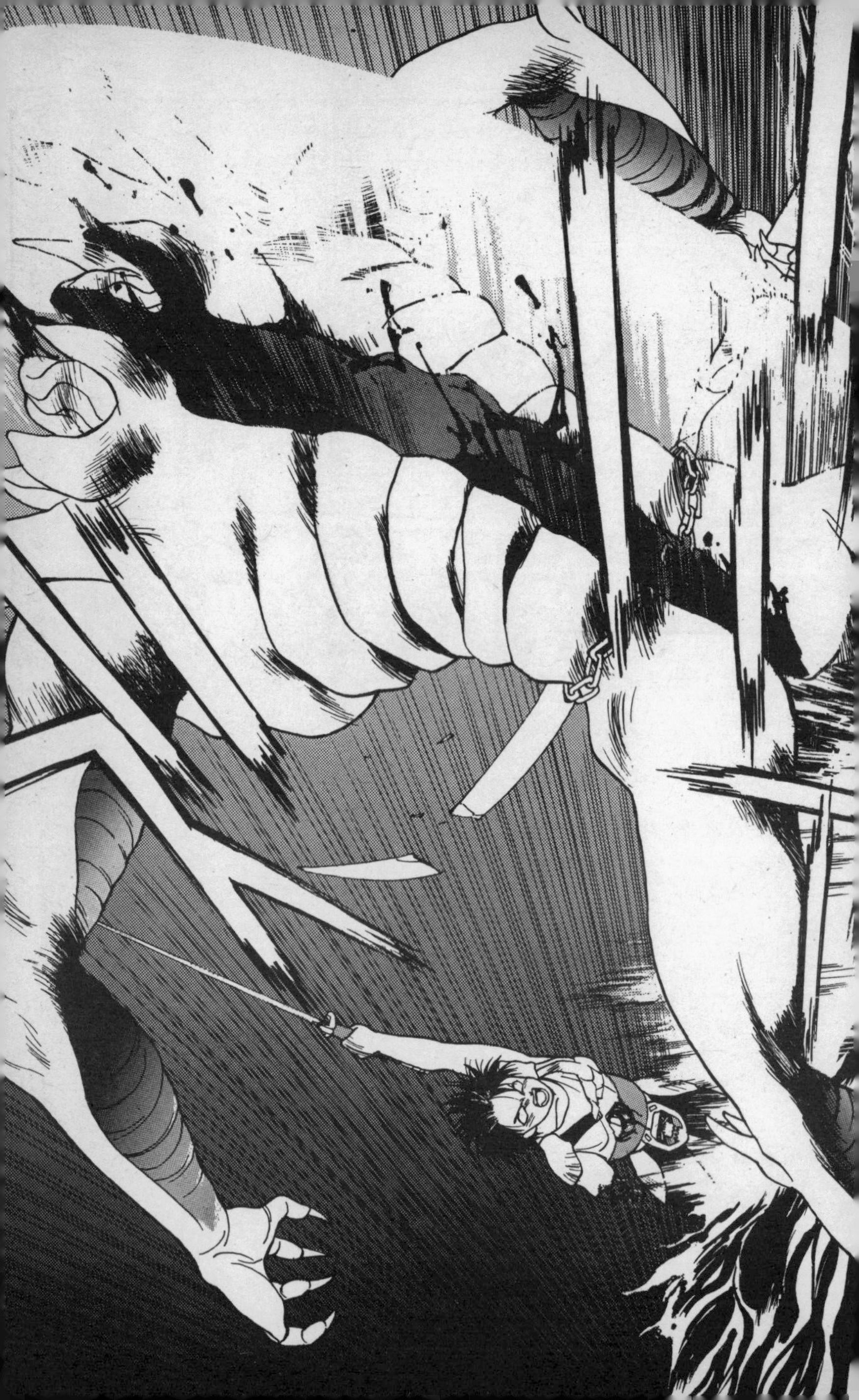

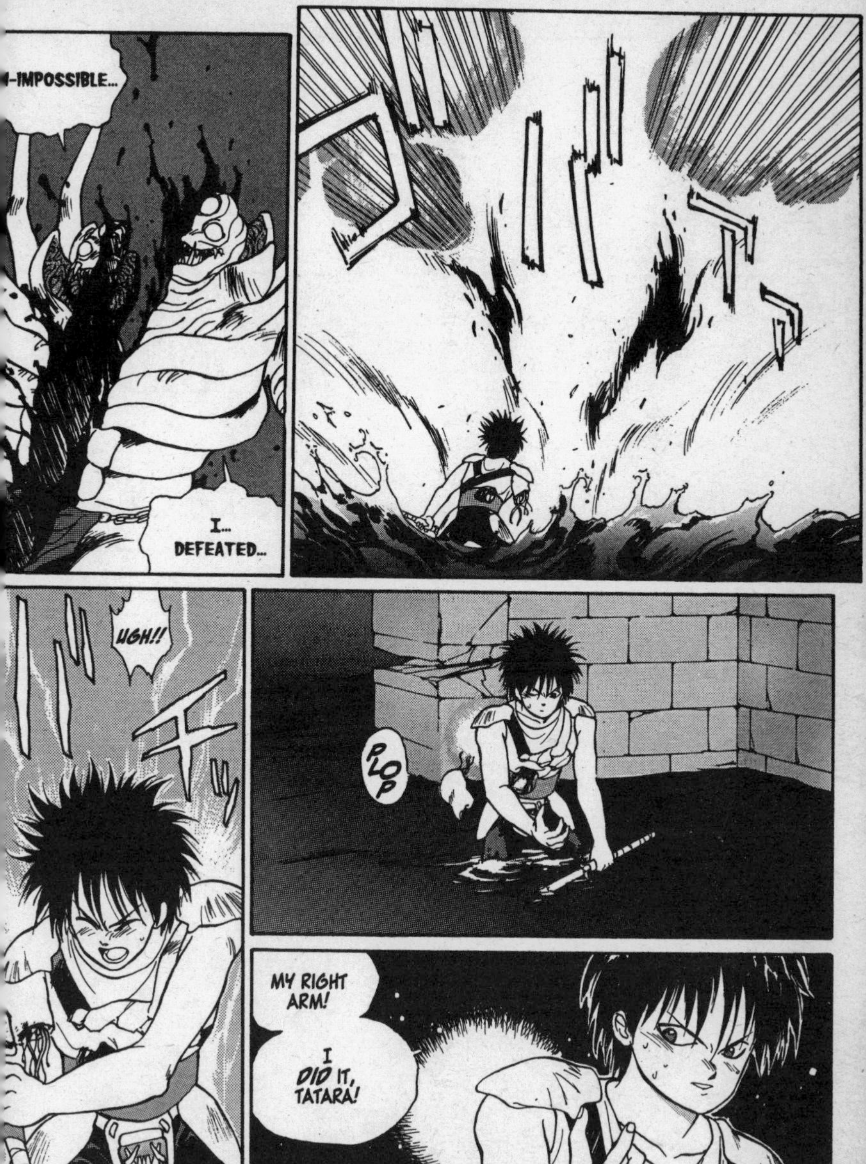

I-IMPOSSIBLE...
I... DEFEATED...
UGH!!
PLOP
MY RIGHT ARM!
I DID IT, TATARA!

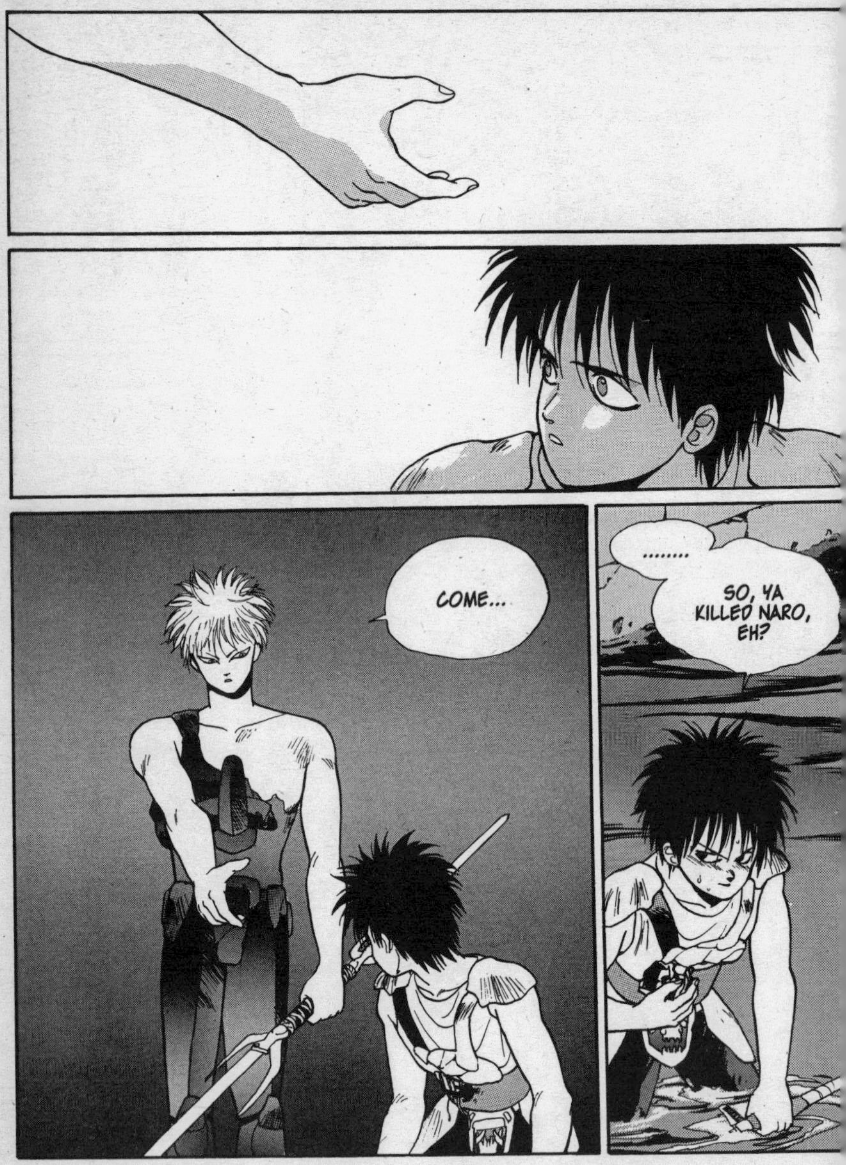
COME...
....
SO, YA KILLED NARO, EH?

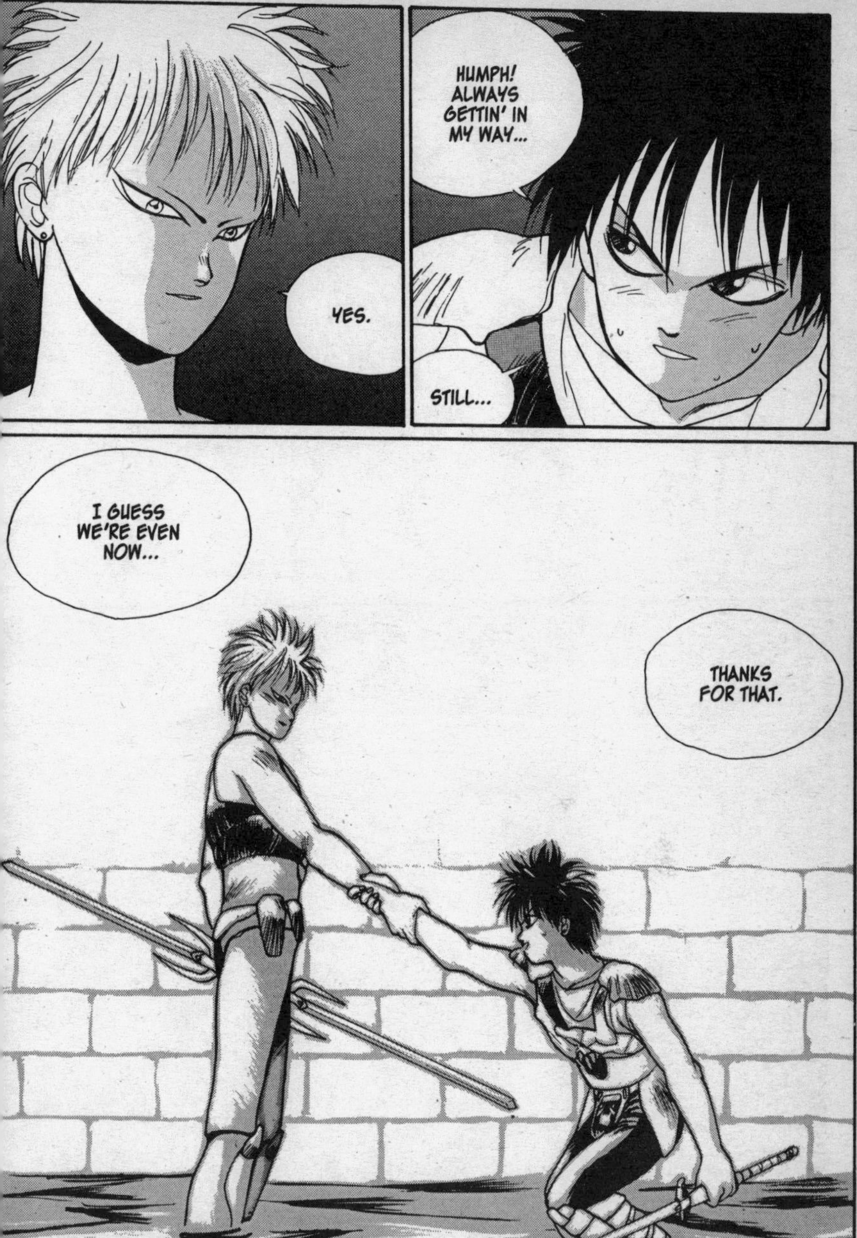
YES.
HUMPH! ALWAYS GETTIN' IN MY WAY...
STILL...
I GUESS WE'RE EVEN NOW...
THANKS FOR THAT.

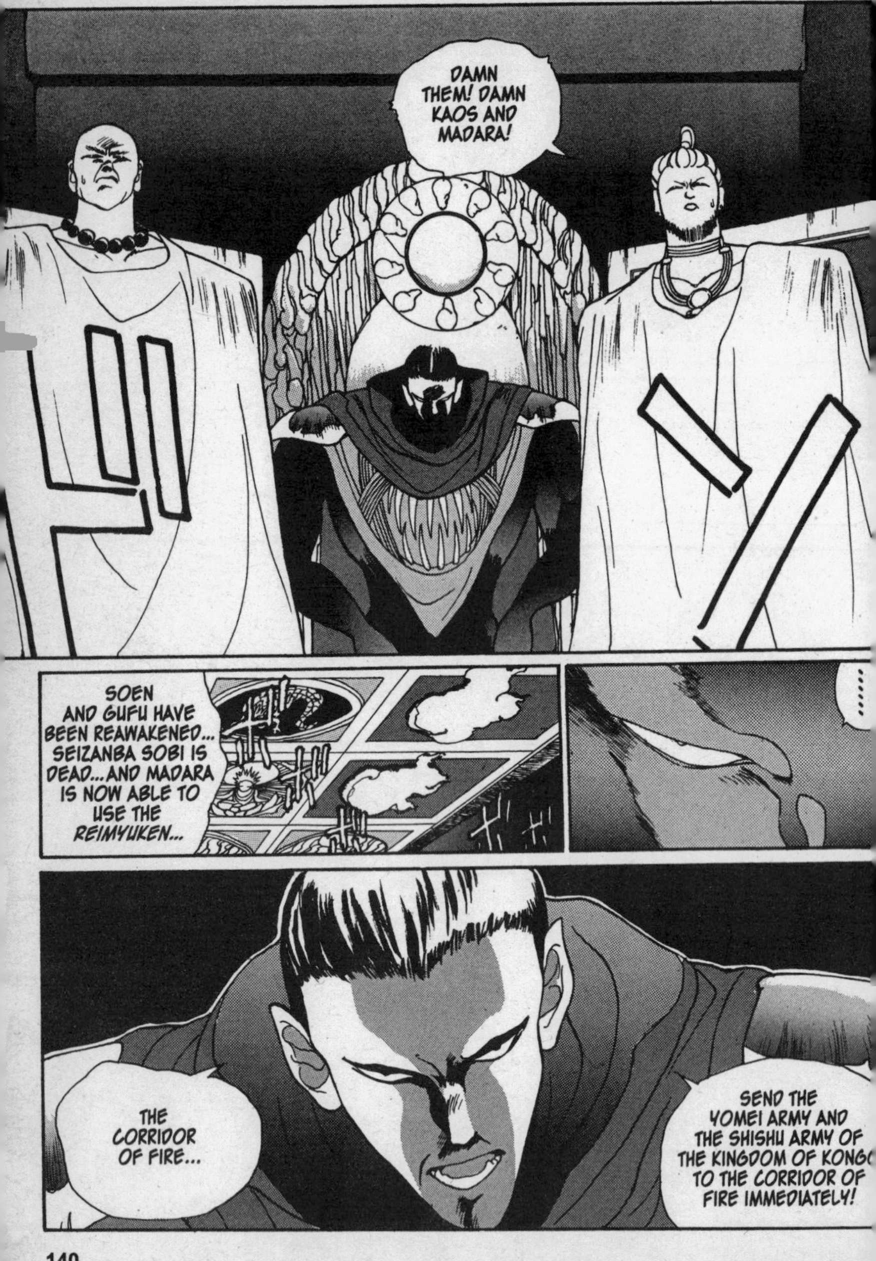
DAMN THEM! DAMN KAOS AND MADARA!
SOEN AND GUFU HAVE BEEN REAWAKENED... SEIZANBA SOBI IS DEAD...AND MADARA IS NOW ABLE TO USE THE REIMYUKEN...
......
THE CORRIDOR OF FIRE...
SEND THE YOMEI ARMY AND THE SHISHU ARMY OF THE KINGDOM OF KONG TO THE CORRIDOR OF FIRE IMMEDIATELY!

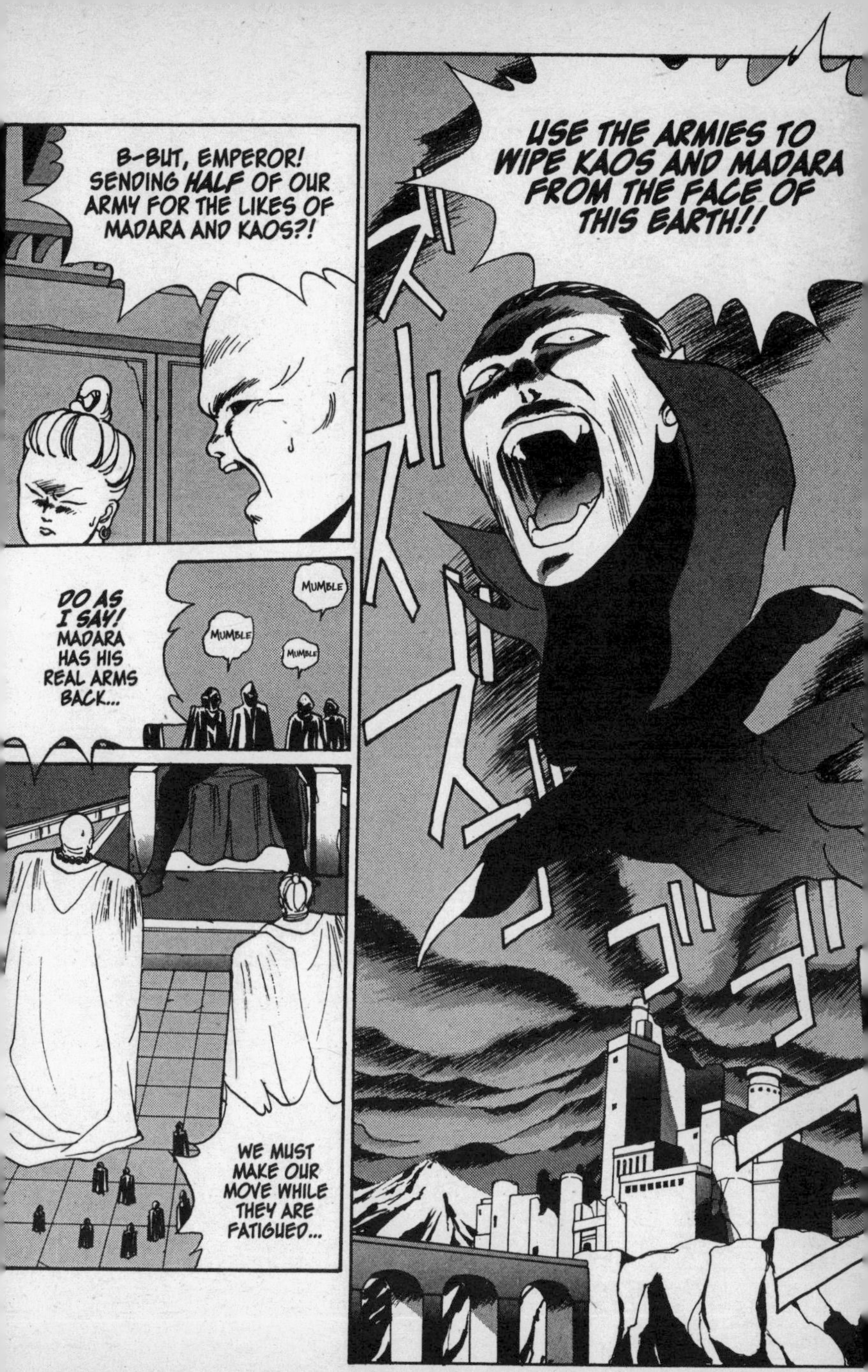
USE THE ARMIES TO WIPE KAOS AND MADARA FROM THE FACE OF THIS EARTH!!
B-BUT, EMPEROR! SENDING HALF OF OUR ARMY FOR THE LIKES OF MADARA AND KAOS?!
MUMBLE
MUMBLE
MUMBLE
DO AS I SAY! MADARA HAS HIS REAL ARMS BACK...
WE MUST MAKE OUR MOVE WHILE THEY ARE FATIGUED...

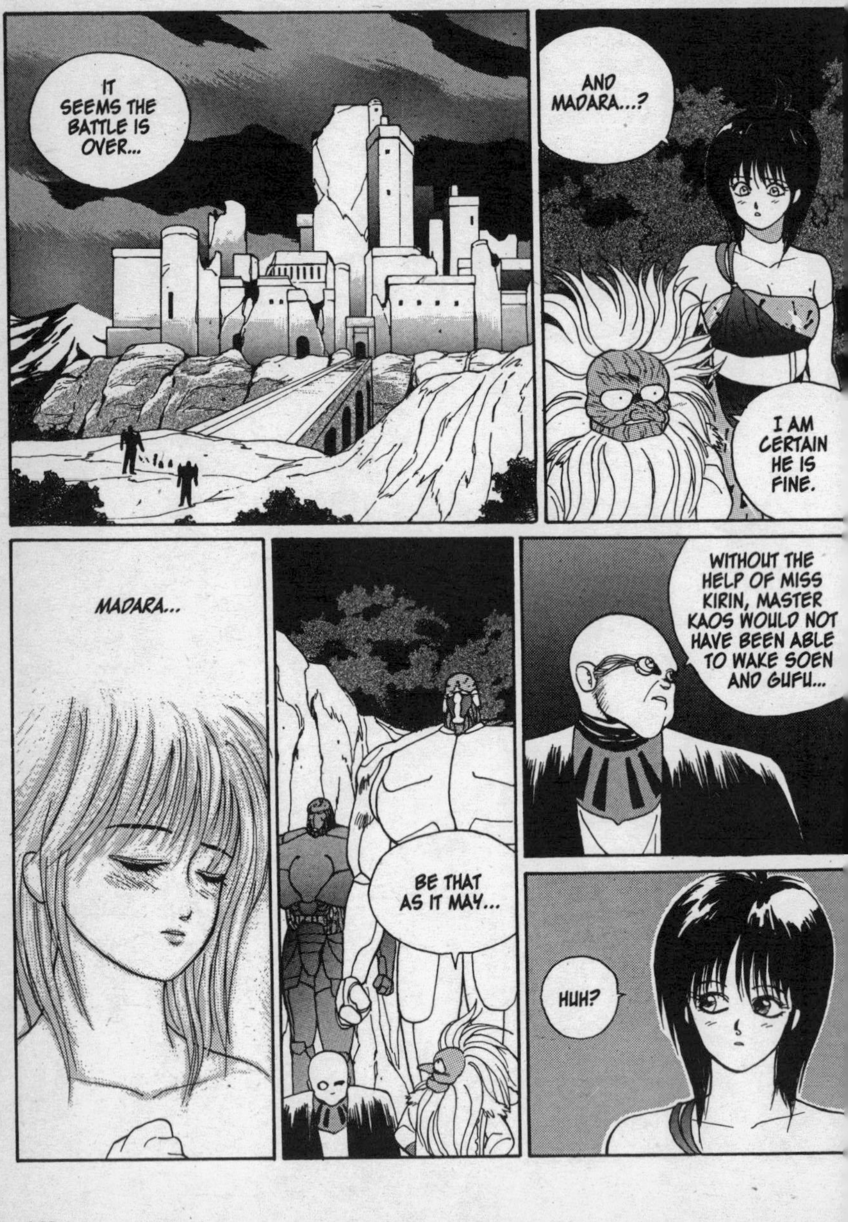
IT SEEMS THE BATTLE IS OVER...
AND MADARA...?
I AM CERTAIN HE IS FINE.
MADARA...
BE THAT AS IT MAY...
WITHOUT THE HELP OF MISS KIRIN, MASTER KAOS WOULD NOT HAVE BEEN ABLE TO WAKE SOEN AND GUFU...
HUH?

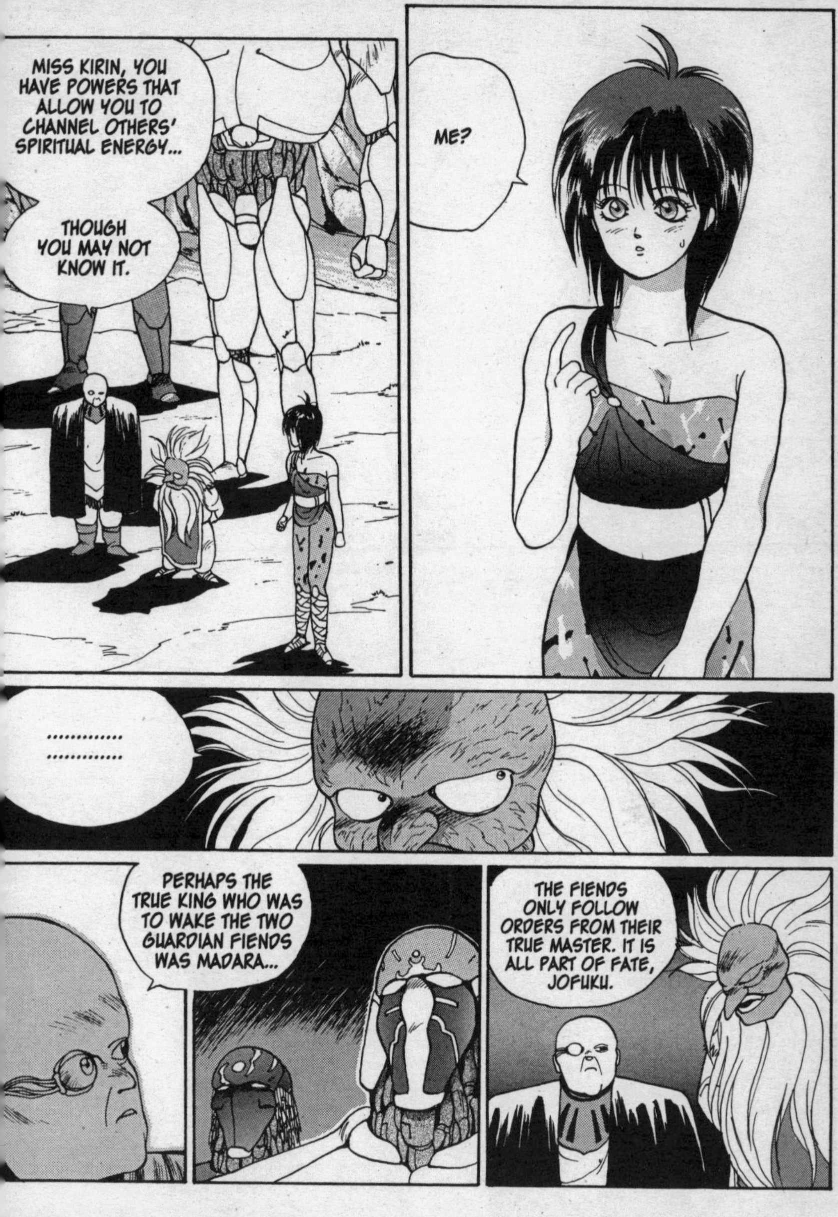
MISS KIRIN, YOU HAVE POWERS THAT ALLOW YOU TO CHANNEL OTHERS' SPIRITUAL ENERGY...
THOUGH YOU MAY NOT KNOW IT.
ME?
....
....
PERHAPS THE TRUE KING WHO WAS TO WAKE THE TWO GUARDIAN FIENDS WAS MADARA...
THE FIENDS ONLY FOLLOW ORDERS FROM THEIR TRUE MASTER. IT IS ALL PART OF FATE, JOFUKU.

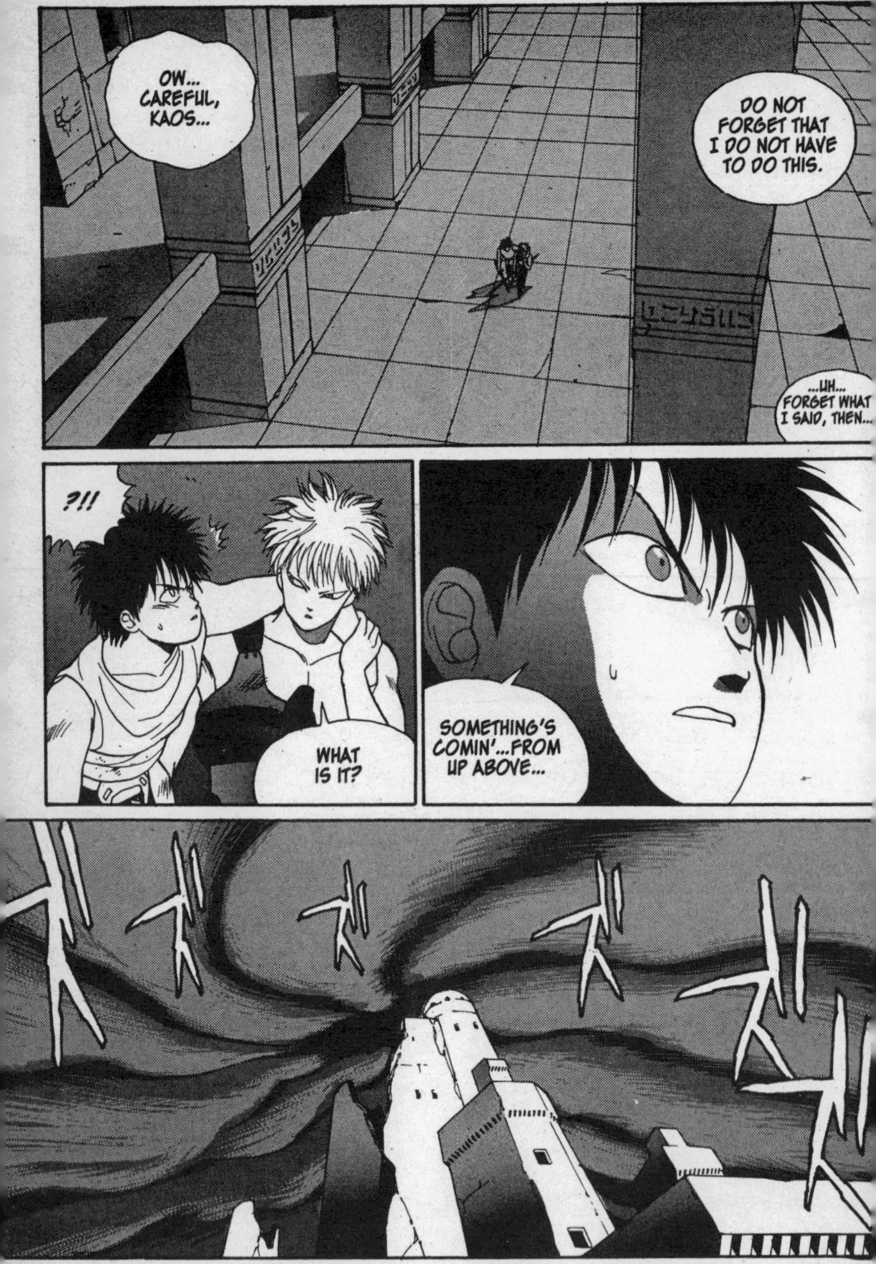

OW... CAREFUL, KAOS...
DO NOT FORGET THAT I DO NOT HAVE TO DO THIS.
...UH... FORGET WHAT I SAID, THEN...
?!!
WHAT IS IT?
SOMETHING'S COMIN'...FROM UP ABOVE...

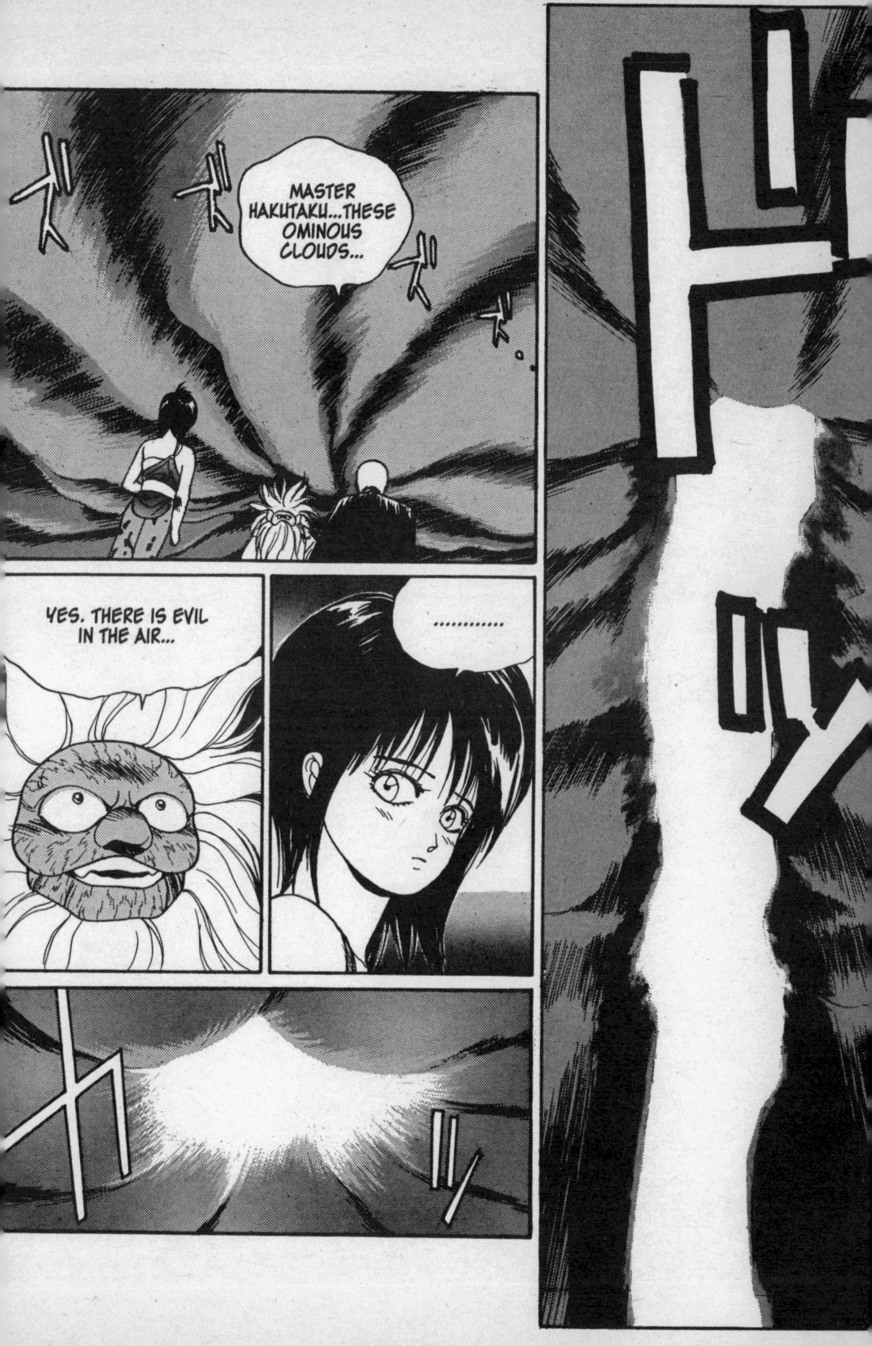
MASTER HAKUTAKU...THESE OMINOUS CLOUDS...
YES. THERE IS EVIL IN THE AIR...
....

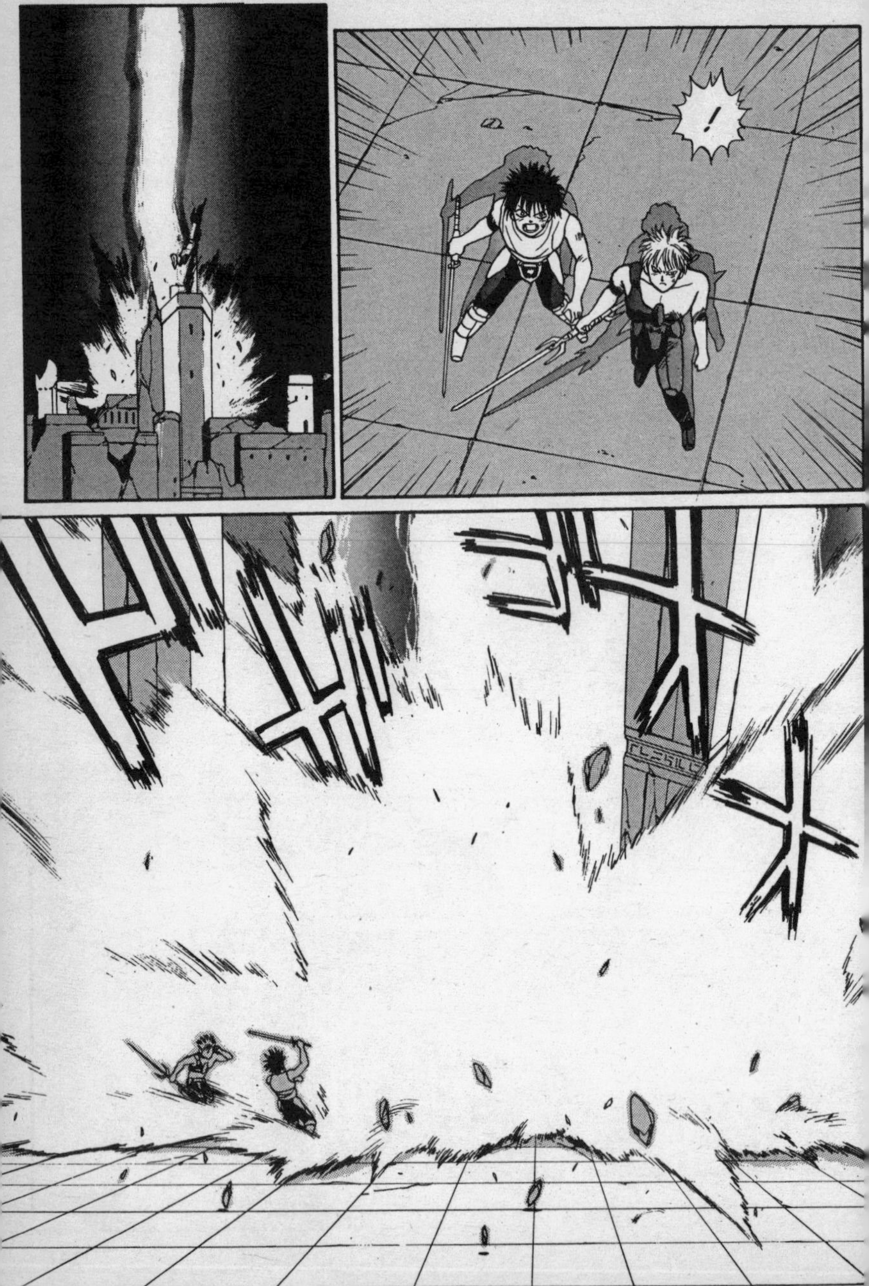
!

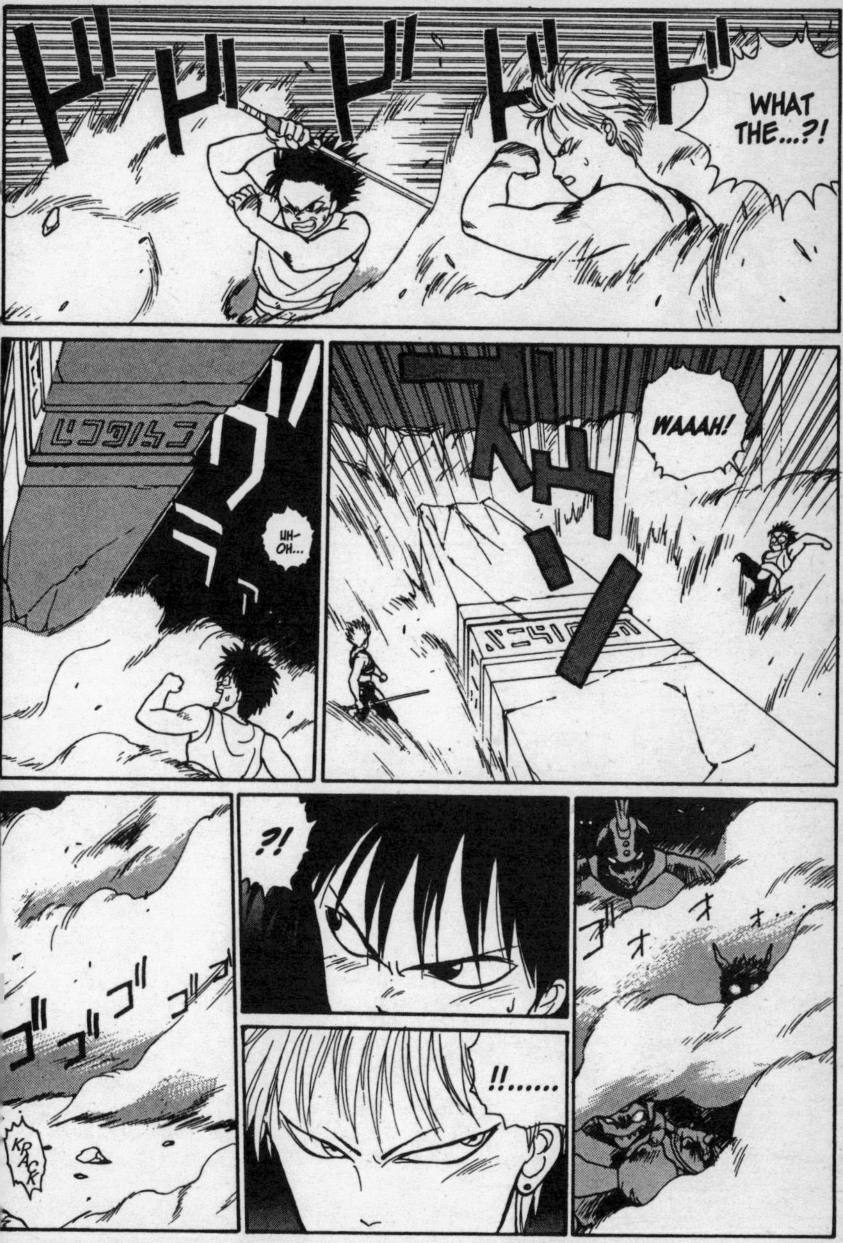
WHAT THE...?!
UH-OH...
WAAAH!
KRACK
?!
!!......

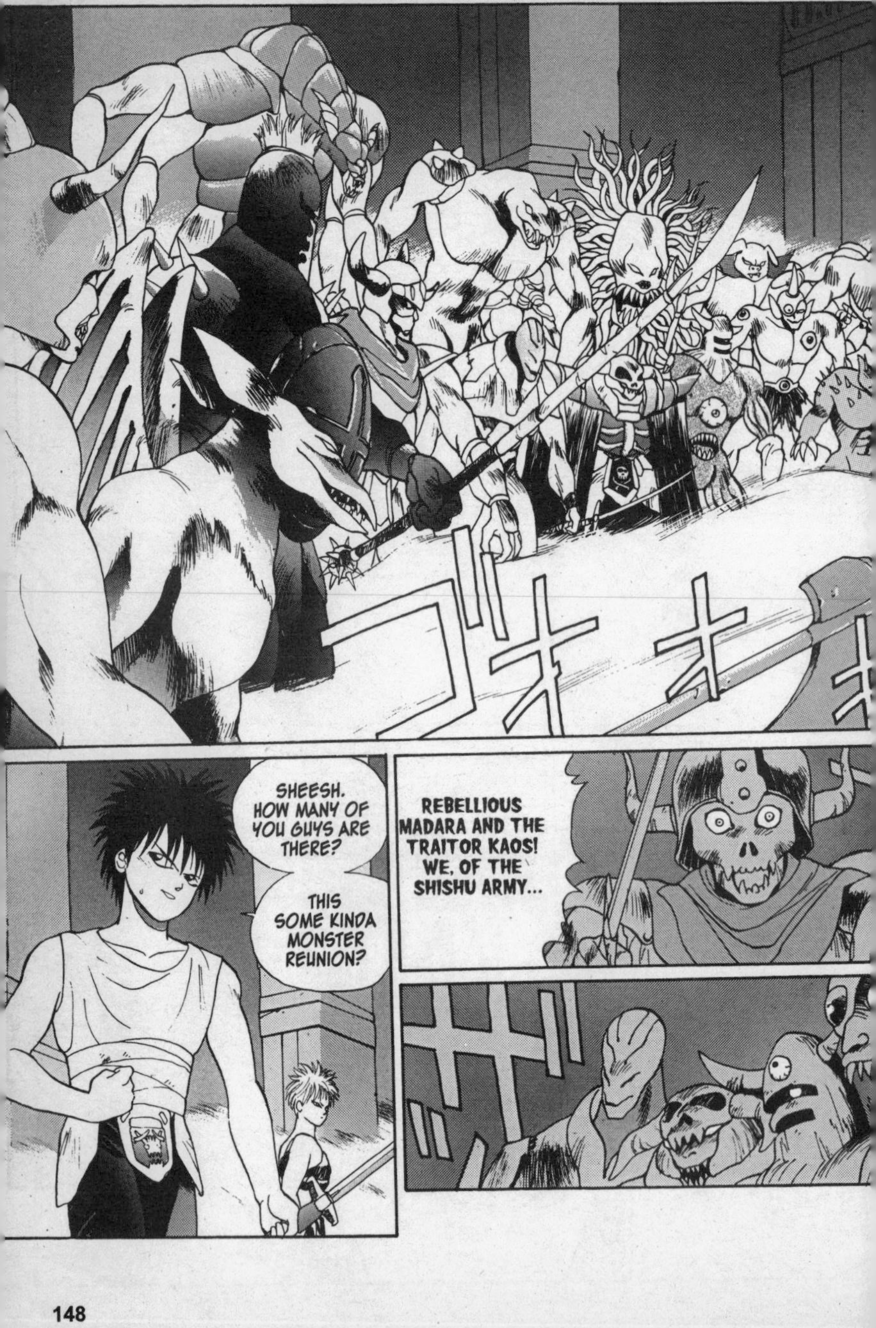
ゴオオオ
SHEESH. HOW MANY OF YOU GUYS ARE THERE?
THIS SOME KINDA MONSTER REUNION?
REBELLIOUS MADARA AND THE TRAITOR KAOS! WE, OF THE SHISHU ARMY...

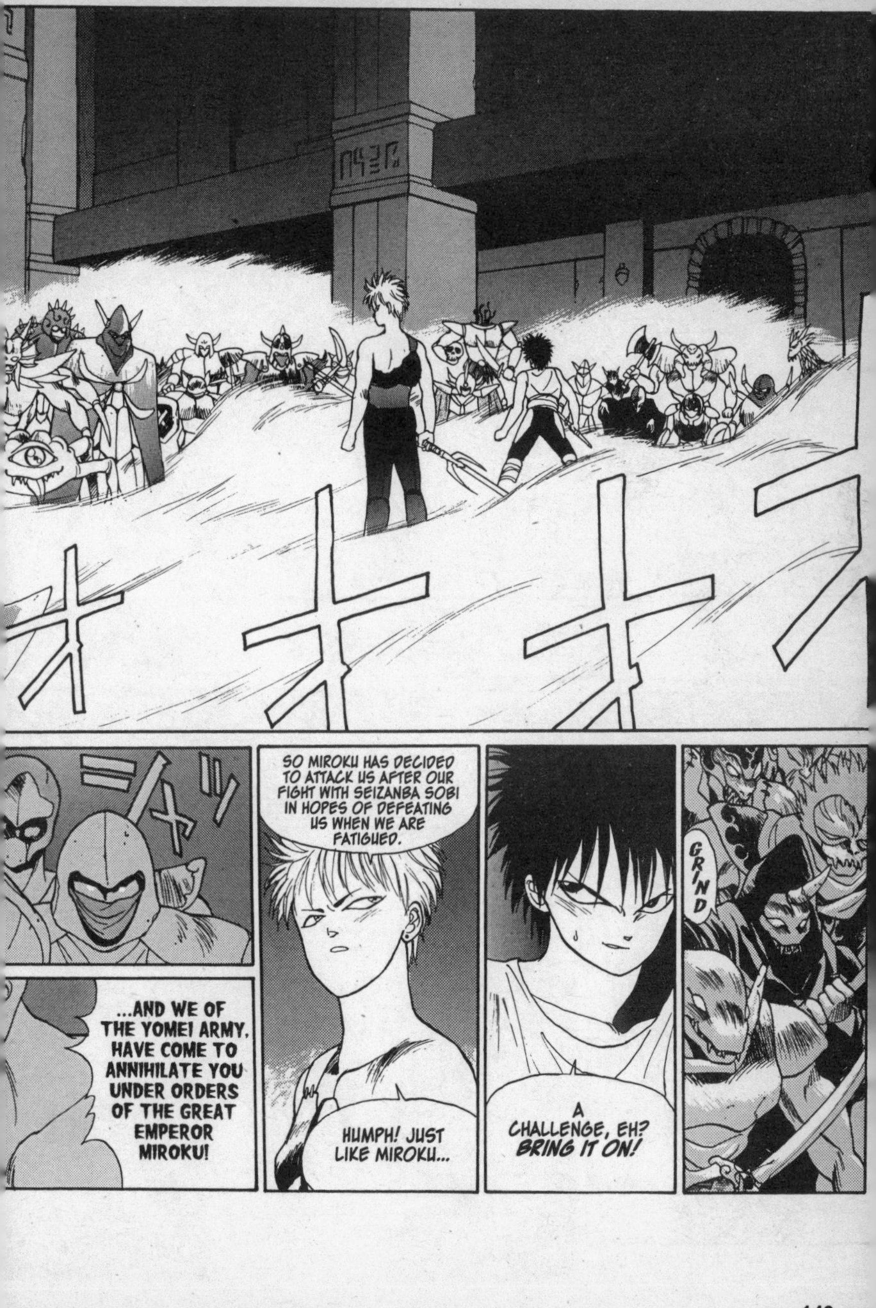
...AND WE OF THE YOMEI ARMY, HAVE COME TO ANNIHILATE YOU UNDER ORDERS OF THE GREAT EMPEROR MIROKU!
SO MIROKU HAS DECIDED TO ATTACK US AFTER OUR FIGHT WITH SEIZANBA SOBI IN HOPES OF DEFEATING US WHEN WE ARE FATIGUED.
HUMPH! JUST LIKE MIROKU...
A CHALLENGE, EH? BRING IT ON!
GRIND

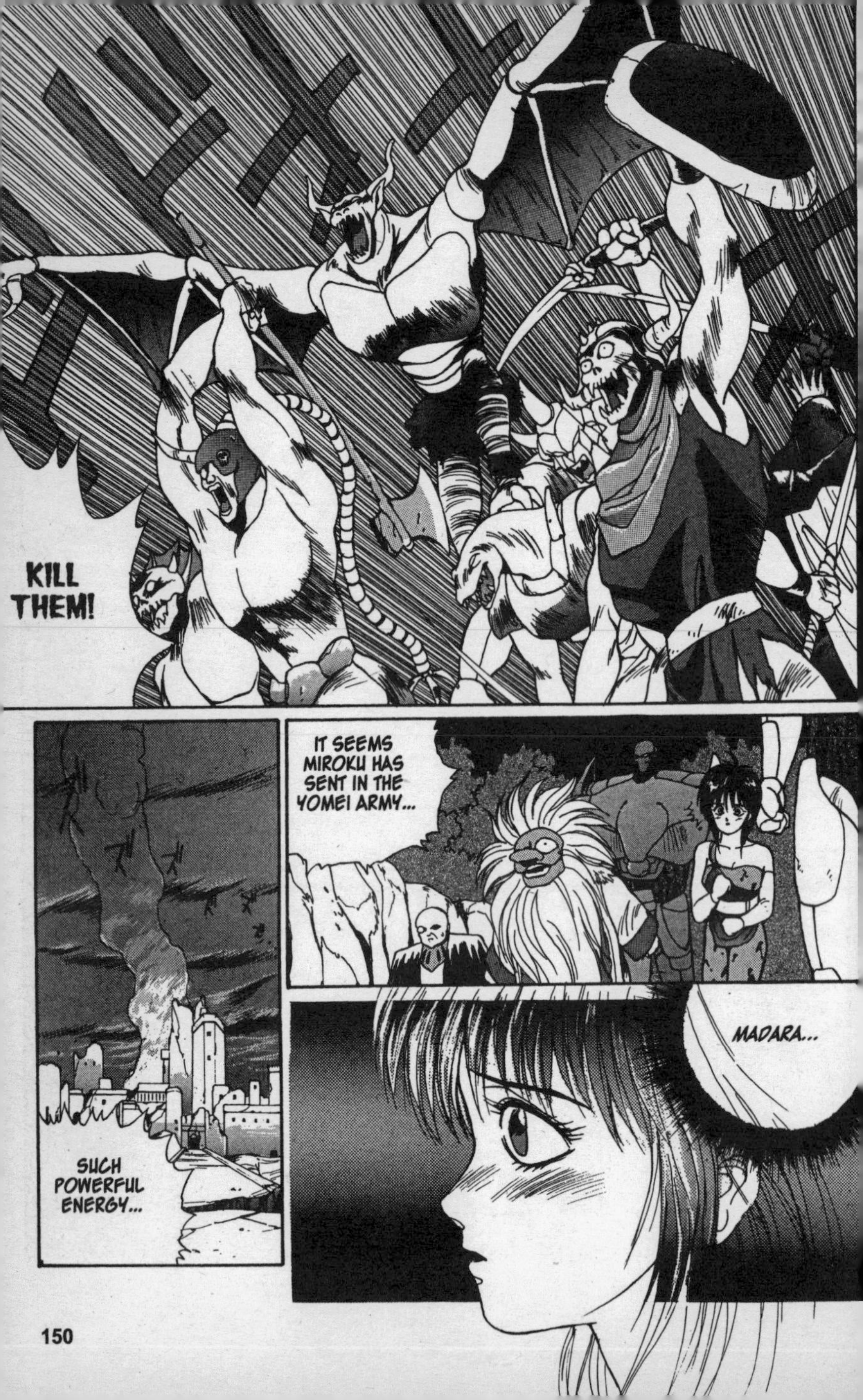
KILL THEM!
SUCH POWERFUL ENERGY...
IT SEEMS MIROKU HAS SENT IN THE YOMEI ARMY...
MADARA...

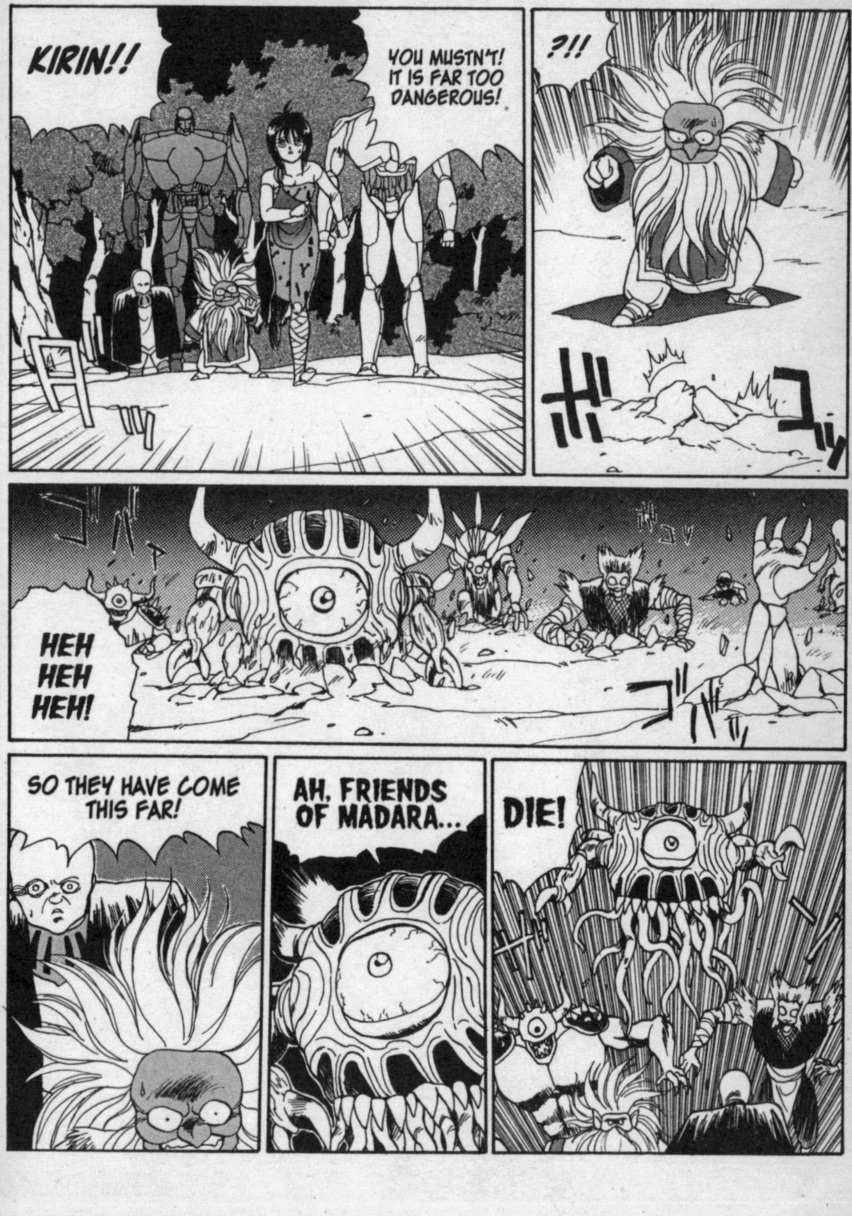
KIRIN!!
YOU MUSTN'T! IT IS FAR TOO DANGEROUS!
?!!
HEH HEH HEH!
SO THEY HAVE COME THIS FAR!
AH, FRIENDS OF MADARA...
DIE!

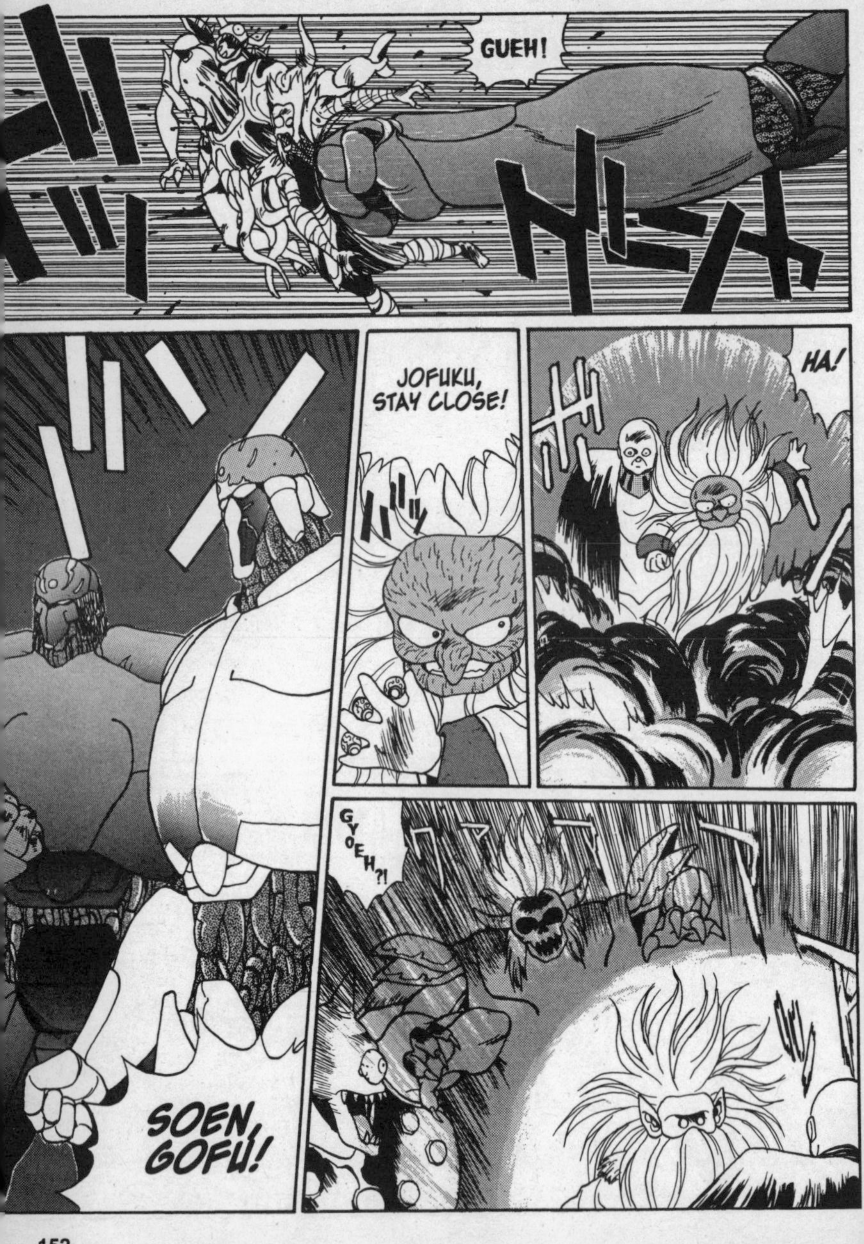
GUEH!
SOEN, GOFU!
JOFUKU, STAY CLOSE!
HA!
GYOEH?!

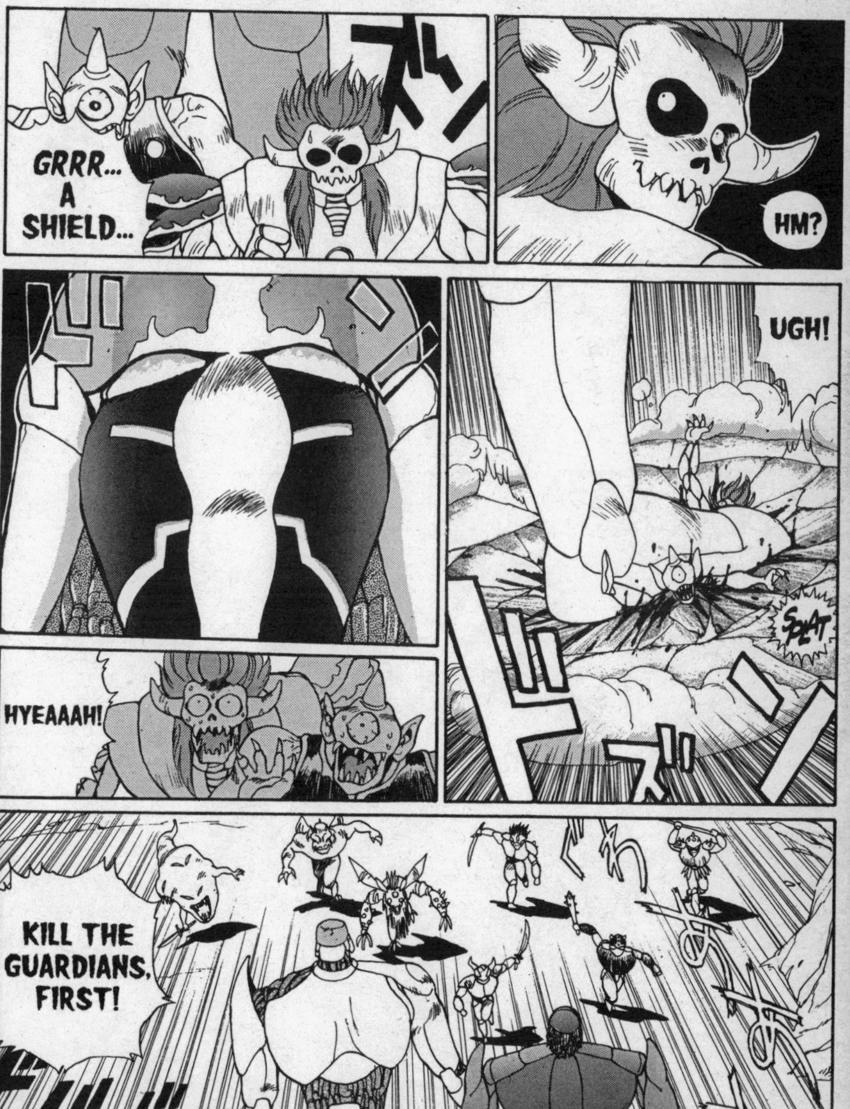
GRRR... A SHIELD...
HM?
HYEAAAH!
UGH!
SPLAT
KILL THE GUARDIANS, FIRST!

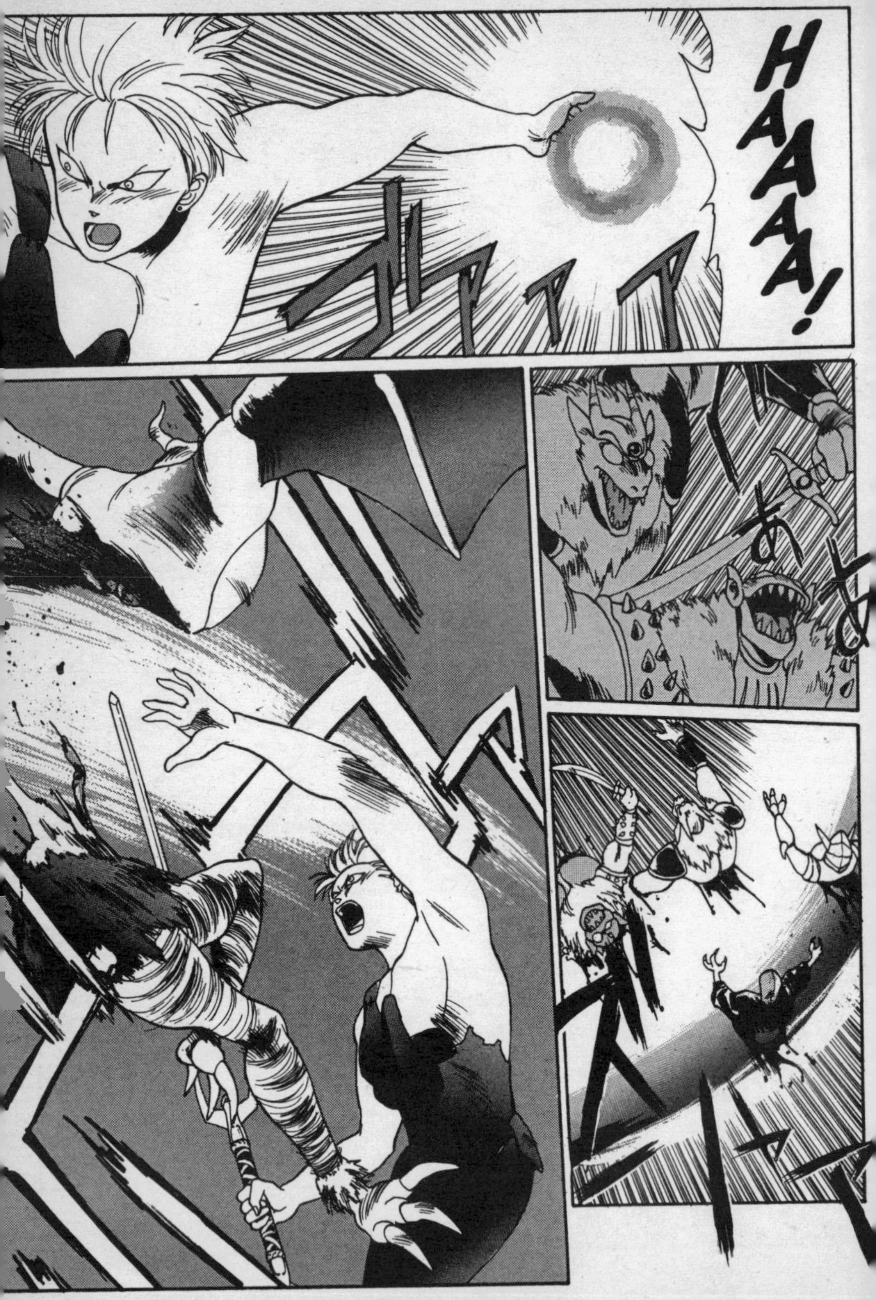
HAAAA!

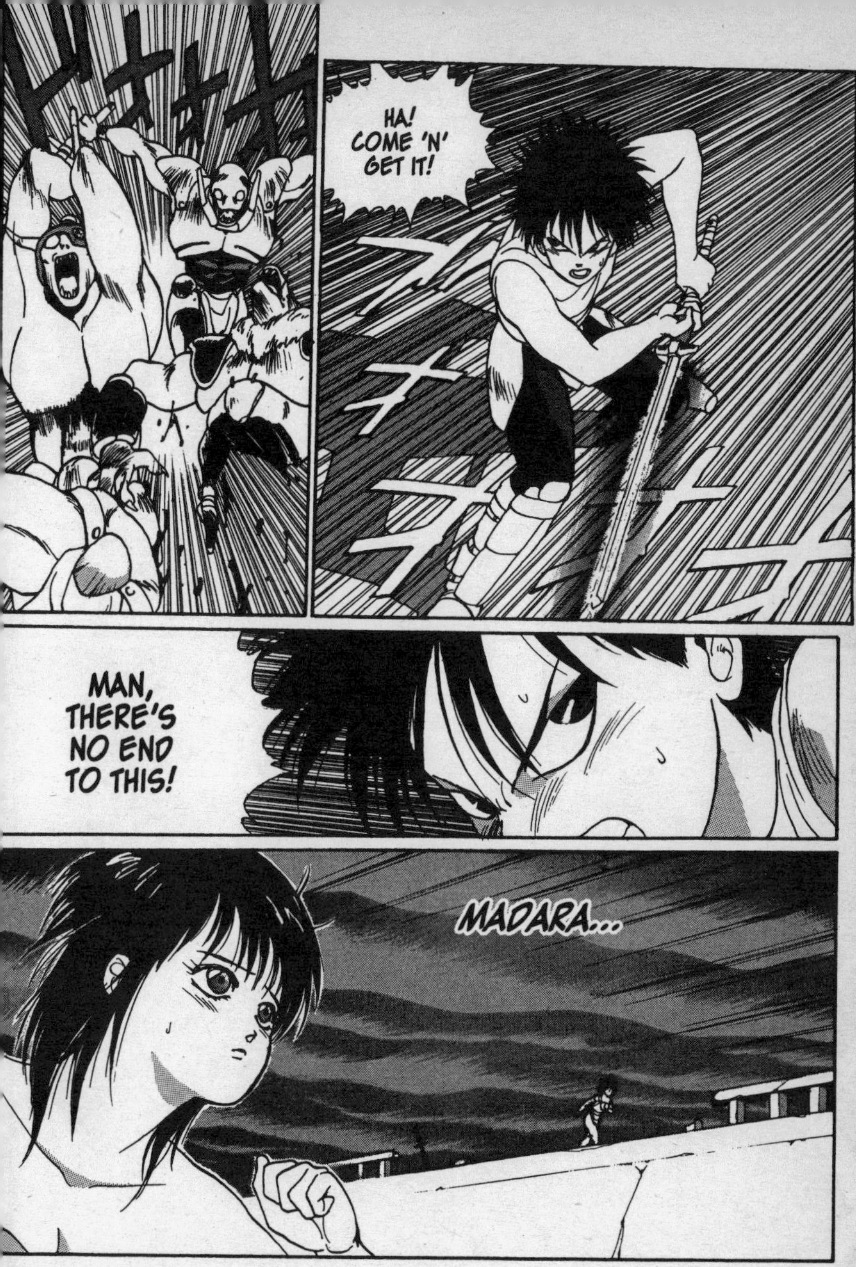
HA! COME 'N' GET IT!
MAN, THERE'S NO END TO THIS!
MADARA...

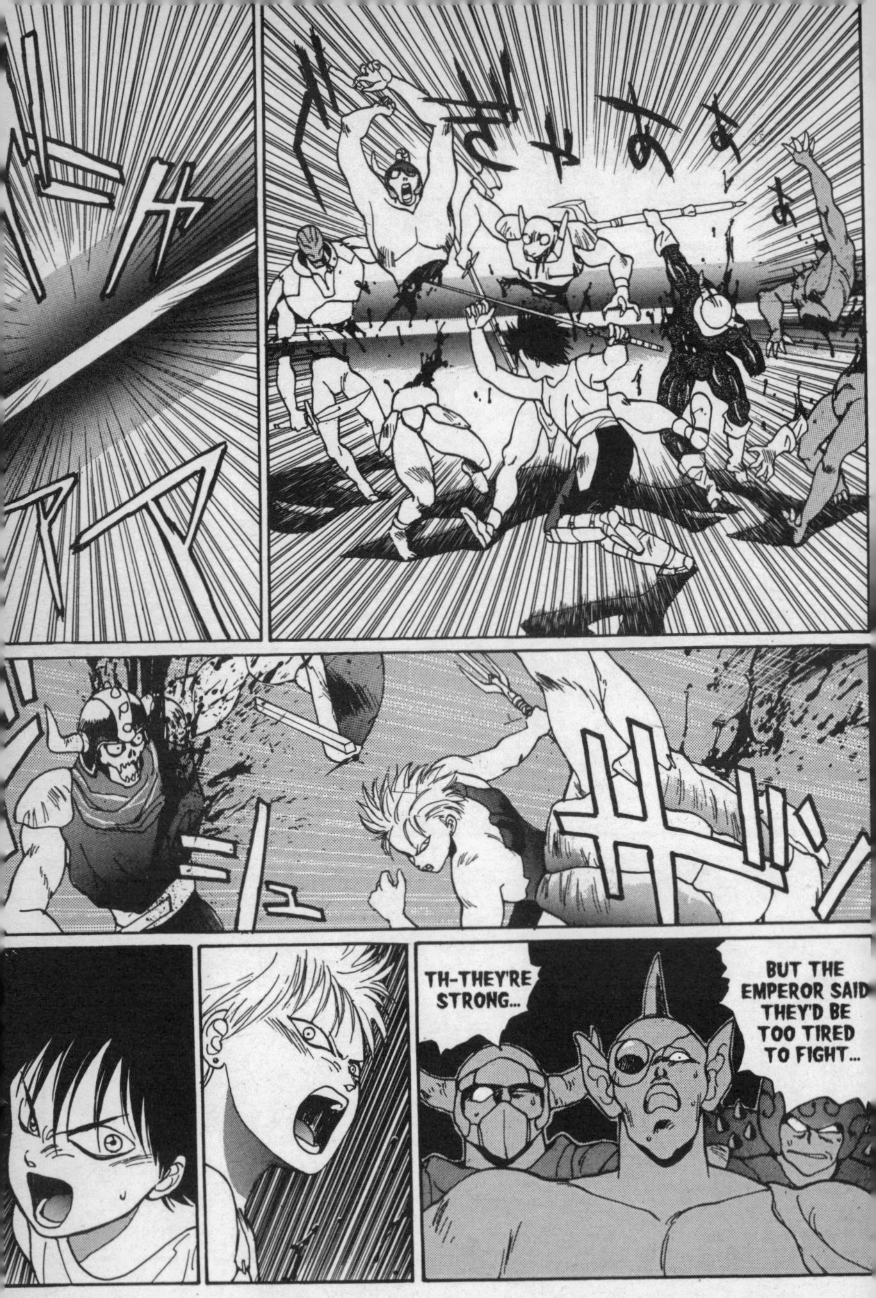
TH-THEY'RE STRONG...
BUT THE EMPEROR SAID THEY'D BE TOO TIRED TO FIGHT...

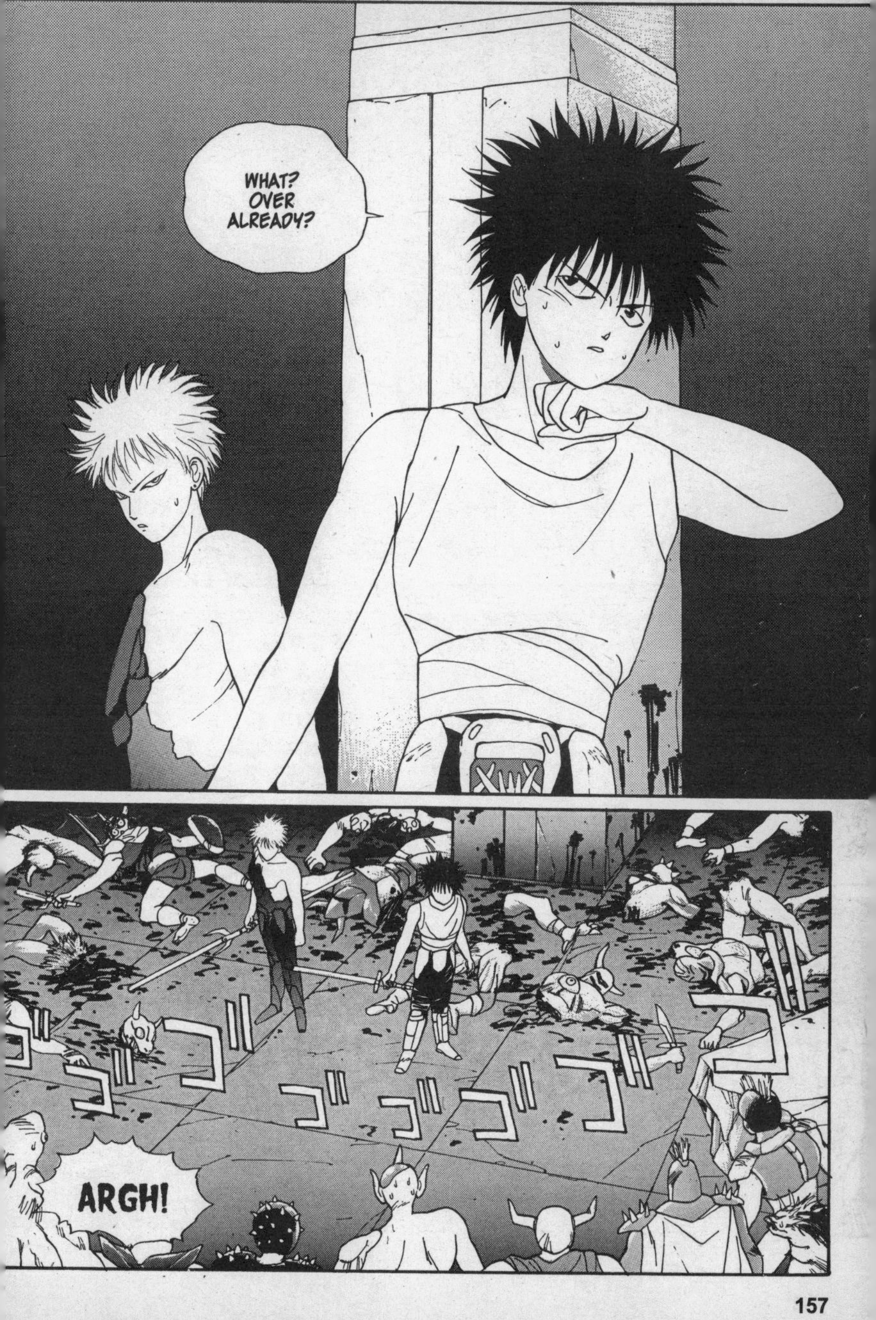
WHAT? OVER ALREADY?
ゴゴゴ
ARGH!

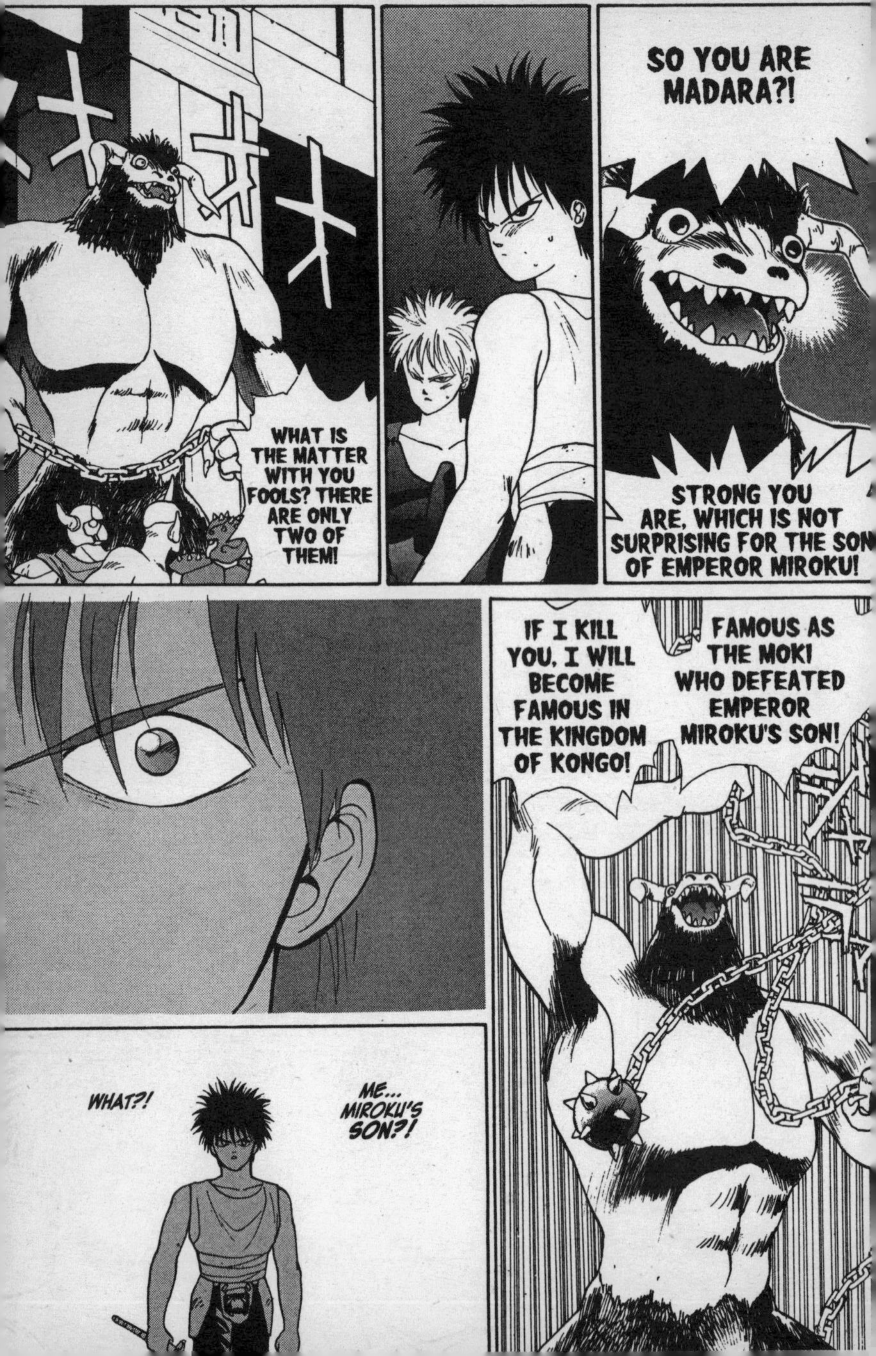
WHAT IS THE MATTER WITH YOU FOOLS? THERE ARE ONLY TWO OF THEM!
SO YOU ARE MADARA?!
STRONG YOU ARE, WHICH IS NOT SURPRISING FOR THE SON OF EMPEROR MIROKU!
IF I KILL YOU, I WILL BECOME FAMOUS IN THE KINGDOM OF KONGO!
FAMOUS AS THE MOKI WHO DEFEATED EMPEROR MIROKU'S SON!
WHAT?!
ME... MIROKU'S SON?!

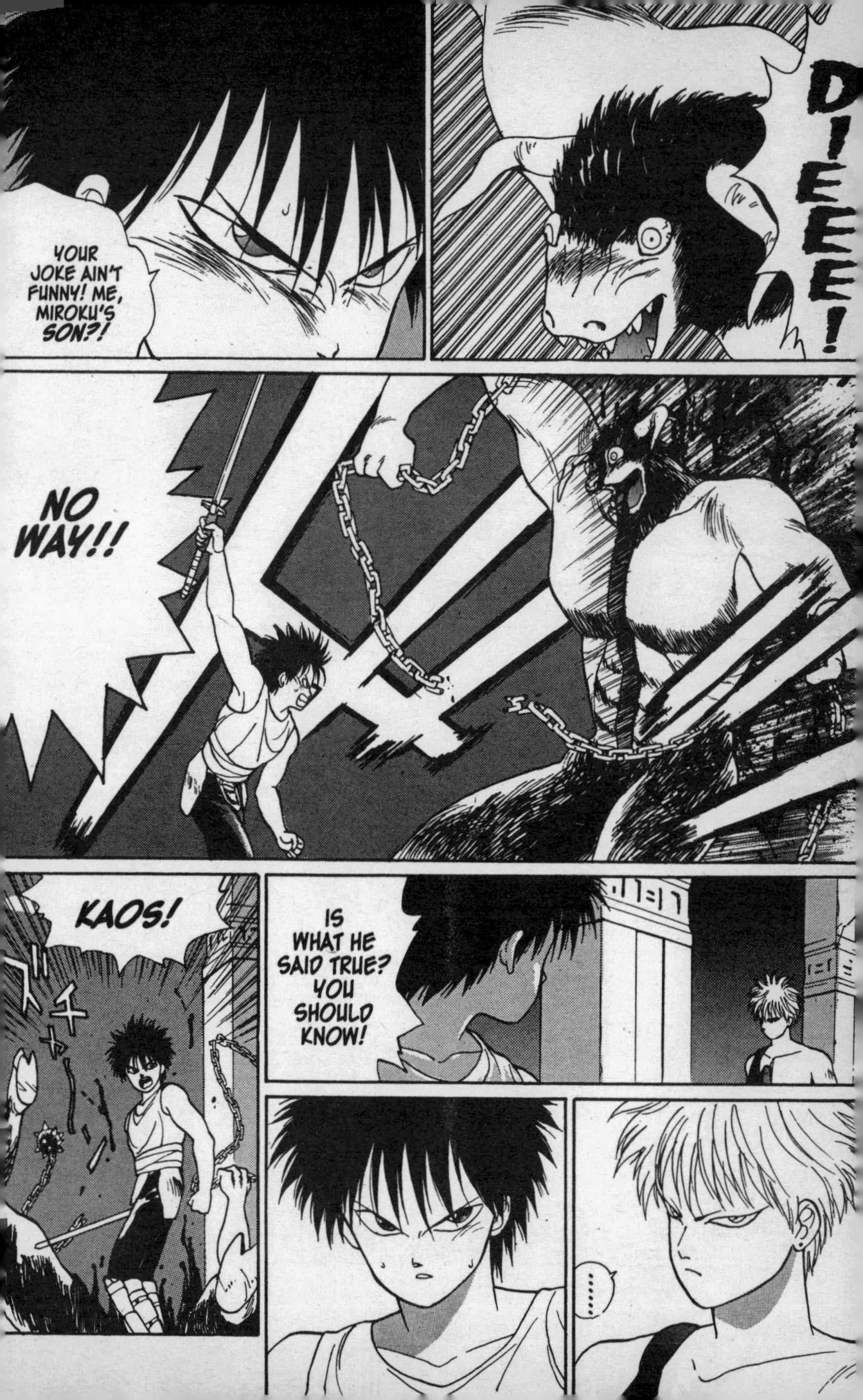
YOUR JOKE AIN'T FUNNY! ME, MIROKU'S SON?!
DIEEE!
NO WAY!!
KAOS!
IS WHAT HE SAID TRUE? YOU SHOULD KNOW!
......

IT IS TRUE.

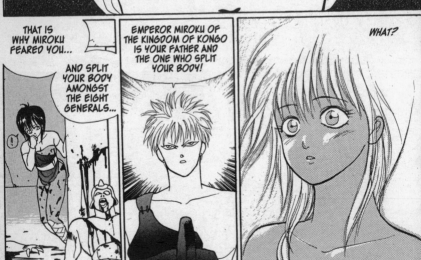

THAT IS WHY MIROKU FEARED YOU...

AND SPLIT YOUR BODY AMONGST THE EIGHT GENERALS...

EMPEROR MIROKU OF THE KINGDOM OF KONGO IS YOUR FATHER AND THE ONE WHO SPLIT YOUR BODY!

WHAT?

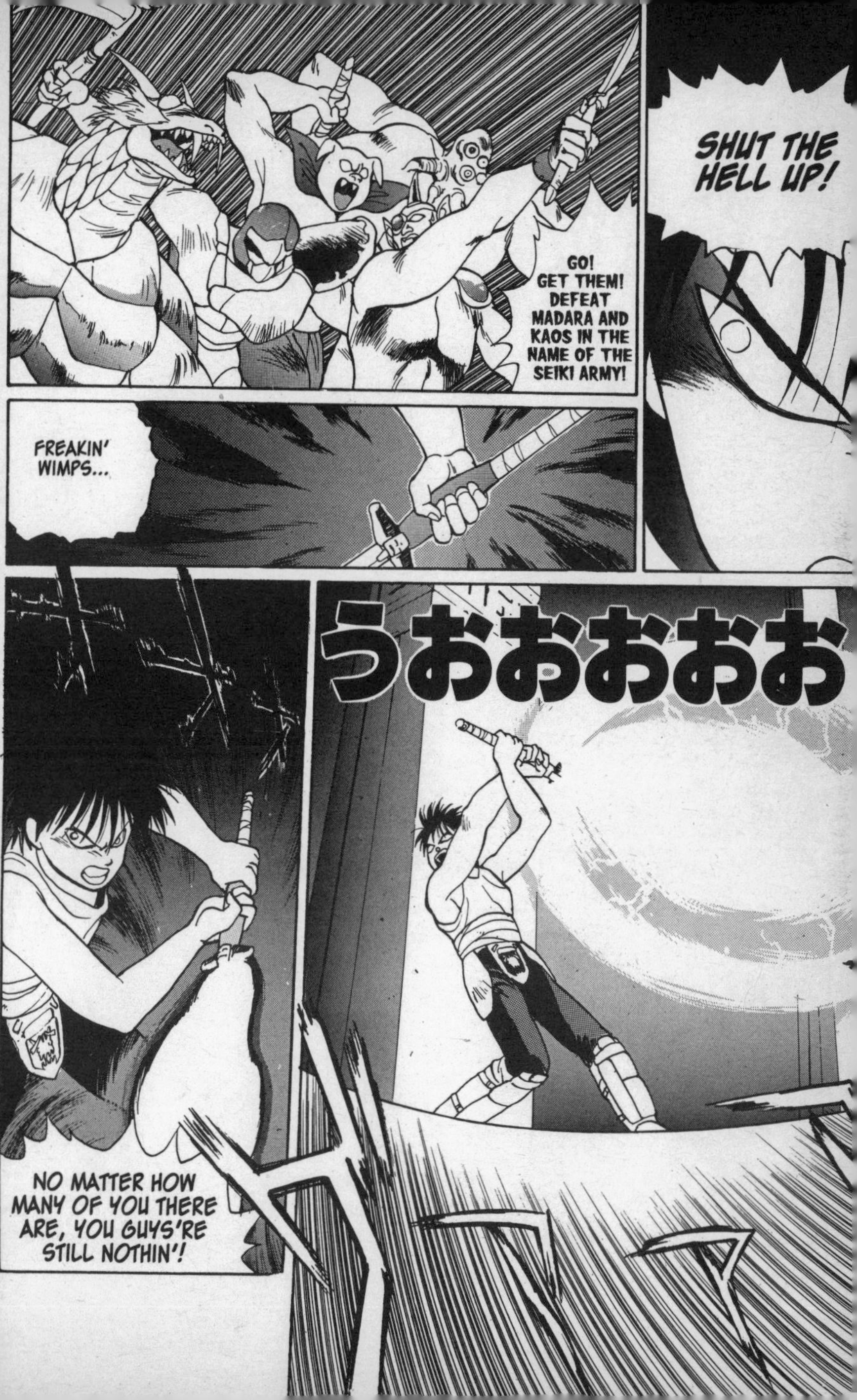
GO! GET THEM! DEFEAT MADARA AND KAOS IN THE NAME OF THE SEIKI ARMY!
FREAKIN' WIMPS...
SHUT THE HELL UP!
NO MATTER HOW MANY OF YOU THERE ARE, YOU GUYS'RE STILL NOTHIN'!
うおおおおおお

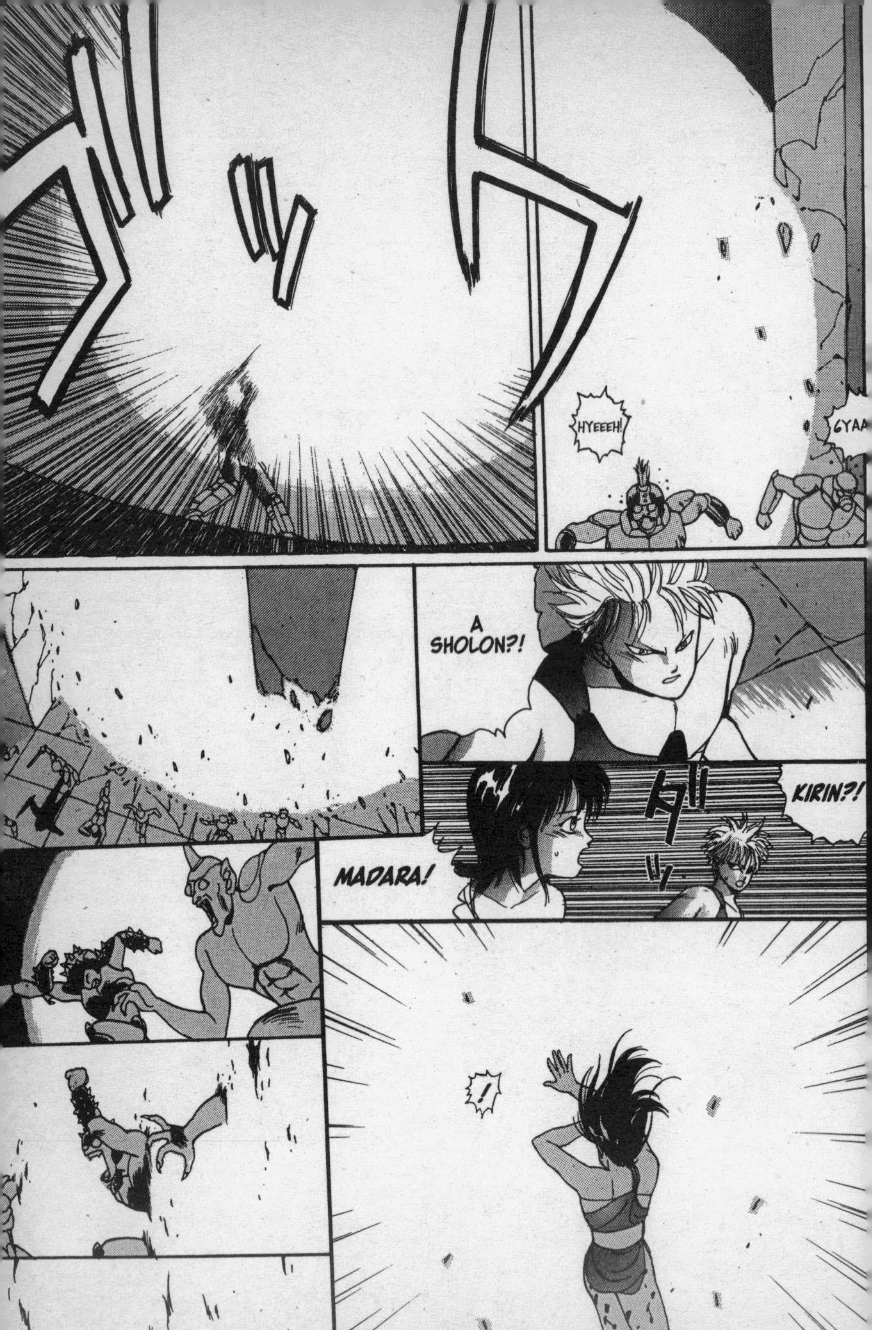
HYEEEH!
GYAA
A SHOLON?!
KIRIN?!
MADARA!
!

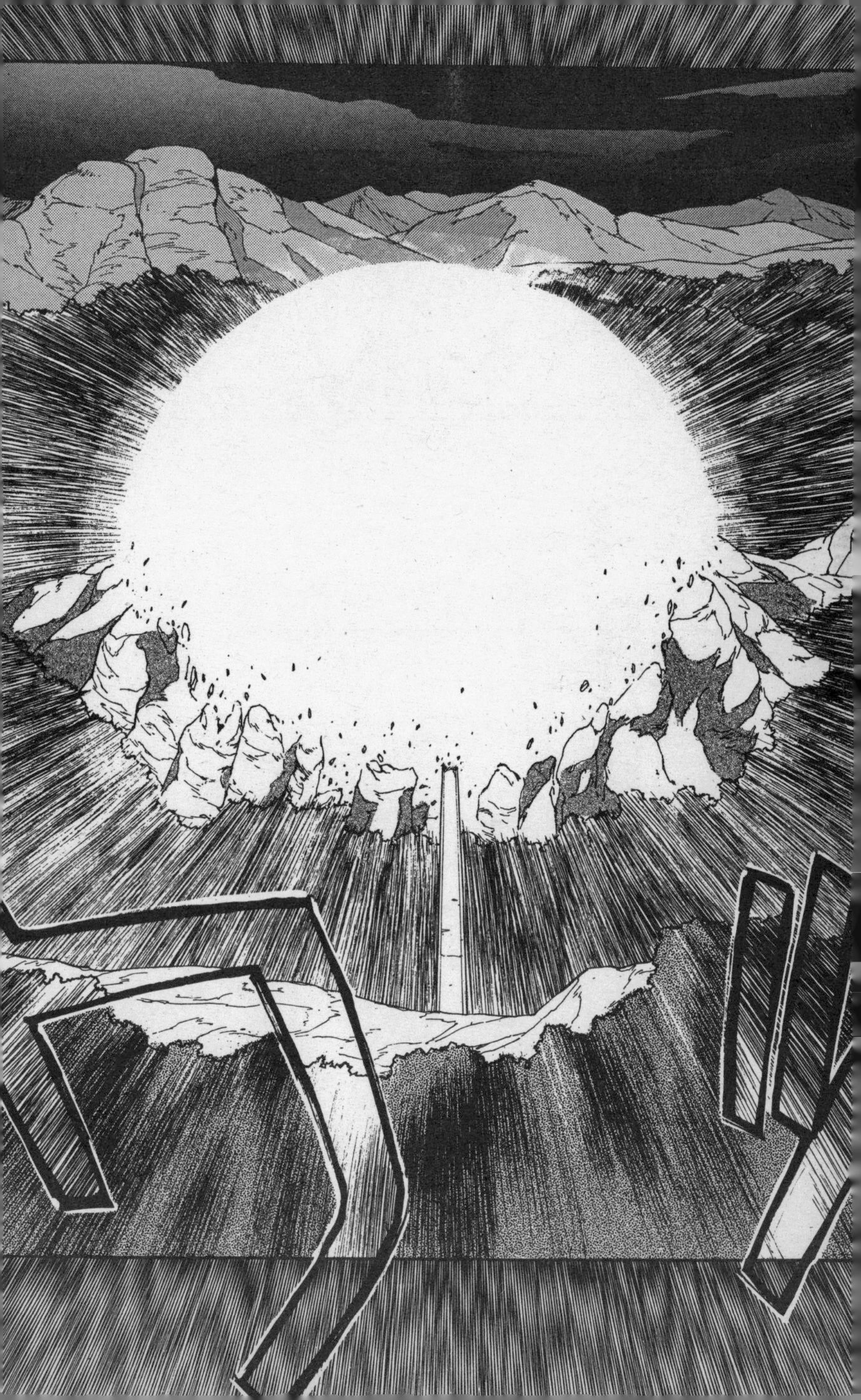

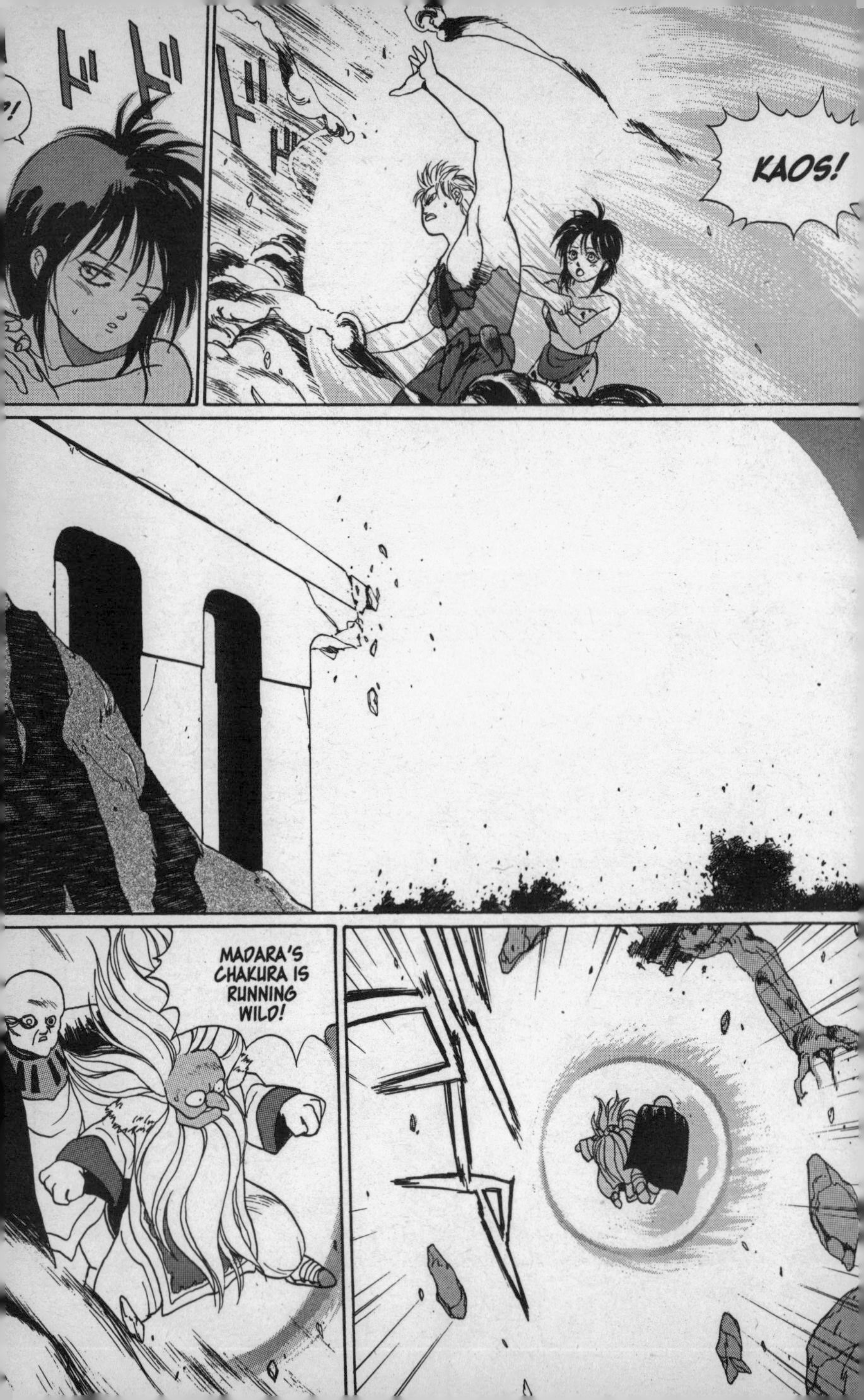
KAOS!
MADARA'S CHAKURA IS RUNNING WILD!

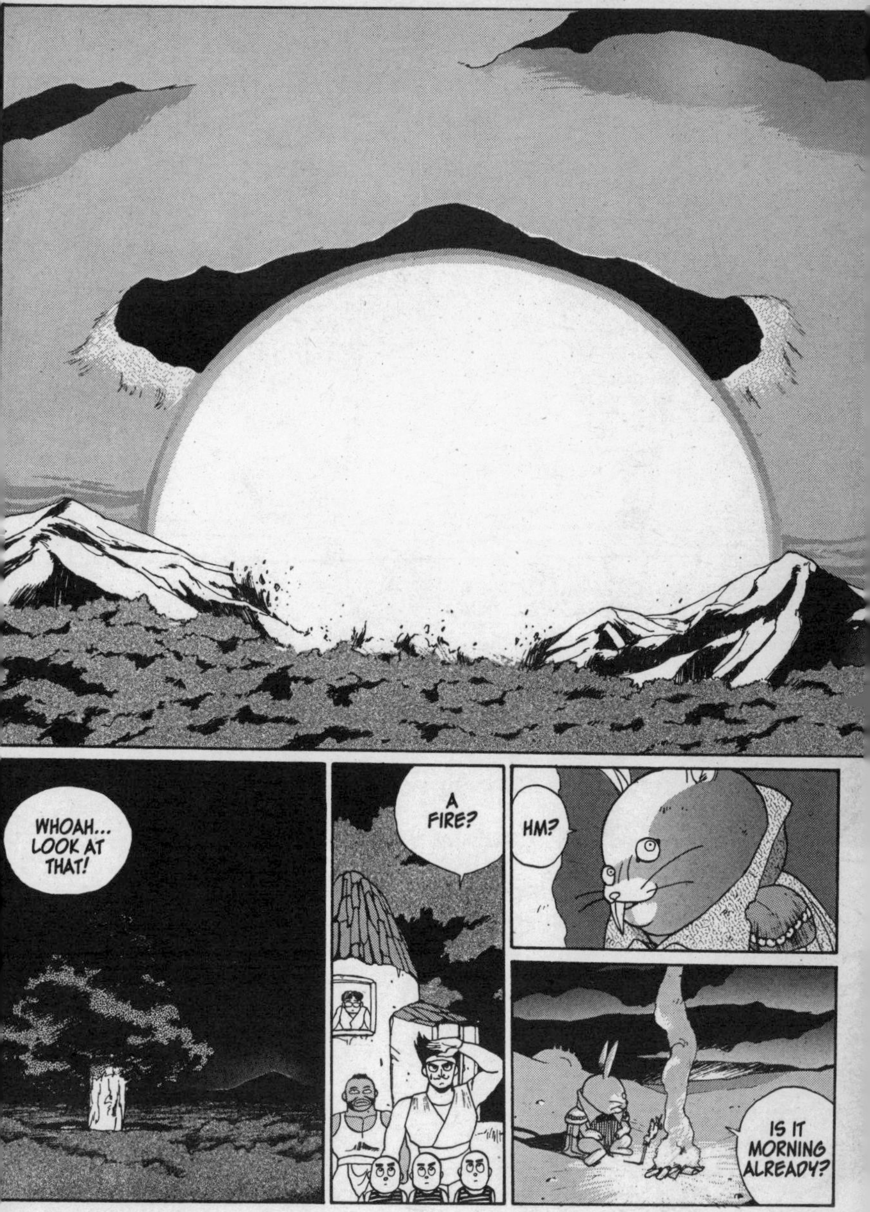
WHOAH... LOOK AT THAT!
A FIRE?
HM?
IS IT MORNING ALREADY?

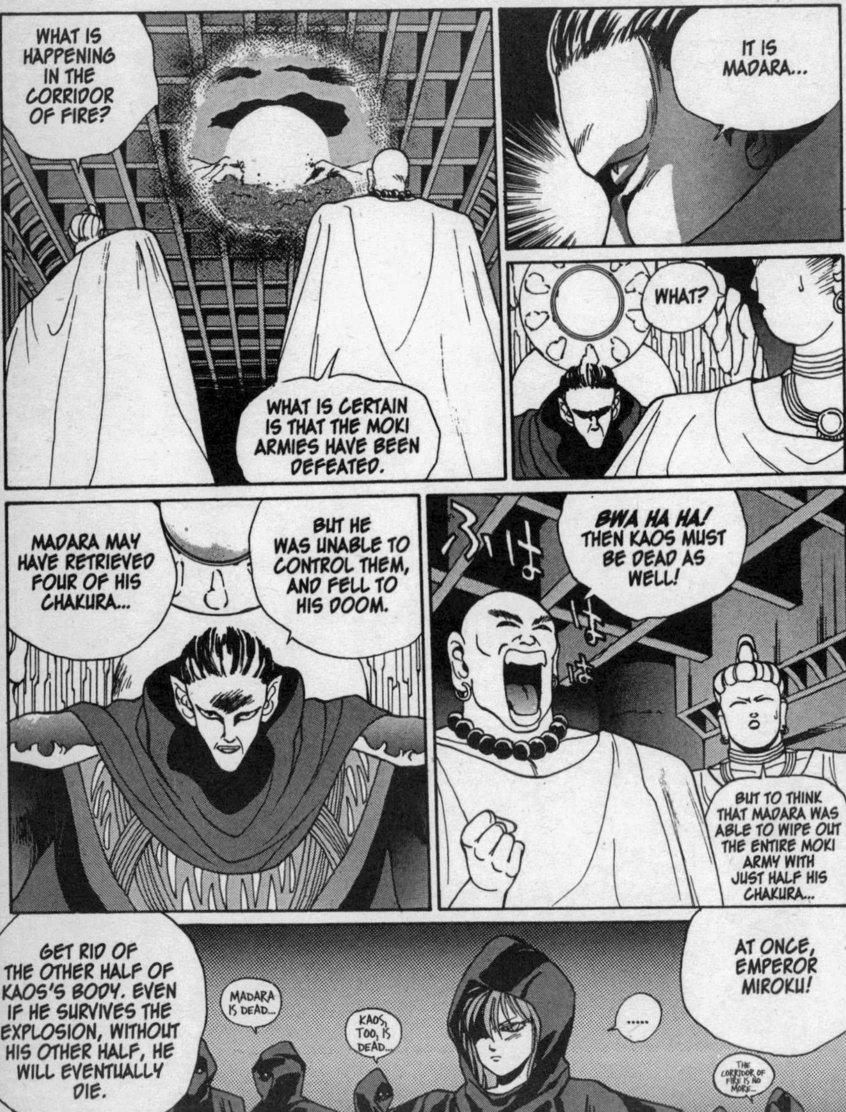
WHAT IS HAPPENING IN THE CORRIDOR OF FIRE?
WHAT IS CERTAIN IS THAT THE MOKI ARMIES HAVE BEEN DEFEATED.
IT IS MADARA...
WHAT?
MADARA MAY HAVE RETRIEVED FOUR OF HIS CHAKURA...
BUT HE WAS UNABLE TO CONTROL THEM, AND FELL TO HIS DOOM.
BWA HA HA! THEN KAOS MUST BE DEAD AS WELL!
BUT TO THINK THAT MADARA WAS ABLE TO WIPE OUT THE ENTIRE MOKI ARMY WITH JUST HALF HIS CHAKURA...
GET RID OF THE OTHER HALF OF KAOS'S BODY. EVEN IF HE SURVIVES THE EXPLOSION, WITHOUT HIS OTHER HALF, HE WILL EVENTUALLY DIE.
MADARA IS DEAD...
KAOS, TOO, IS DEAD...
......
AT ONCE, EMPEROR MIROKU!
THE CORRIDOR OF FIRE IS NO MORE...

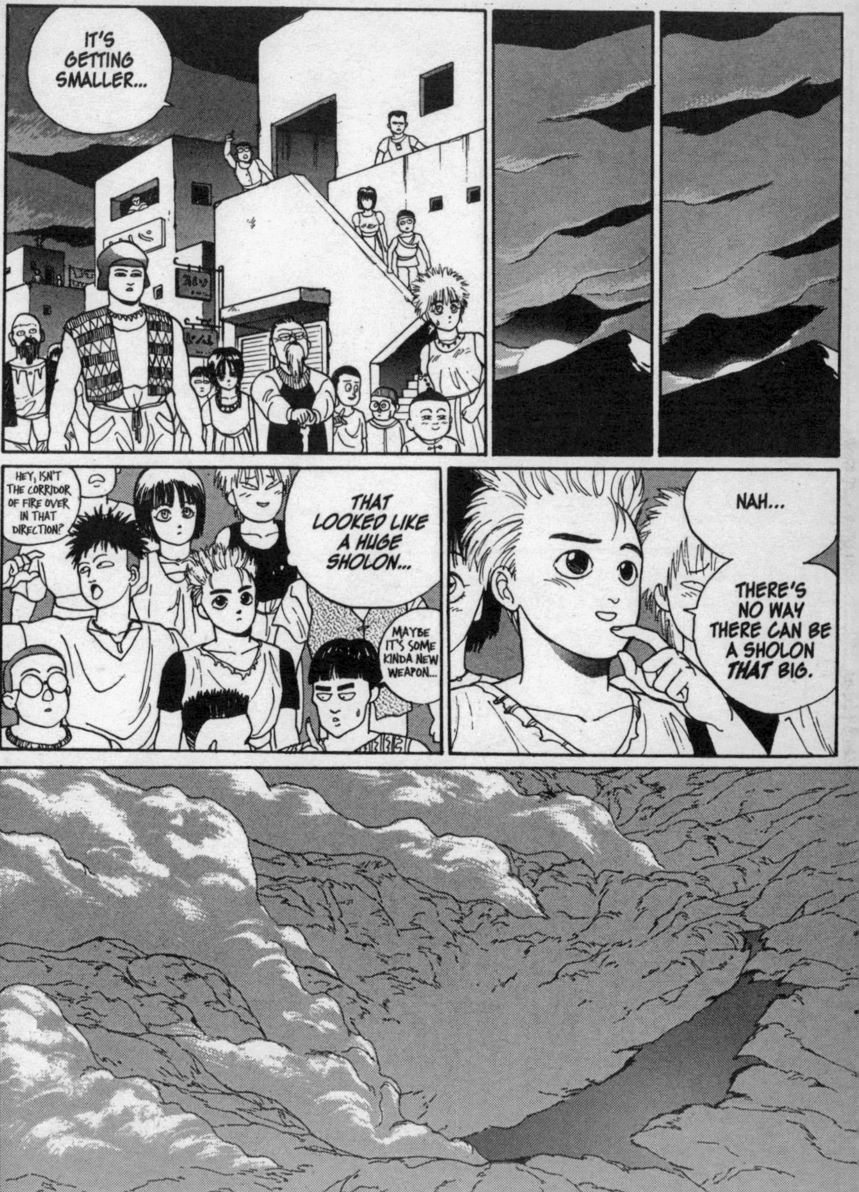
IT'S GETTING SMALLER...
HEY, ISN'T THE CORRIDOR OF FIRE OVER IN THAT DIRECTION?
THAT LOOKED LIKE A HUGE SHOLON...
MAYBE IT'S SOME KINDA NEW WEAPON...
NAH...
THERE'S NO WAY THERE CAN BE A SHOLON THAT BIG.

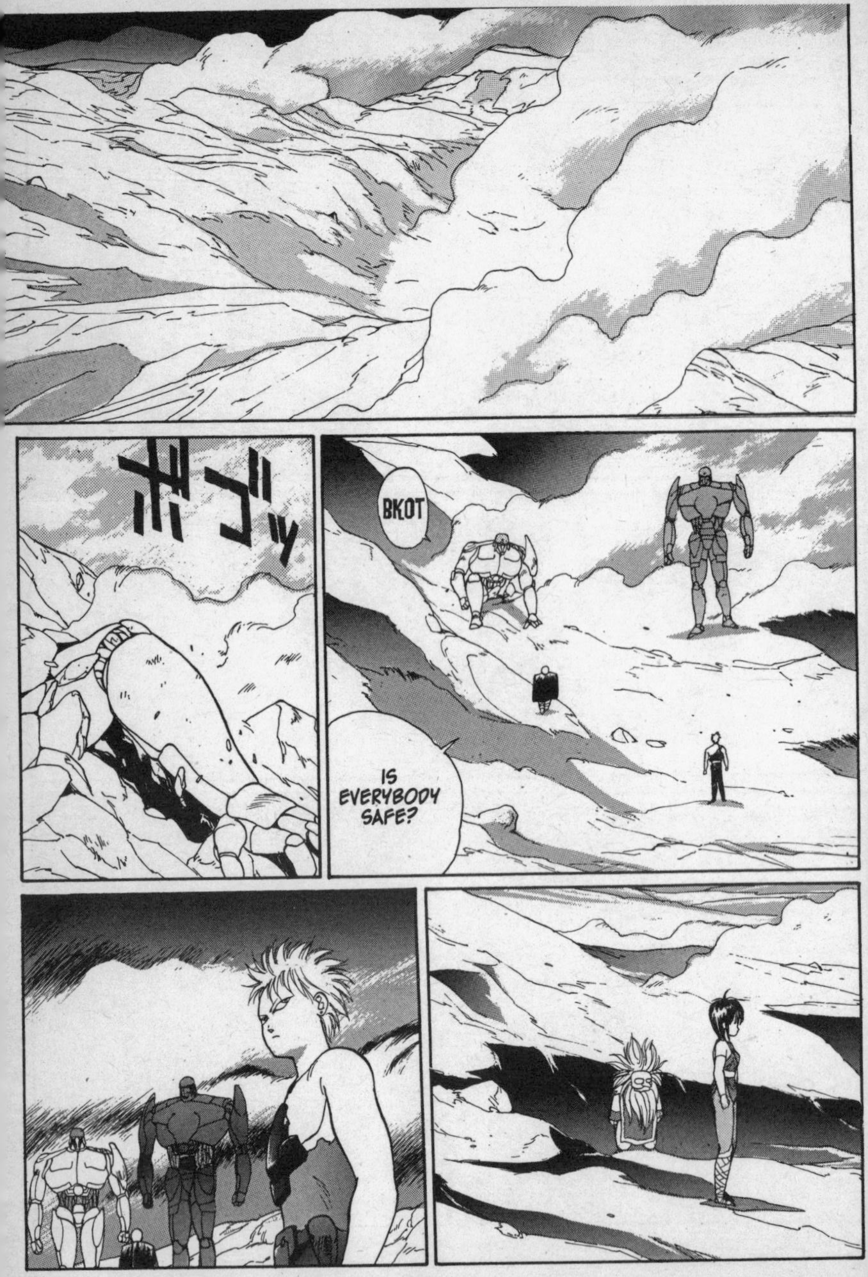
ボゴッ
BKOT
IS EVERYBODY SAFE?

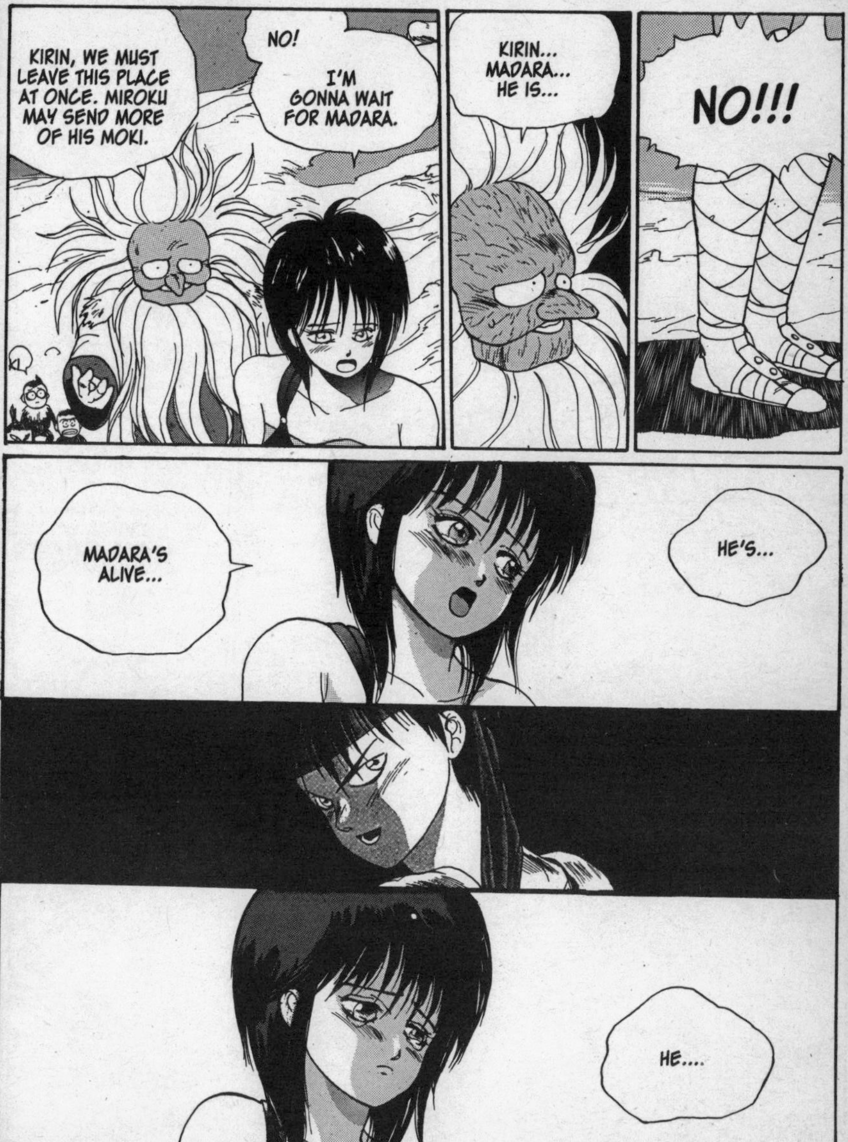
KIRIN, WE MUST LEAVE THIS PLACE AT ONCE. MIROKU MAY SEND MORE OF HIS MOKI.
NO!
I'M GONNA WAIT FOR MADARA.
KIRIN... MADARA... HE IS...
NO!!!
MADARA'S ALIVE...
HE'S...
HE....

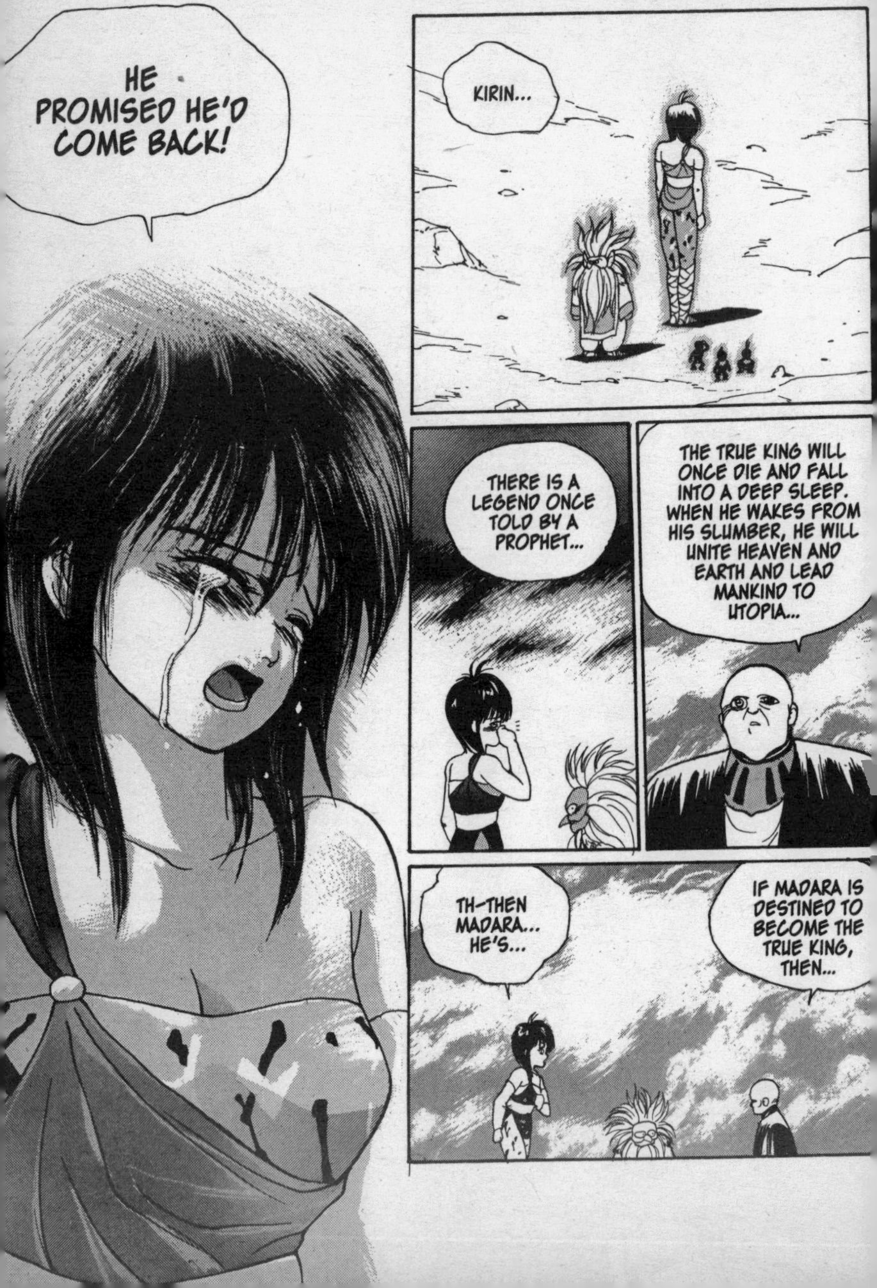
HE PROMISED HE'D COME BACK!
KIRIN...
THERE IS A LEGEND ONCE TOLD BY A PROPHET...
THE TRUE KING WILL ONCE DIE AND FALL INTO A DEEP SLEEP. WHEN HE WAKES FROM HIS SLUMBER, HE WILL UNITE HEAVEN AND EARTH AND LEAD MANKIND TO UTOPIA...
TH-THEN MADARA... HE'S...
IF MADARA IS DESTINED TO BECOME THE TRUE KING, THEN...

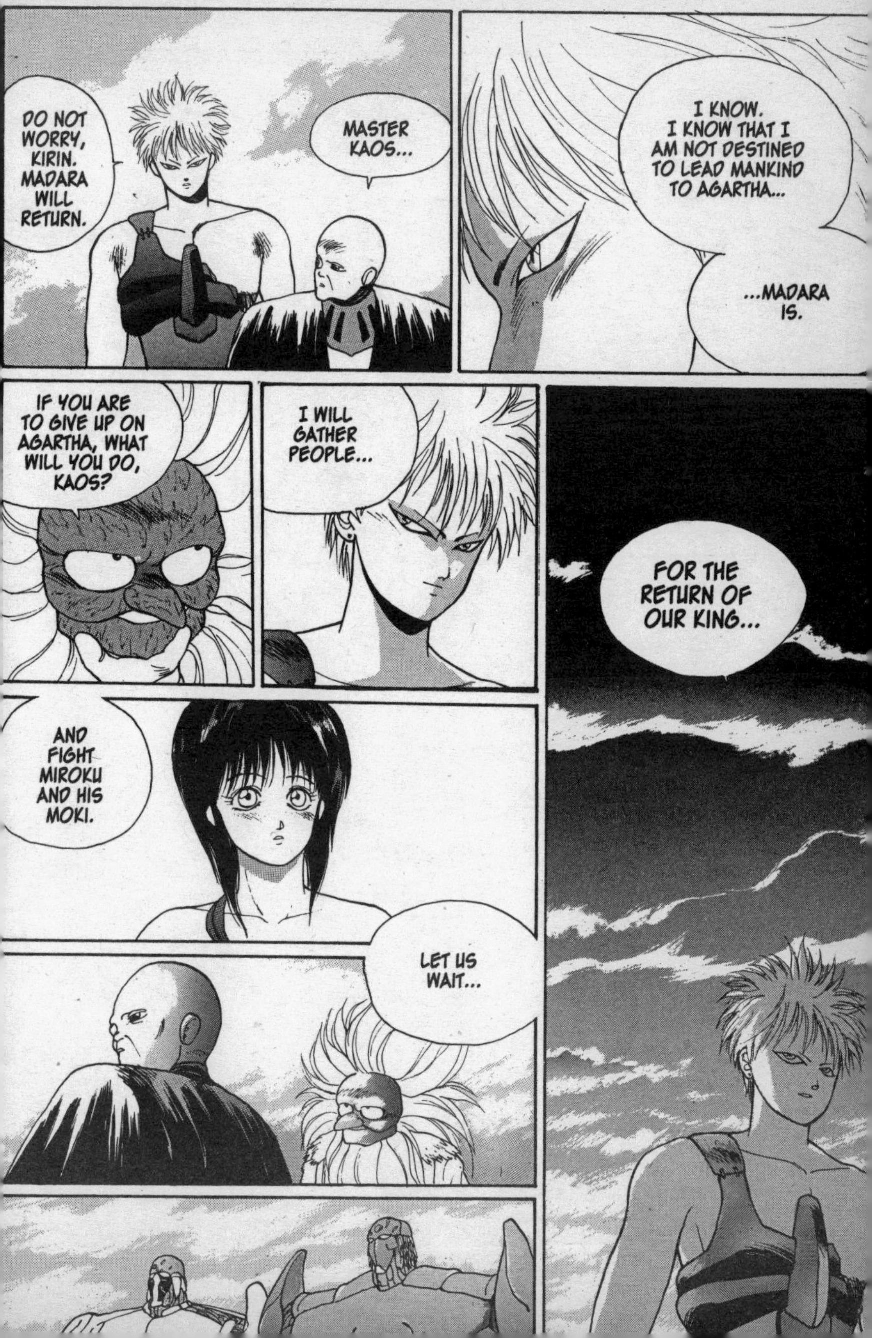
DO NOT WORRY, KIRIN. MADARA WILL RETURN.
MASTER KAOS...
I KNOW. I KNOW THAT I AM NOT DESTINED TO LEAD MANKIND TO AGARTHA...
...MADARA IS.
IF YOU ARE TO GIVE UP ON AGARTHA, WHAT WILL YOU DO, KAOS?
I WILL GATHER PEOPLE...
FOR THE RETURN OF OUR KING...
AND FIGHT MIROKU AND HIS MOKI.
LET US WAIT...

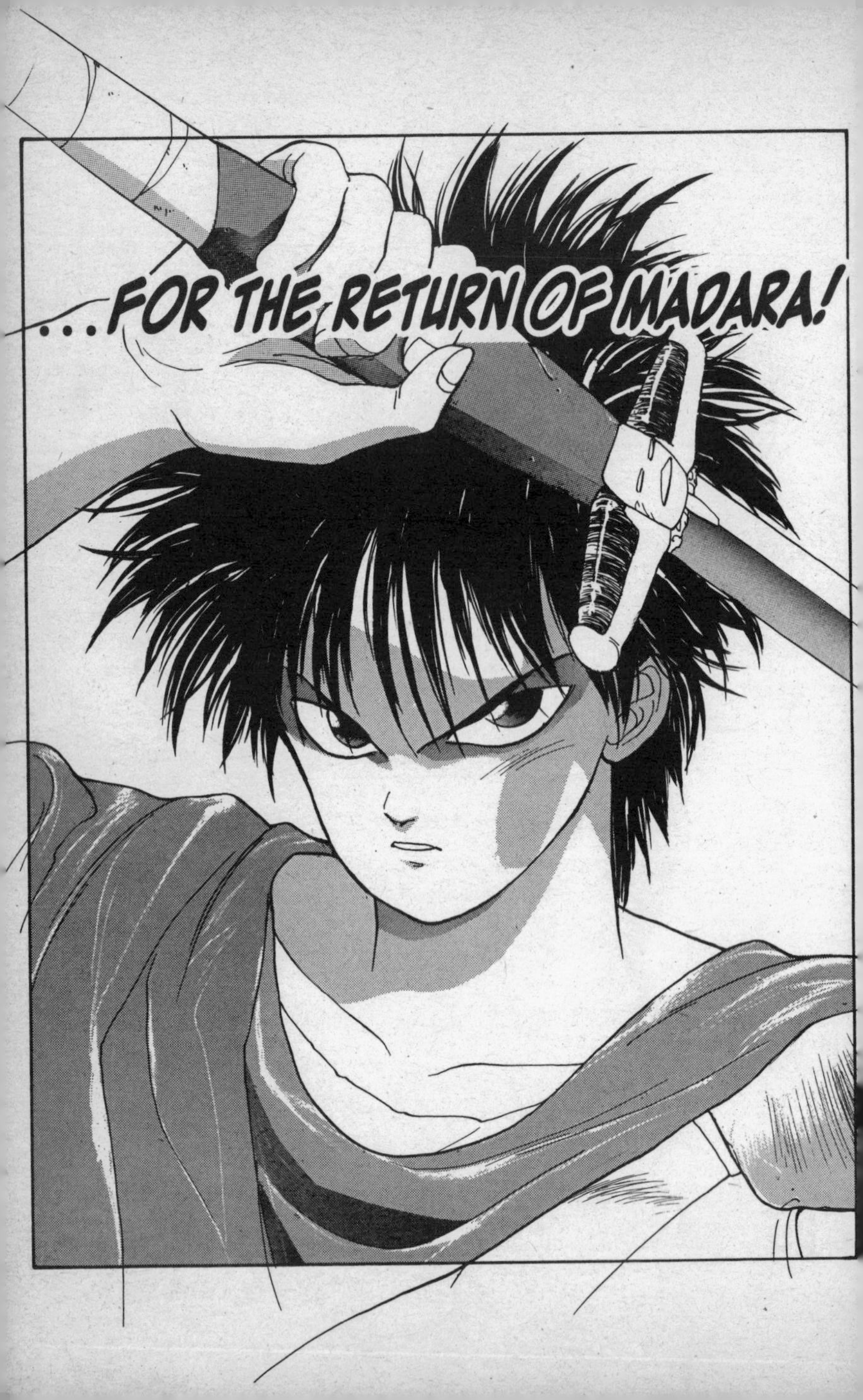
...FOR THE RETURN OF MADARA!

To be continued...

cmx

MADARA

3

In Stores April 2005
MADARA, Vol. 3
By Sho-u Tajima & Eiji Otsuka

Kirin and Kaos return to the river village, where Loki and his people prepare to
fight the remainder of the emperor's forces. But how will they stand now that
Madara has vanished?

CMX ALSO AVAILABLE

FROM EROICA WITH LOVE, VOL. 2

By Aoike Yasuko

As Eroica pursues a jade Buddha, Klaus chases a Russian spy who aims to seduce the Buddha's owner, Yanis Phaerikis. When Phaerikis company executives set their own plot in motion, chaos ensues! Later, Klaus looks forward to a less stressful assignment at a peace summit of world leaders. But the International Association of World-Class Criminals is holding its annual conference at the exact same location—hosted by Dorian! on sale in january!

EROICA YORI AI WO KOMETE © 1976 Yasuko Aoike/AKITASHOTEN.

LAND OF THE BLINDFOLDED, VOL. 2

By Tsukuba Sakura

Kanade can sometimes see the future, and Arou can always see the past. Even with the chemistry they feel, it's impossible to forecast what will become of their relationship. Adding to the tension, Namiki develops a crush on Kanade. on sale in january!

MEKAKUSHI NO KUNI © 1998 Sakura Tsukuba/HAKUSENSHA Inc.

GALS!, VOL.1

by Fujii Mihona

Kotobuki Ran is the toughest of the Japanese high school girls that rule the streets of Shibuya in Tokyo. Follow the adventures of this sassy young girl as she and her friends deal with the challenging issues facing the urban youth of Japan. on sale in february!

GALS © 1998 Mihona Fujii/SHUEISHA Inc.

TENJHO TENGE, VOL. 1

by Oh! great

In one unusual Tokyo high school, education takes a backseat to brawling, as warring school clubs wreak havoc in the hallways and cause chaos in the classrooms, all in a bid to be the baddest team around! on sale in february!

TENJHO TENGE © 1997 by Oh! great/SHUEISHA Inc.

FLIP IT!!

We know what you're thinking. "Real manga reads right to left! This is supposed to be the front of the book, not the back! This manga has been...**flipped!**"

In *Madara*, artist Sho-u Tajima and writer Eiji Otsuka wanted to experiment with creating a comic book in Western format, just like their great European and American counterparts. The pages read left to right and most of the balloons are horizontal.

The entire *Madara* series will be printed in this same format...just like it was in Japan.

CMX: pure manga

The Story so far:

Madara was cast into a river at birth; rescued by humble villagers, only the false limbs created by his adoptive father, Tatara, allow him the ability to move at all.

On his fifteenth birthday, after demons attacked, Tatara told the story of his true origin. Fearful of Madara's tremendous powers, Emperor Miroku cut up his body and divided the parts amongst the generals of the Kongo army.

Now *Madara* and his companion Kirin set off to fight the demons and reclaim his true body parts—and his destiny!